"This workbook is stronger and more effective than any medication I know of for treating chronic pain."

—**L. Stephen Long, MD**, pediatric anesthesiologist; medical director of complex pain, UCSF Benioff Children's Hospital Oakland

"Although there are a few excellent resources for parents on how to understand and help their child with chronic pain, until the publication of this book, there were no equivalent books for the teens themselves struggling with this problem. This practical workbook by a highly experienced clinician helps reframe chronic pain for teens who are struggling with it, and offers accessible strategies that they can use to help themselves. Although its tone is casual and friendly, the advice offered is highly sophisticated and evidence-based without being pedantic. One can almost hear Dr. Z's soothing, optimistic, and experienced voice emerge from the pages to say, 'Here are things you can do to help yourself. We can get through this.' Words that are truly welcome to the frustrated, often hopeless, teens struggling with chronic pain. It contains numerous scenarios, examples, and scripts that ring true, and are easily adaptable to the situations of most teens and their families. The additional materials that can be downloaded to support this volume are an added bonus. One can foresee that the use of this workbook will soon be a standard recommendation by pediatric pain clinics across the country, and it will be a valuable resource for teens in the throes of this challenging problem."

—**Neil L. Schechter, MD**, director of the Chronic Pain Clinic at Boston Children's Hospital; associate professor in the department of anesthesiology at Harvard Medical School; and coeditor of *Pain in Infants, Children, and Adolescents*

"This phenomenal workbook aimed at strategies for empowering teens with chronic pain to take control of their path toward well-being is based on both clinical experience and a foundation in science. Rachel Zoffness has created a strong self-help workbook that is a 'must-read' and 'must-use' for all youth suffering from chronic pain. It is a highly impactful workbook for any teen with chronic pain and for their parents."

—**Lonnie Zeltzer, MD**, former director of the University of California, Los Angeles (UCLA) pediatric pain and palliative care program; UCLA distinguished professor in the department of pediatrics, anesthesiology, psychiatry, and biobehavioral sciences; pain researcher; and author

"I was sure that I would spend the rest of my life miserable with migraines, yet you taught me how to cope with pain rather than wallow in it. I can't express in words how much you helped me. You gave me the hope to start striving to live my life with or without chronic migraines."

—Teen chronic pain survivor and cognitive behavioral therapy (CBT) program graduate

"Rachel Zoffness's workbook is an engaging how-to manual for teens struggling with chronic pain. She presents concepts in a down-to-earth way that will help youths master the techniques necessary to improve their function, decrease their pain, and, most importantly, get their lives back. It reinforces many of the themes we emphasize in our clinics. It will be a great resource for our patients!"

—**William T. Zempsky, MD, MPH**, head of the division of pain and palliative medicine at Connecticut Children's Medical Center, and professor in the department of pediatrics at the University of Connecticut School of Medicine

"This is a terrific and engaging workbook for teens with chronic pain that provides instruction in core behavioral and cognitive skills for pain management. Rachel Zoffness masterfully uses humor and patient stories that should appeal to teens who are either using this workbook independently or with a therapist. It is a must-have addition to the pain practitioner's library."

—**Tonya M. Palermo, PhD**, professor in the department of anesthesiology and pain medicine at the University of Washington; clinical psychologist; author of *Cognitive-Behavioral Therapy for Chronic Pain in Children and Adolescents*; and coauthor of *Managing Your Child's Chronic Pain*

"This workbook is an outstanding and much-needed self-help guide for youth who are suffering from chronic pain. Dr. Z uses teen-friendly language to explain how the body feels pain, and to teach ways to manage pain and help teens take charge of their lives. Each chapter builds new coping skills with engaging exercises and examples. There are so many choices to pick from so that teens should have no trouble finding their own favorite set of skills! Parents and pain clinicians will undoubtedly learn a lot from this workbook as well."

—**Susmita Kashikar-Zuck, PhD**, professor in the department of pediatrics at the University of Cincinnati College of Medicine and Cincinnati Children's Hospital Medical Center; licensed clinical psychologist; and nationally recognized researcher in pediatric pain

"Every teen who struggles with chronic pain and illness will find something helpful in *The Chronic Pain and Illness Workbook for Teens*. The author speaks to teens with understanding and compassion while presenting practical and effective methods to help teens suffer less. I highly recommend this highly readable book on a topic that receives too little attention."

—**Michael A. Tompkins, PhD, ABPP**, codirector of the San Francisco Bay Area Center for Cognitive Therapy; assistant clinical professor in the department of psychology at the University of California, Berkeley; and coauthor of *The Relaxation and Stress Reduction Workbook for Teens*

"Teenagers have a hard time dealing with chronic pain. This interactive, educational workbook will significantly help teens understand and manage their pain. It is a unique and valuable resource."

—**Myles B. Abbott, MD**, general pediatrician in Berkeley and Orinda, CA; clinical professor in the department of pediatrics at the University of California, San Francisco (UCSF) School of Medicine; and former board member of the American Academy of Pediatrics and the American Board of Pediatrics

"What a fantastic resource for anyone caught in the miserable 'stuckness' of chronic pain! With her innately fearless, humorous, and eminently readable voice, Dr. Z leads her readers on the journey to discovering their own fearlessness in the face of debilitating pain."

—**David Becker, MD, MA, LMFT**, behavioral pediatrician; clinical professor in the UCSF department of pediatrics; and co-medical director of the UCSF IP3 Pain Management Clinic

the chronic pain & illness workbook for teens

cbt & mindfulness-based practices to turn the volume down on pain

RACHEL ZOFFNESS, PhD

Instant Help Books

An Imprint of New Harbinger Publications, Inc.

Distributed in Canada by Raincoast Books

Copyright © 2019 by Rachel Zoffness
        Instant Help Books
        An imprint of New Harbinger Publications, Inc.
        5674 Shattuck Avenue
        Oakland, CA 94609
        www.newharbinger.com

INSTANT HELP, the Clock Logo, and NEW HARBINGER are trademarks of New Harbinger Publications, Inc.

The exercise "Going Grey" is adapted from *Cognitive Behavioral Therapy for Chronic Pain in Children and Adolescents* by Tonya Palmero. © 2012 Oxford University Press. Used by permission.

Pacing for Pain and Fatigue diagrams are © 2019. Adapted with permission from Psychology Tools, psychologytools.com.

Cover design by Amy Shoup

Acquired by Tesilya Hanauer

Edited by Karen Schader

All Rights Reserved

Library of Congress Cataloging-in-Publication Data on file

Book printed in the United States of America

21   20   19

10   9   8   7   6   5   4   3   2   1   First Printing

To the amazing teens who walk through my door showing bravery and determination in the face of pain. You are the reason I do what I do!

To Victor and Marie-Helene Yalom, beloved mentors and friends, who provided countless hours of invaluable support and consultation; to Amanda Silver, my soul sister; and to the memory of Marjorie and Norman Alexander, who are always with me.

Contents

Foreword

Benjamin Franklin said the only things certain in life were death and taxes, but he could more accurately have said pain, death, and taxes. Pain is one of the most certain things in life unless you are unlucky enough to be born with the rare condition in which pain does not exist, the congenital indifference to pain. Unlucky because we need pain to survive; it alerts us to life-threatening danger.

So there is a fascinating philosophical paradox: why does something without which we will certainly die early give us so much misery and suffering? One answer is that pain in fact does not have to give us unending, unmanageable misery and suffering. And there is the crux of Dr. Zoffness's book, lessons on how to tame pain with your brain: how to turn down the volume; how to redefine the meaning of pain from something terrible and fearful to something protective; in short, how to learn to coexist with pain, if medical science cannot make it go away. And sadly, medical science is a long, long way from making illness painless.

Chronic pain, the subject Dr. Z focuses on, is pain that lasts for several months or more. That children and young adults should suffer from chronic pain is a terribly unjust thing. Therefore to give children the tools to manage their pain, to master their pain, is a noble undertaking; it is righting a terrible wrong. And here is how Dr. Z does it:

The first chapters take on the very common misperception that the body and the mind are two different things. This wrongful way of thinking is a holdover from the mid-seventeenth-century thinking of French philosopher René Descartes, who believed that humans had minds or souls that were completely distinct from their bodies. But modern philosophers and scientists understand that in fact the mind and the body are one. They are inseparable; they are both the result of cells working together, chemical reactions, energy. And they influence and even control each other in the most powerful and profound ways. The mind can turn the intensity of pain up or down, and the body exerts an equal effect on the mind, sometimes distorting thoughts, riling emotions, depressing moods. To understand that the mind is part of the body, and that the mind can change the body and how it feels, is the first and perhaps most critical step to understanding that the mind can be a tool with which pain can be not just understood, but controlled, and perhaps eliminated.

And that leads to the following chapters by Dr. Z—how to use the power of the mind and its emotions to control the experience of pain. She explores coping; setting goals for school and play; relaxation strategies; mental imagery; mindfulness and meditation; lifestyle; and very importantly, thoughts: what thoughts are, where they come from, the effects of negative thoughts and positive thoughts. Her advice on lifestyle includes ideas about work/play balance, exercise, and the importance of sleep, nutrition, and friendship.

This book is not a diagnostic aid, nor is it a substitute for medical care; there are doctors and surgeons for that job, and they should be used. But rarely can the best medicines and doctors eliminate chronic pain. What one needs then are the strategies that Dr. Zoffness brings to this book. When medical and surgical care cannot stop pain cold in its tracks, what are you going to do? Are you going to crawl into bed, turn on your laptop, and give up? Or are you going to master your pain and your life, and get on with the things that are important? With this book, Dr. Zoffness shows the way to begin the mastery of pain, to learn how to put it in its proper context and place, and when necessary, to coexist with it.

—Elliot J. Krane, MD

Professor, Departments of Anesthesiology, Perioperative & Pain Medicine, and Pediatrics

Stanford University School of Medicine

Introduction and Welcome

Oh, hello!

My name is Dr. Rachel Zoffness—call me Dr. Z!—and I'm a clinical psychologist. I work with teens coping with pain and medical issues. Helping teens find their way back to health is one of my favorite things. (I also really like raptors and ice cream, but that's not what this book is about.)

This workbook is for any teen who's ready to learn how to cope more effectively with pain and illness, as well as providers working with chronic pain clients just like you. The main goals of this workbook are to

- help you regain control of your brain and body (they're yours, take 'em back!);

- reduce pain intensity and frequency, and reduce the impact of illness on your life;

- manage triggers so that you have fewer episodes and flare-ups;

- teach you to cope more effectively with pain episodes once they start;

- improve your quality of life, so you can live a life you love even if you have pain.

You can start achieving these goals by learning to be the boss of how you think, feel, and act in response to pain and illness.

Sometimes teens with chronic pain wonder if this workbook, cognitive behavioral therapy (CBT), or mindfulness has been recommended because they're "crazy" or "it's all in their heads." The answer is *no*! You aren't, and it isn't. Your pain is real, and it can be confusing when a doctor or health provider suggests that you'd benefit from therapy. Here's why this workbook can help: because research shows that medical treatment, while important, often isn't sufficient on its own. How you feel physically and how you feel emotionally are inextricably intertwined: each affects the other, all the time. In fact, pain is *always* influenced by thoughts and feelings! You'll soon learn about your "pain dial," the pain-control center that lives in your brain and spinal cord and controls pain volume. This book will give you tools to turn the volume down on pain and regain control of your body.

Because some people don't understand pain, they can attach stigma and shame to therapy or a workbook like this one. But just as going to the gym to exercise your body doesn't necessarily mean there's something wrong with your body, going to therapy to exercise your mind doesn't mean there's something wrong with your brain! Rather, it's the opposite: exercising your body makes you stronger and healthier, just as therapy, or brain exercise, makes your mind stronger and healthier. Moreover, if it's okay to use crutches when you break your leg, it's certainly okay to use a "pain coach" when you have pain or illness. Just as a soccer coach helps you get better at soccer, a pain coach—like a therapist, or this workbook!—can help you get better at coping with pain.

Pain and illness take away your power. It's time to take that power back. In this book, you'll learn all sorts of skills and facts: the purpose of pain, how the brain works, and how changing thoughts and emotions can change your pain. (*What!* Yes, it's true.) These skills will give you more control over your body so that pain and illness have less power over your life. The most important thing for you to know is this: the more you use this book, the more you'll get out of it. *It only works if you work it.*

The activities in this book are rooted in research, fun to learn, and easy to practice. Some will resonate with you more than others, so find the ones that are best for you. There are also activities and references available for download at the website for this book: http://www.newharbinger.com/33522. I'll be with you every step of the way, rooting for you!

Chapter 1

Pain and Your Brain

What Is Pain?

The generally accepted definition of pain is "an unpleasant sensory and emotional experience." This means that pain is both physical *and* emotional, 100 percent of the time. It is never just one or the other.

Pain = Physical + Emotional

In fact, if pain weren't horrible, it wouldn't get your attention—and that is pain's job. Pain that isn't bothersome fails to change your behavior enough to protect you. Consider the words used to describe pain and health conditions; for example, I describe my chronic leg pain as burning, shooting, miserable, and frustrating. What words describe your pain?

_____

_____

Did you use both physical and emotional words in your description, like I did? That's because pain isn't just physical—it's also emotional! Not convinced? Consider this: rather than having a single "pain center" in your brain, you have multiple sites that contribute to the experience of pain. These include the parts of your brain responsible for:

- emotions (limbic system)

- thoughts (cerebral cortex)

- attention (prefrontal cortex)

This means that how you *think and feel* significantly affects your experience of pain, not just some of the time—but all the time. In fact, you hurt more when you're stressed, scared, angry, or sad.

What's the Point of Pain?

We can all agree that pain isn't much fun. Why do we even have pain?

Pain is your body's *warning system*. Pain tells you when there's a threat to your safety or well-being. It tells you when you've stepped on a nail and need to pull it out, to run from a hive of wasps after you get stung, and to rest after hitting your head during a football game. By giving you unpleasant feelings, pain buys you time to heal and teaches you to avoid dangerous situations. Believe it or not, pain is a good thing. It's your body's way of keeping you safe and alive. In fact, pain is essential for survival.

How Pain Works

Even though we experience pain in our bodies, pain is actually processed in the brain. Your brain is part of your *central nervous system* (CNS), which is made up of your brain and spinal cord. There is always two-way traffic in the spinal cord sending information up from body to brain, and back down from brain to body.

Here's how this works: Receptors in your body pick up information about things like movement, texture, temperature, and pressure from the world around you. This information is sent up your spinal cord to your brain. Your brain then interprets these signals and decides how to respond. Is it an emergency, or a false alarm? Do you need to run, duck, hide, or stand still? Or can you do nothing and go about your day? If there's a good reason to think that protection is required, *your brain makes pain*. Even if there isn't an actual threat to your safety, as long as you *believe* you're in danger, your brain will try to protect you. Put another way, pain is not an accurate indicator of tissue damage. It is an interpretation, your brain's best guesstimate based on available information.

Say, for example, you break your ankle after tripping on a run. Receptors in your body send *warning messages*, alerting your brain to possible danger—from your ankle—up through your spinal cord—to your brain. This information is shared with various parts of the brain, including your emotion center, which all work together to reach a conclusion about context (fell on concrete!), how to interpret the warning messages (injury!), what to do (stop!), and what you're feeling (PAIN!).

The brain then sends signals back down to your body, saying: *"Danger! Pain! Yeeeouch, stop running!"* This pain response protects your body and prevents further damage to bone and tissue. Pain is *adaptive*—that means it helps us survive. It may sound wonderful to never feel pain, but without it, you'd have seriously damaged your leg on that run, because you wouldn't be motivated to stop.

But ongoing pain and health issues can also be a pain. They can make us feel stressed, anxious, angry, and sad. They can get in the way of doing things we want to do. They can stop us from seeing friends, playing sports, going to school, even going outside.

Types of Pain

Pain comes in all shapes and sizes. Some pain comes and goes quickly. This type of pain is called *acute* pain. Other pain is stubborn and hangs around for a while. If pain endures beyond expected healing time, typically defined as three to six months, it's called *chronic* or *persistent* pain. Both acute and chronic pain can be anywhere in your body—head, leg, kidney, elbow.

But do not despair, my friend...you're on the right path! Understanding pain is the first step toward managing pain. Read on!

Pain Questionnaire

To get a better picture of your pain, complete the following questionnaire.

Circle the condition(s) you are coping with and use the blank lines to add others.

abdominal pain/GI condition

anxiety

amplified pain (amplified muscu-
loskeletal pain syndrome [AMPS],
including complex regional pain
syndrome [CRPS], fibromyalgia,
neuropathic pain, myofascial pain)

autoimmune disease

back pain

blood disease

cancer

cardiovascular disease

cerebral palsy

chronic fatigue

cystic fibrosis

depression

diabetes

headache

liver or kidney disease

Lyme disease

migraine

neurological disorder

neuromuscular disease

pancreatitis

post-concussion syndrome (PCS)

postural orthostatic tachycardia
syndrome (POTS)

respiratory condition

rheumatological disease

sports injury

seizure disorder

sleep difficulties

traumatic brain injury (TBI)

_____

_____

_____

(For a more complete list, see http://www.newharbinger.com/33522.)

When did your pain or illness start? _____

What triggered it?

_____

_____

How often do you have pain (for example, once a month, once a week, all day)?

_____

What's your average level of daily pain on a scale of 0 to 10? (0 = none, 5 = moderate, 10 = severe)

_____

What's your average mood on a scale of 0 to 10? (0 = saddest you've ever been, 5 = neutral, neither happy nor sad, 10 = happiest you've ever been)

_____

What's the *lowest* your mood reached in the past two weeks on a scale of 0 to 10? (0 = saddest you've ever been, 5 = neutral, neither happy nor sad, 10 = happiest you've ever been)

_____

How high is your stress about pain or illness and the impact it's having on your life? (0 = none, 5 = moderate, 10 = extreme)

_____

How well are you coping with pain, and the issues that come with it, on a scale of 0 to 10? (0 = not coping well, feel like I'm crashing, 5 = getting by; sometimes I can cope, sometimes I can't, 10 = thriving even though I have pain)

_____

Which aspects of your pain or illness are most difficult to deal with? (Circle all that apply and use the blank lines to add others.)

physical

emotional

missing school

missing friends

falling behind socially

falling behind academically

giving up hobbies

impact on sleep

changes in mood and stress

staying home and inside

impact on family

medications and doctor's appointments

surgeries or medical procedures

_____

_____

The Brain Learns Pain

Your brain is *amazing* at learning. If you want to become good at something—playing checkers, riding your bike, drawing unicorns—just practice it over and over, and your brain will get better at it. For example, when I was twelve, I wanted to be a superb piano player. After a few months of practice, it was like my fingers knew the songs! I didn't need to think—my fingers just played the music. How did this happen? Well, the more I practiced, the more I used the "piano pathway" in my brain. Just as bicep muscles get bigger and stronger the more you lift weights, brain pathways also get bigger and stronger with use. So the more I used the "piano pathway" in my brain, the stronger that pathway got, and the better I became at playing!

What are some things you've practiced and become good at over time?

1. _____

2. _____

3. _____

Just as the brain can become good at piano, checkers, or unicorn drawing, your brain can also become really good at *pain*. When you have pain for weeks, months, and years, your brain "practices" pain.

The longer you practice pain, the more you use the "pain pathway" in your brain, and the bigger and stronger that pathway gets. The stronger the pathway gets, the better your brain gets at pain! When this happens, we say your brain has become *sensitive*. Your central nervous system (CNS; your brain + spinal cord) and peripheral nervous system (the rest of your body) can both become sensitive.

Your Body's Warning System

If you're sensitive to odors, you pick up faint scents that other people hardly notice, so smells seem magnified and you pick up on them more. Some animals, like dogs, are sensitive to sound—they detect sounds humans can't even hear.

Teens with chronic pain have become sensitive to *warning messages*. To you, these messages seem magnified, and your brain picks up on them more. When your pain pathway has gotten big and strong, pain volume is very "loud." Small signals from your body now sound—and feel—huge, so warning messages are interpreted as signs of danger even when your body is safe. In other words, your warning system has become highly reactive.

Chronic pain = False alarm

As with any alarm system, there can be false alarms. When you have chronic pain, your body's warning system "goes off" even when nothing's wrong—like when the fire alarm at school goes off even though there's no emergency. Sirens wail, lights flash…but no fire.

This is what happens when you have chronic pain. Your brain sounds the pain alarm, when in truth, despite your very real pain and discomfort, you're not actually in danger! These signals no longer serve as a warning, nor do they protect you. Your nervous system has simply learned to be good at pain, so your pain response is louder.

Activities That Hurt May Not Be Harmful

It's easy to believe that if something *hurts*, it's *harming* your body. Indeed, the pain system exists to tell us if and when something is wrong. But pain is not always an indicator of danger or harm. Let's define our terms:

Hurt: the uncomfortable sensation of pain; for example, the hurt you feel after your brother pinches you.

Harm: physical damage to your body; for example, the purple bruise left behind by that pinch, evidence of crushed capillaries.

When you have acute or short-term pain, "hurt" is an important indicator of danger. Take, for example, that broken ankle: If you try to keep running, your brain will respond with a strong message that says *stop!* This pain grabs your attention and tells you to sit and rest—because if you run on a broken ankle, you'll further damage the bones, muscle, and tissue in your leg, and significantly harm your body. With acute pain, hurt is typically a signal of harm.

However, when pain becomes chronic, it isn't always a reliable signal of danger or harm. Instead, you experience a false alarm that leads you to believe you're in danger, even when you're not. When you sense danger, your body responds with stress and fear. As you'll soon learn, stress and fear further sensitize your pain system, making pain worse.

For these reasons, it's important to understand that, when you have chronic pain, *the pain you feel isn't necessarily a signal that you're in danger of harm*. For example, going for a walk when you have daily migraines might hurt, but it isn't going to harm your head. Having a picnic in the park when you have fibromyalgia might hurt, but it will not harm your body. Riding a stationary bike when you're fatigued and achy might make you feel tired, but it isn't harmful. In fact, the opposite is true: movement and exercise help retrain your pain system!

Before you can turn off this false alarm, you must first understand when you're at risk of actual harm—like stomach pain after eating something you're allergic to, warning you of a dangerous reaction—and when you're *not* at risk of harm, like while walking during recovery from complex regional pain syndrome (CRPS) and noticing pain in the affected foot. For many painful conditions and illnesses, like headaches, migraines, abdominal pain, irritable bowel syndrome, rheumatoid arthritis, post-concussion syndrome, fibromyalgia, CRPS, and other health issues, pain is *not* necessarily a signal that your body is in danger of harm.

How to Retrain Your Pain System

The good news is this: your brain and body are capable of change, and you can start rewiring your pain system…today! One way to help your sensitive nervous system is to *desensitize* it. When you desensitize your pain system, you reduce your level of sensitivity so that you feel less and react less.

Here's another way of thinking about it: When I was in high school, my friend's maniacal little brother loved to scare people. The first time he jumped out of the closet, I screamed and leaped three feet into the air. My heart raced, my eyes bulged, and my face turned tomato-red. I was terrified, and my reaction was huge. The second time, he managed to scare me again (how annoying). But can you guess what happened the four hundredth time he jumped out of the closet?

Nothing. Nothing happened. My heart didn't race, my eyeballs didn't bulge, I didn't become a tomato-face. I had no reaction at all.

This, my friends, is desensitization. Over time, I became less sensitive to his scare tactics, and got so used to him jumping out of the closet that it eventually stopped bothering me. My brain stopped reacting to him.

One way to help a highly sensitive nervous system become less sensitive is to gradually expose it to small (not big!) doses of activities and stimuli that initially get a big pain reaction, like walking with leg pain or studying with a headache, until over time the pain response gets lower…

and lower…

and lower…

until, like my brain, your brain just stops alarm-ing!

Over time, as you slowly get used to small amounts of activity and stimulation, your nervous system will desensitize. Your brain will learn that "hurt" doesn't necessarily mean "danger" or "harm." Pain and discomfort will go down. In this way, desensitization rewires your nervous system, turning the volume down on those big warning signals so that they're smaller and less loud.

Desensitization is a critical part of breaking the pain cycle.

An important way to accomplish this is by doing things: going outside, moving, seeing friends, and stimulating your powerful and amazing brain!

It sounds counterintuitive, I know. When you have pain, it's normal to think that you're supposed to stay home and rest. That's what most of us do in response to pain and illness. And it's true that sometimes you need short-term rest to recover from a procedure, sickness, or injury.

But staying home and not moving when you have chronic, long-term pain or illness is a *trap*. Missing activities for long stretches of time makes pain worse because your nervous system stays sensitized to, and focused on, the pain. The false-alarm system keeps shrieking loudly with nothing to control its volume. In fact, the longer you stay home and avoid activity, the longer your brain will stay in this sensitive, protective state, and the longer your pain will last.

Before learning to retrain your nervous system—and you will!—you first need to know how thoughts and feelings affect pain.

Thoughts and Feelings Affect Pain: Your Pain Dial

Pain processing is a complicated system. To help you understand it, here's an analogy: Imagine you have a *pain dial* in your CNS that controls pain volume. The function of this dial is to protect you from harm. Anytime your brain believes your body is in danger, the pain dial is turned way up, so pain volume is very loud—loud enough to grab your attention and get you out of harm's way. However, if your brain determines that your body is safe, the dial is turned down—so pain volume is lower, and warning signals are quieter.

Body in danger = Volume turned up = Pain high

Body safe = Volume turned down = Pain low

Your pain dial can be turned up or down by multiple factors, including

1. stress and anxiety,

2. mood, and

3. attention.

Specifically, when you're feeling *stressed and anxious*—

your body is tense and tight,

you're having worried thoughts, and

you believe your body is in danger,

your cerebral cortex and limbic system (which control thoughts and feelings) send signals to your pain dial, turning it way up.

Your brain, interpreting this as an emergency, generates loud signals that sound like this:

PAIN!!!!!!!!!! PAIN!!!!!!!!!!

PAAAAAAIIIIIINNNNN!!!!!!!!!!!!!!!

The pain dial is also controlled by negative emotions like sadness, anger, and frustration.

When your *mood* is low and thoughts are negative,

your brain amplifies pain signals

so that pain volume is pushed way up,

making pain feel worse.

This is also true when *attention* is focused on pain.

When you're home in bed,

missing school,

and focused on your pain,

> your prefrontal cortex (which controls attention) sends signals to your pain dial

> turning it way up,

> making pain feel worse.

But have no fear…the opposite is also true!

When *stress and anxiety* are low—

you're feeling relaxed,

your thoughts are calm,

you believe your body is safe,

> your cerebral cortex and limbic system send signals to your pain dial,

> lowering the volume on pain,

> so that pain feels less bad.

And when your *mood* is high—

you're engaged in pleasurable activities,

your thoughts are positive,

and you're feeling happy,

> your brain determines little protection is needed

> so pain volume is reduced.

And finally, when you're *distracted*—

your attention is focused on things other than pain, like watching funny movies with friends and shoving your face full of popcorn,

the pain dial is pushed down!

Pain volume is reduced, making pain feel less bad.

This means that when you're *relaxed, happy, distracted, and believe your body is safe,* pain is quieter. Signals sound like this:

PAIN. PAIN.

PAIN.

The pain is still there—it hasn't magically disappeared—but it *feels less bad.*

This means that thoughts, beliefs, and emotions can adjust pain volume.

It worked this way for Nicolette:

Nicolette, a star athlete, had double-knee surgery. Her daily pain was a ten out of ten. She was on crutches for months, sidelined from sports, and worried she'd never run again. One day, friends invited her over to watch funny movies. They sat together giggling, scarfing popcorn and chocolate, engrossed in the movie... and when the lights came on a few hours later, she stood and tried to walk because she'd completely "forgotten" about her pain! The combination of friends, distraction, laughter, and relaxation was like a magic medicine that turned down her pain dial without her even realizing it.

Describe a time when you were distracted, happy, relaxed, or having fun, and your pain felt a little less bad:

_____

_____

_____

_____

_____

If your thoughts, beliefs, and emotions can amplify and muffle pain, *this means that you have more control over your pain than you realized!* In fact, you can take control of your pain dial by managing (1) stress, (2) anxiety, (3) mood, and (4) attention. Download this pain dial review at http://www.newharbinger.com/33522. Print a copy and put it on your fridge!

PAIN DIAL REVIEW

Volume high = Pain feels worse

Stressed or anxious

Body tense and tight

Worried thoughts

Believing your body is in danger

Negative mood

Attention focused on pain

Staying inside/in bed for long periods

Volume low = Pain feels less bad

Relaxed

Body loose and stress-free

Calm thoughts

Believing your body is safe

Positive mood

Distracted, attention focused elsewhere

Going outside, moving, and engaging in activities

Lower Your Pain Volume

To take power back from pain, brainstorm activities that improve your mood, relax your body and mind, and distract you. These will help reduce pain volume. In order to heal, your nervous system needs exposure to sunlight, real-world activities, and people, so try to choose activities that don't center on screens. See Lisa's example:

What lifts your mood?

Lisa's list:

1. reading Calvin and Hobbes

2. watching my cat try to figure out the dripping faucet

3. shopping with my sister Stacy

4. inviting friends over to make sundaes

Your list:

1. _____

2. _____

3. _____

4. _____

What relaxes your body?

Lisa's list:

1. a hot bath

2. going for a nature walk outside

3. getting a back massage

4. stretching and yoga

Your list:

1. _____

2. _____

3. _____

4. _____

What relaxes your mind?

Lisa's list:

1. telling myself that everything is going to be okay

2. imagining I'm at my favorite beach

3. listening to thunderstorms on a relaxation app

4. practicing mindfulness

Your list:

1. _____

2. _____

3. _____

4. _____

What distracts you?

Lisa's list:

1. puzzles and brainteasers

2. reading about hawks

3. drawing and painting

4. counting backward from two hundred by sevens

Your list:

1. _____

2. _____

3. _____

4. _____

Pain Dial Worksheet

List five things that *raise* your pain volume and make pain worse. Include activities and beliefs that make you feel stressed or worried, trigger negative emotions like sadness or anger, and focus attention on pain instead of away from it. See Chris's example:

Chris's list:

Five things that increase my pain volume:

1. when people ask about my pain (increased attention on pain)

2. doing nothing at home, especially when friends are having fun without me (high stress, low mood, increased attention)

3. a pile of work that feels too big to finish (high stress)

4. believing that leg pain means I'll never walk again (belief that my body is in danger, high stress, low mood)

5. when I stop playing baseball because I'm in pain (low mood, increased attention)

Your list:

1. _____

2. _____

3. _____

4. _____

5. _____

Now list five things that *lower* your pain volume. Include ideas from the last activity that lift your mood to make you feel happier, help you feel relaxed and calm, and distract you from pain. Remember, these activities don't magically cure pain; they simply turn down the volume on loud signals so that pain feels less bad!

Chris's list:

Five things that lower my pain volume:

1. reading a fun book (relaxed, good mood, distracted)

2. going for a walk in the sun and petting friendly dogs (relaxed, good mood, distracted)

3. eating ice cream with friends (relaxed, good mood, distracted)

4. watching baseball games under my favorite blanket (relaxed, good mood, distracted)

5. reminding myself that hurt doesn't equal harm (belief that my body is safe, relaxed)

Your list:

1. _____

2. _____

3. _____

4. _____

5. _____

Pain Control 101: The Biopsychosocial Model

The causes of—and most effective treatments for—chronic pain and illness are *biopsychosocial*. This means that there are three interconnected domains to target in order to feel better and get back to life: *biology* ("bio"), *psychology* ("psych"), and *social* functioning. Remember, your brain is always connected to your body, so emotional and physical health necessarily impact one another. The more pieces of this puzzle we put together, the better you're likely to feel!

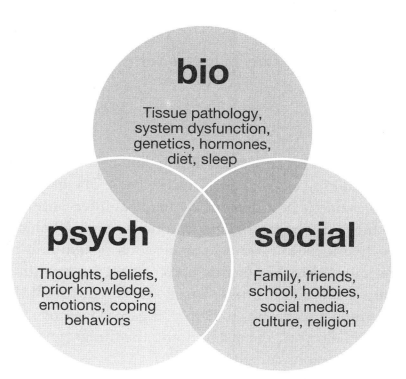

Figure 1. Biopsychosocial model

Biological components of health and wellness focus on pathology in tissues and the pain transmission system, genetics, and hormones, and are often treated with medical interventions. By now, you've probably found a stellar medical team, had multiple tests and procedures, and tried various medications.

Psychological components of health include emotions that turn up the pain dial like depression, anxiety, and helplessness that commonly—and understandably—occur when we're sick or in pain. This domain also addresses negative thoughts, beliefs, and predictions that frequently accompany pain, such as *I'll never get better* and *I can't do anything*, which make you feel worse. It also targets coping behaviors, or how you behave in response to pain and illness.

The third domain is *social*. Research shows that social support—or lack of it—can significantly impact pain and wellness. Social components of pain include family, friends, school, social media, community, and culture. For example, spending less time with friends, missing school, falling behind, quitting hobbies and teams, and isolating at home are social factors that can exacerbate pain. When you improve your social functioning and quality of life, you also improve how you feel!

Conclusion

Once you realize that pain isn't always a sign of damage and may instead be a false alarm, you can start taking steps to get your life back. The biopsychosocial model of pain suggests that this is best done using medical interventions *plus* psychosocial strategies to target thoughts, beliefs, emotions, coping behaviors, and social functioning. Effective tools to retrain your nervous system and turn down your pain dial can be found throughout this book. You'll learn skills from cognitive behavioral therapy (CBT), mindfulness-based stress reduction (MBSR), and other scientifically supported approaches to help you gain power over pain and illness. These strategies will help you get back to doing the things you love! We'll start by learning about how emotions can change pain.

Chapter 2

Emotions and Pain

The Inextricable Link Between Physical and Emotional

The experience of pain is influenced by multiple parts of your brain, including your limbic system—your brain's "emotion center." This means that pain is never just physical, it's also emotional. To effectively treat pain, we must address thoughts and feelings in addition to physical symptoms.

Cognitive behavioral therapy (CBT) is a scientifically supported treatment for chronic pain and illness, sleep, depression, anxiety, and other issues. CBT teaches us that

> how we *think*
>
> affects how we *feel* (emotionally and physically), and
>
> affects how we *act* (behavior).

These four things—thoughts, emotions, physical feelings, and behaviors—all influence each other, and also affect pain. These interconnected relationships are outlined in the CBT cycle diagram below.

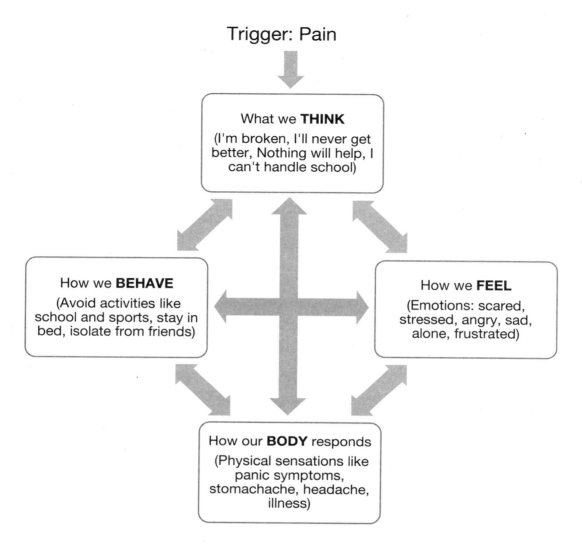

Figure 2. CBT Pain Cycle

The CBT cycle starts with a *trigger,* which is a difficult situation or event. Triggers can be anything from a pain flare-up to an argument with your brother. Triggering events then generate thoughts, feelings, body sensations, and behaviors, which all affect one another. For this example, our trigger will be pain.

Say you have a pain flare-up that prevents you from going to school on an important day. The next thing that happens is that your brain generates a thought. These thoughts happen so quickly that we call them *automatic*. With pain or illness, automatic thoughts are often (and understandably!) negative. Some common automatic negative thoughts that occur when we have pain are *Nothing can help me*, and *I can't deal with this*. You'll learn more about these thoughts in chapter 5.

Negative Emotions Amplify Pain

The next step in the CBT cycle is to notice how these thoughts make you *feel*. Not surprisingly, negative thoughts lead to negative emotions. Thoughts about pain might make you feel scared, angry, or sad.

When you think about your pain or illness, what words describe how you feel? (Circle all that apply and add your own.)

angry	resigned	numb	grieving
upset	worried	guilty	unsupported
stressed	panicky	unmotivated	afraid
worried	sad	checked out	left behind
frustrated	dissatisfied	self-protective	invisible
annoyed	scared	stuck	alone
confused	ashamed	disappointed	tense
furious	avoidant	rageful	tearful
paralyzed	exhausted	hopeless	overwhelmed

Other words that describe how you feel:

_____

_____

_____

Emotions Live in Your Body

Here's an important thing to know about emotions: they aren't just in your head. Emotions also live in your body. For example, anxiety before a big test might come out as "butterflies," a stomachache, or even vomiting. When you're watching a scary movie, fear can come out as goose bumps, dry mouth, or a racing heart. Sadness can make you walk and talk slo-o-o-wly and make your body feel heavy. Stress can cause rashes or acne, trigger headaches and illness, and even make your hair fall out!

How do stress and anxiety come out in *your* body? (Circle all that apply and add your own.)

feeling like you're not getting enough air

bouncing legs, tapping feet, drumming fingers

biting nails, picking fingers

shallow or rapid breathing

dizziness

headaches

tightness in chest

desire to escape or avoid

dry mouth

sweating

light-headedness

irritability

fatigue, exhaustion

stuttering

muscle tension

rapid heartbeat

feeling edgy

feeling restless

butterflies

trouble making decisions

indigestion

stomachaches

nausea, vomiting

fidgeting, twitching

gassiness

trouble concentrating

blushing

acid reflux

mind going "blank"

talking fast

tight jaw, neck, shoulders

difficulty sleeping

rashes, hives, eczema, break-outs

cold hands and feet

trouble making eye contact

mind racing

high energy

difficulty finding words

gulping, swallowing hard

sweaty palms

trembling, shaking

trouble sleeping, night-awakenings

body or muscle pain

grinding teeth

crying

diarrhea, constipation

bloody nose

weight loss or gain

Other ways stress and anxiety come out in your body:

_____

_____

_____

Pain Causes a Mood Crash

Many people feel sad or depressed when they're sick or in pain. Being in pain is no fun. Just like stress and anxiety, sadness shows up in the body in many different ways.

How does sadness come out in *your* body? (Circle all that apply and add your own.)

crying, tearfulness

getting less pleasure out of things than you did before

irritability

heavy feeling in body and limbs

headaches

urge to "hole up" or hide

stomachaches, nausea, vomiting

walking and talking slower

fatigue, lethargy, physical exhaustion

diarrhea, constipation

sleeping more or less

less activity

change in appetite, eating more or less

muscle aches, joint pain, unexplained body pain

lower motivation

decreased desire to go out or socialize

trouble concentrating

feeling like you can't get up

trouble making decisions

staying in bed or inside

loss of interest in activities

isolating from friends

Other ways negative emotions come out in your body:

_____

_____

_____

Coping Affects Pain

The CBT cycle then spins back 'round: when we think negative thoughts and feel negative feelings, we then *behave*, or act, in certain ways. These behaviors are attempts to *cope*, or deal with, pain and illness. A behavior can be something we do—like going to the doctor—and it can also be something we stop doing. For example, some teens stop going to school because they feel sick and can't concentrate, or stop exercising because it hurts. Some stop seeing friends or make a completely new group of friends. Some dial back on hobbies and activities and spend extra time in bed.

What are some things you've started or stopped doing to cope with pain? (Circle all that apply and add your own.)

resting more

visiting doctors

going outside less

spending more time in bed

dropping old hobbies, picking up new ones

having less social interaction (fewer plans, activities, and parties)

taking medicine

sleeping during the day

missing school

using screens more

doing less homework

eating meals in bed

staying in pajamas during the day

taking part in fewer afterschool activities

exercising less

Other coping behaviors:

_____

_____

_____

Vampire Mode

What we *do* then circles around to affect how we *think* and *feel*, both emotionally and physically. Take a moment to consider what happens when

you stay home, day after day?

stop seeing friends?

miss school?

reduce favorite hobbies and after-school activities?

stop exercising and moving?

get less sunlight and fresh air?

You probably know: Your mood crashes! You start feeling miserable. Stress and anxiety spike as you fall behind socially and academically. As mood goes down and stress rises, *the pain dial is turned way up, making pain feel even worse.*

This cycle is familiar to Zia, a high school student who struggles with chronic head and stomach migraines. She calls her CBT pain cycle "going into vampire mode." Says Zia:

> On bad pain days, the light hurts my eyes so I close the blinds to keep the sunlight out. I put on my favorite hoodie, climb into bed, and pull the covers over my head. I don't go to school because I'm in pain and can't concentrate. I stop seeing friends, going outside, and exercising. I dial back on hobbies like soccer and sewing. I feel like a vampire because I come out of my room only when it's dark. After a few days, my mood crashes and I start feeling depressed. This makes my head and

stomach feel worse. My stress and anxiety skyrocket because I'm falling behind in school. The makeup work piles up—it's more than I can handle, and I feel like I'll never catch up. I start thinking I'm going to fail, that my bad grades will affect my chances of getting into college. Every time I think about school, my migraines spike.

On top of that, my friends are having fun without me. I worry about being left out of everything and losing them. The anxiety triggers nausea and I vomit. After a while, I feel like I can't go back to school because I'm so behind that I won't understand what the teacher is talking about. Plus, none of the kids understand what I'm going through. One of them even accused me of faking.

After a few weeks in bed, I have no motivation to leave my house. I'm miserable and my body feels weak. I start thinking that if my medications haven't worked yet, nothing will work. I start believing that the rest of my life is going to be like this, that I'll be in vampire mode forever, that no one and nothing will ever help me. The more stressed and sad I get, the worse my body feels.

If this sounds even a little bit familiar, you're in good company—this is a common example of how thoughts, feelings, and behaviors interact when teens are sick or in pain. But here's the good news: now that you're familiar with this cycle, *you have the power to break it.* That's exactly what CBT can help you do! As you learn about your own cycle of thoughts, feelings, and coping behaviors, you'll develop new skills to control your pain dial—just as Zia did (she's doing awesome, by the way).

Triggers: What Sets Off Your Pain?

The first step in this CBT cycle is to identify the things that trigger—or set off—your pain. A *trigger* is a difficult emotion, situation, or event that causes pain to increase. Difficult situations and events (*situational triggers*) can trigger difficult thoughts and emotions (*emotional triggers*), and vice versa. For example, Adam was recovering from back surgery. He got into a big fight with his sister about the car (*situational trigger*) and became angry (*emotional trigger*). He felt the anger in his body; his muscles got hot and tight and his back started spasming. Gina is an example of the reverse. She believed that nothing could cure her fibromyalgia, which made her feel depressed and hopeless (*emotional trigger*). She stayed home for weeks on end without school, friends, or distractions (*situational trigger*), and started feeling worse.

What *emotions* trigger your pain? (Circle all that apply and add your own.)

frustration

anger

stress

anxiety

loneliness

sadness

_____

_____

_____

_____

What *situations* trigger your pain? (Circle all that apply and add your own.)

not getting enough sleep

arguing with family members

having piles of homework

missing fun events because I'm sick

thinking about upcoming exams

doctors' appointments and hospital visits

_____

_____

_____

_____

Know Your Pain Recipe

Have you ever baked brownies? (Mmmm!) Baking requires following a specific, detailed recipe to get your brownies juuuust right. If you don't follow the recipe or skip steps, you'll have gross, not-delicious brownies, and nobody wants one of those.

Well, pain works the same way. Just as there's a recipe for brownies, there's also a recipe for pain. Your high-pain recipe is a list of all the ingredients, or triggers, that go into creating a high- pain day. These can be situations, emotions, activities, thoughts, sleep, even foods. Everyone's pain recipe is different, but when combined, these ingredients combust to exacerbate pain.

Just as you have a high-pain recipe, you also have a low-pain recipe. A low-pain recipe is all the ingredients—situations, emotions, activities, thoughts, food, and sleep, for example—that go into creating a low-pain day. How can you exert some control over which kind of day you're going to have? One technique is to closely examine your low- and high-pain days, and notice the ingredients for each.

For example, let's look at Emma's recipes. Over a couple of weeks, Emma noticed that certain situations, thoughts, feelings, and events contributed to feeling awful, while others contributed to feeling pretty good. She listed the following pain ingredients:

Emma's High-Pain Recipe

- Skipping meals (poor nutrition)

- Being out of balance: hungry, tired (insufficient sleep), overworked (doing homework until 11:00 p.m.)

- Overcommitting (too many afterschool activities, clubs, and extra-credit work)

- High stress

- Anxiety and frustration about pain

- Not having time to relax, exercise, or have fun

Emma's Low-Pain Recipe

- Three meals a day plus snacks (well-fed, nutritious diet)

- Being balanced: eating regularly, sleeping well, balanced workload

- Saying no, limiting extra work and activities

- Low stress

- Using coping strategies to manage anxiety and frustration about pain

- Scheduling time to engage in self-care: exercising, relaxing, knitting, embroidery, creating art, journaling

Emma noticed that her overly busy life frequently resulted in a recipe for high pain. What changes could she make to replace some high-pain ingredients with low-pain ingredients? These were her ideas:

- Schedule protected "relaxation time" after school and on weekends to walk and draw.

- Set an alarm at mealtimes to prevent skipping meals.

- Go to bed earlier, sleep in on weekends.

Enter your high-pain and low-pain recipes (bonus brownie recipe!):

Brownie recipe	High-pain recipe	Low-pain recipe
1.5 cups flour		
2 cups sugar		
4 eggs		
¾ teaspoon baking soda		
½ teaspoon salt		
1 cup butter		
½ cup cocoa powder		

List some ideas for replacing high-pain ingredients with low-pain ingredients:

_____

_____

_____

_____

_____

How Stress and Anxiety Affect Pain and Health

Emotions like stress and anxiety play a significant role in pain and health. *Stress* is a temporary response to an existing, external stressor; it typically abates once the threat is gone. *Anxiety* is a sustained stress response, typically disproportionate to the threat of the stressor, and often focused on future events that haven't even happened yet.

Sometimes teens with pain and illness say: "Oh, but I don't have any stress or anxiety." Newsflash: Having pain or illness is a *huge stressor* on your brain and body. In fact, pain is one of the biggest stressors there is!

Stress, anxiety, worry, and fear are all members of the same emotion family. These emotions are your body's adaptive response to danger. Remember, if something is *adaptive*, that means it functions to help you survive.

Back in the day, humans were hunters. While we hunted for our dinner, other animals hunted us! Your body therefore developed a system to manage emergencies: when a hungry lion approached, your body's stress-response system, including your *sympathetic nervous system* (SNS)—the system that readies your body for action—released stress hormones like adrenaline into your bloodstream.

Adrenaline sends your body into a state called *fight or flight*. This immediately readies your body to either (1) fight the lion, or (2) flee from the lion, and run away as fast as you can! Adrenaline affects your body in many ways: it accelerates heart and respiration, halts digestion, tenses muscles, makes you feel restless, triggers feelings of fear… In fact, many of the items on the anxiety and stress checklist in the "Emotions Live in Your Body" section can be attributed to adrenaline.

However, in today's modern world, we no longer need to hunt for our dinner with spears. Instead we buy food at the grocery store, and there aren't many lions there. But sometimes your body releases adrenaline anyway, and at inconvenient times— like when you're standing onstage trying to sing, taking a test in class, or thinking about an upcoming medical procedure.

Because there's not much difference in your stress response whether you're being hunted or taking a test, you experience similar symptoms: hammering heart, churning stomach, rapid breathing, sweaty palms, pounding head. But you're just sitting in class, onstage, or on your couch, with the urge to flee and nowhere to go. (*Hmm. Thanks, body, but I don't need to fight-or-flight right now!*) This fight-or-flight response is what we call anxiety and stress. In these situations, whether you're at school or on your couch, it's no longer adaptive or useful. Instead, it's a false alarm that causes great distress.

If you've ever wondered why pain seems to be triggered or exacerbated by stress, one reason is that pain activates your SNS stress response. Stress, anxiety, and fear of pain sensitize your nervous system. Thinking there's an emergency—an activated stress response suggests danger!—your brain turns up your pain dial to make pain. The more pain volume increases, the more stressed you become—and so the stress-pain cycle persists.

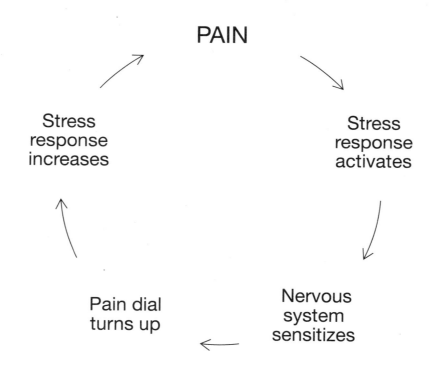

Figure 3. The Stress-Pain Cycle

Stress and Your Immune System

When you're stressed, like when you have pain or illness, your body releases an additional stress hormone called *cortisol*. If you've ever doubted whether emotions directly affect health, consider this: Cortisol suppresses your immune system. Your *immune system* is your body's defense against sickness and infection, fighting off harmful pathogens like viruses and bacteria. When stress and anxiety are high, you're less able to fight off infection and more likely to get sick. You're also more likely to get sicker if you're already sick.

High stress → High cortisol → Weakened immune system

Control Your Stress Response

When you're the boss of stress and anxiety, you're able to turn off your fight-or-flight response, break the stress-pain cycle, and turn down pain volume. Skills like relaxation and mindfulness, which you'll learn in chapter 4, can help you do this. These skills turn on your *parasympathetic nervous system* (PNS), your body's *relaxation system*. The PNS slows your heart rate, allows your body to rest, and promotes healing. Added bonus: when you decrease stress and increase relaxation, you turn off the false alarm system—and lower pain volume.

Stress → SNS on, PNS off → Pain volume high

Relaxation → SNS off, PNS on → Pain volume lower

Release Negative Emotions: How to Tea-Kettle

Regulating emotions and releasing stress can help you effectively regulate pain. One way to do this is to *tea-kettle*. What is tea-kettling, you ask? Well, first answer this:

Q: What would happen to a teakettle if it didn't have a whistle to release the steam?

A: The steam would have nowhere to go. The pressure inside the teakettle would rise…and rise…and rise…until…POP! It exploded.

Similarly, negative emotions need a place to go. If we don't find healthy outlets to release these feelings, they find ways to come out on their own. Negative emotions can come out in your body as muscle tension, stomachaches, vomiting, skin break-outs, or a headache that just won't quit. A great way to cope is to tea-kettle: let out, or express, your emotions in a healthy way (this is why it's called "venting"!). This way, pent-up emotions won't come out as pain. Better yet, they won't get stuck inside you to begin with!

Here are some great ways to tea-kettle:

- Write or journal—writing takes emotions out of your body, translates them into words, and releases them onto paper.

- Dance—dancing and moving help channel emotions into creative physical expression.

- Create art—drawing, painting, and other art transform emotions into colors, shapes, and images.

- Exercise—moving and sweating release emotional energy.

- Talk to someone—putting feelings into words releases them.

Additional tea-kettling ideas:

_____

_____

_____

Conclusion

Understanding the various parts of the CBT cycle—triggers, thoughts, emotions, body sensations, and coping behaviors—gives you the power to change the cycle, making *you* the boss of your pain. Now that you have insight into how negative emotions impact physical health, let's learn some behavioral strategies that can change pain.

Chapter 3

Strategies for Changing Pain

Coping with Pain and Illness

There are healthier and less healthy ways to cope with pain and illness. This is why the *B* in CBT stands for *behavior,* or how you act as a result of thoughts and feelings. The strategies in this chapter turn the volume down on pain by soothing stress, distracting you from pain, and helping you gradually resume activities and get back to life.

Act First, Feel Changes Later: How to Work Backward

It's understandable to think pain needs to resolve first, before you can resume activities. But to start feeling better, you actually need to work backward and resume activities first! Once you start getting sunlight, moving, exercising, seeing friends, catching up in school, and reengaging in hobbies and pleasurable activities, your mood is more likely to go up, stress and anxiety to go down, and pain volume to gradually decrease. Here's how it worked for Evan:

Evan struggled with rheumatoid arthritis that caused joint pain and required surgery. He'd stopped rock climbing and attending social events, and was getting tutored at home. He missed climbing and the friends he'd made at his climbing gym. He figured he'd have to wait for the pain to go away—presumably, after surgery— before he could go back. But once he learned the strategy of working backward, he decided he'd waited long enough. He missed enjoying his life.

Evan decided to try physical therapy along with CBT to regain strength, muscle tone, confidence, and calm. After a few weeks, he texted his climbing partner to ask if he could join him at the gym, even if he had to go slowly. His friend, who'd been concerned about him, was glad to hear from him and said yes. Going back to the climbing gym felt like medicine. Evan enjoyed being around friends, and resuming activity actually made his pain feel less bad!

Engaging in activities by working backward helps you break the cycle of pain and illness. So how do you decide where to start? The first step is to *establish a goal*.

Goal Setting

No matter what your goals are—be they medical, physical, social, or academic— make them more achievable by following these steps. First, state your goals in terms of what you *do* want instead of what you *don't* want. For example, "I don't want to be trapped at home" keeps your brain stuck and lacks a plan for forward motion. Instead try: "Go outside more." Then, follow these goal-setting steps:

- Be realistic.

  Make your goals realistic and achievable. Setting unrealistic goals only results in frustration. For example, instead of "Feel completely better by Friday," try "Use three CBT strategies today."

- Be specific.

  State your goal using units of *measurement*—time of day, quantity, and duration. For example, instead of "Be more social," which is broad and vague, try "Text one friend on Friday at 4 pm." Instead of "Go back to school," try "Attend school for one hour three days this week."

- Break your big goal into smaller steps.

  Dream big! Just make sure to break your big goals down into smaller steps. This makes them less intimidating and more achievable. Small steps are also more trackable, so you can see where you've been and where you're going. For example: "Week 1—bike 10 mins daily at 1 pm. Week 2—bike 15 mins daily at 1 pm. Week 3—bike 20 mins daily at 1 pm."

- Pick a practical starting point.

  Identify an easy starting point that doesn't sound overwhelming. Starting small gives your brain and body a chance to gradually adjust to change. For example, if your goal is to resume cross-country running, don't start by running five miles after a month of not moving. Your body won't be used to it, and overexertion leads to pain. Instead, set a small, measurable starting goal, like "Walk 15 mins every day for one week."

- Measure progress.

  Keep a chart to track daily progress. It's rewarding and encouraging to watch your improvement. Feel proud of each small accomplishment!

- Anticipate obstacles.

  Anticipate obstacles before they happen, and troubleshoot solutions in advance. This way, you're ahead of the game. Ask yourself, *What might get in the way of achieving my goal?*

- Earn rewards!

  Rewards help motivate us and move us forward. For example, some teens work hard to earn money, while others work hard to get into a stellar college. Some teens will work for chocolate! Rewards are different for different people. Set up a system with your parents to earn rewards for accomplishing each small goal. Rewards can be screen time, going to a concert, money toward a guitar, shopping with your mom, or points toward a larger reward.

Add your goals in the space below. Use Lily's example to guide you.

Lily's big goal: Go back to Irish dance

Your big goal: _____

Lily's first small step (goal 1): Attend one dance rehearsal this week and just watch

Your first small step (goal 1): _____

41

When Lily will take that first step: After school today at 4 pm

When you'll take that first step: _____

Lily's next three realistic, specific steps (goals 2–4):

2. Email dance teacher today at noon

3. Attend weekly dance rehearsals Fridays at 4 pm

4. Practice dancing at home for 10 minutes 3 days this week

Your next three realistic, specific steps (for goals 2–4, include date, time, and units of measurement):

2. _____

3. _____

4. _____

Lily's Progress Chart (X = complete)

	Mon	Tues.	Wed.	Thurs.	Fri.	Sat.	Sun.
Goal 1: Attend rehearsal, just watch	X						
Goal 2: Email teacher	X						
Goal 3: Weekly rehearsal					X		
Goal 4: Dance 3 days for 10 mins		X	X			X	

You can download a copy of this chart at http://www.newharbinger.com/33522.

Your Progress Chart

	Mon	Tues.	Wed.	Thurs.	Fri.	Sat.	Sun.
Goal 1:							
Goal 2:							
Goal 3:							
Goal 4:							

Lily's potential obstacles and solutions: The teacher might not email back; if she doesn't, I'll go to her office. I may get tired and have pain; I'll take frequent breaks and bring an ice pack.

Your potential obstacles and solutions:

_____

_____

_____

_____

Lily's reward ideas: New recipe book and mixing bowl

Your reward ideas:

_____

_____

_____

Pacing: How to Resume School and Activities

One of the most important, effective strategies for desensitizing your sensitive nervous system and managing pain and illness is called *pacing*. You can use this skill to resume a physical activity or hobby (*activity pacing*) or an academic activity (*academic pacing*), or even to return to school.

Some teens protect themselves from pain by resting, reducing activity, and staying home. This can last for an afternoon, a month, or more than a year. While this seems reasonable and understandable, resting for too long actually makes it harder to return to the activities you love. Motivation decreases, your body gets stiffer and less fit, your nervous system stays sensitive, and movement and activity become even more painful. The cycle of inactivity as a result of pain looks like this:

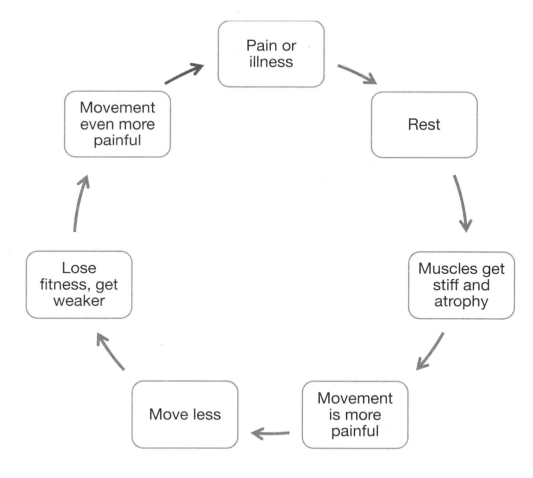

Figure 4. Pacing: inactivity and pain

On a low-pain day, some teens do the opposite. They're so excited to have less pain that they try to do as much as possible. They go for a run, play basketball, do as much homework as they can, then spend the rest of the day with friends. But what happens when you push yourself too hard?

Ugh. Pain. You may crash and not be able to get out of bed for hours or days. This cycle of intense overactivity and underactivity *decreases* your overall functionality. This is the dotted line you see in the diagram below. This boom-and-bust, up-and-down cycle actually results in less activity over time rather than more, because it wears out both your body and your resolve.

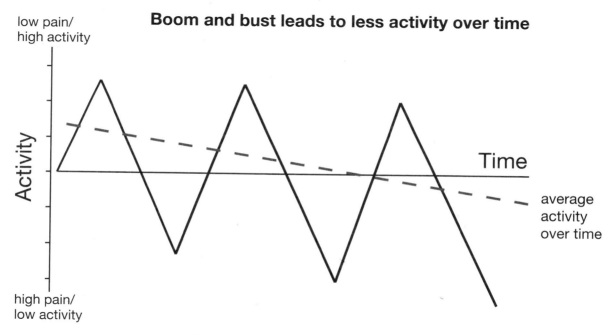

Figure 5. Pacing: boom and bust

One way to find a balance between doing too little and too much is to try *pacing*. When you pace yourself, you engage in a regular, daily level of activity somewhere between doing nothing (too little) and doing everything (waaay too much). This results in a gradual increase in activity and functioning over time.

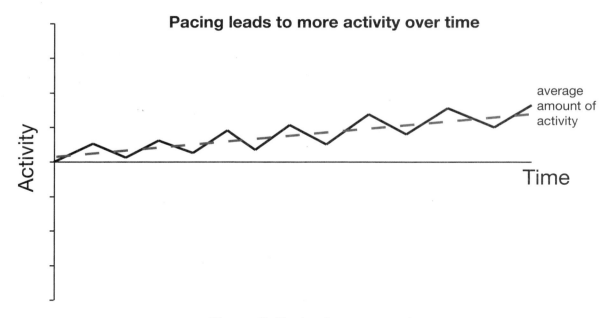

Figure 6. Pacing improvement

Pacing is like warming up an old car after it's been sitting outside in the winter snow for too long. The engine has become cold and clunky from disuse and needs to warm up before it can perform well. Your sluggish car can't drive cross-country the instant you turn it on! First it needs to warm up in the driveway, then do some practice laps around the block. Once the engine is warm and used to moving, it can go longer distances. This is true for you, too. Think of pacing as a way to warm up your brain and body.

Pacing = Brain- and body-warming

Even if you've been inactive for weeks or months, you can warm your brain and body starting today. *Now.* Pick any activity! You can pace to train for a sport or to restart your favorite hobby. You can pace to get back to Irish dance (hi, Lily!), soccer (hi, Jack!), even sewing (hi, Zoe!). Lily, Jack, and Zoe all used the pacing plan to return to activities they used to love before they got sick. It's real and it works!

Pacing Brainstorm

What activities are you willing to try this week? Circle some ideas:

audiobook	walk in a park	yoga
hike	math	trampoline
lift light weights	soccer	walk to the mailbox
basketball	dance	school
walk the dog	write	swim
ride a bike	run	build robots
read	jumping jacks	drive
trapeze	see friends	go grocery shopping
ballet	spelling	do homework

Add your own ideas for pacing:

_____

_____

_____

_____

Activity Pacing

The trick to pacing is to set realistic, measurable goals, and slowly work your way up to them—bit by bit. For this exercise, first check with your doctor to make sure pacing is right for you. Next, pick an activity you'd like to try but have been unable to do because of pain or illness. Then create a *pacing plan*.

Here's Dr. Z's example:

Step 1. Set a goal. Pick a physical activity you'd like to resume or try.

Hula-hooping!

Step 2. State your ultimate goal for this activity using specific measurements like time, duration, and frequency.

Hula-hoop for one hour daily, 7 days a week.

Step 3. Measure the length of time you can do this activity comfortably on a low-pain day, and then on a high-pain day.

On a low-pain day, I can hula-hoop for 20 minutes. On a high-pain day, I can hula-hoop for only 4 minutes.

Step 4. Calculate the average by adding these together, then dividing the total by two.

20 (low) + 4 (high) = 24 minutes (total)

24 (total) ÷ 2 = 12 minutes (average)

Step 5. Once you have an average amount of time you can do this activity, subtract a few minutes to give yourself a cushion. This will be your *daily baseline,* or the amount of time you do this activity every day—whether it's a high-pain day or a low-pain day.

12 minutes (average) – 2 minutes (cushion) = 10 minutes (daily baseline)

Step 6. Each week, add five or more minutes to your activity until you reach your ultimate goal. This is your weekly *activity increase.*

I will increase hooping by 5 minutes weekly until I reach my goal (one hour of hula-hooping, woo-hoo!). Next week, I'll hoop for 15 minutes, and the following week, I'll hoop for 20 minutes.

Daily baseline = Daily activity goal

Your *daily baseline* is the amount of time you should try this activity every day—on low-pain *and* high-pain days. Don't do more, and don't do less. This will prevent you from becoming inactive and also from overexerting yourself. Most importantly, it will help your brain desensitize. Over time, your brain will respond a little less to those loud, false-alarm warning messages you've been getting all the time, because you're slowly warming it up like an engine. It will unlearn the emergency response to harmless stimuli, like walking or hula-hooping, that make you *hurt* but don't cause *harm*. Your body will get used to moving; your muscles will get stronger and fitness will increase. You'll get better at tolerating whatever activities you choose, even on days when you feel sick or have some pain. That's the magic of pacing!

For example, I'll hula-hoop for ten minutes every day during week one, regardless of my pain level. There will be times I want to hoop more (on days I feel awesome), and times I want to stay in bed and not hoop at all (on days I feel terrible). But I'll use my pacing plan to accomplish ten minutes of activity every day, which will help my brain rewire and enable my body to get healthy and strong again.

Taking breaks is also an important part of pacing. If your pain starts increasing, rest for a few minutes. Drink water, take deep breaths, listen to music, stretch. It's also helpful to get support by asking someone to do this pacing activity with you! For example, if I'm having a tough high-pain day, I'll ask friends to hoop with me for company and cheer me on.

Now create your own activity pacing plan.

Step 1. Set a goal. Pick a physical activity you'd like to resume or try.

_____

Step 2. State your ultimate goal for this activity using specific measurements like time, duration, and frequency.

_____

_____

Step 3. Measure the length of time (in minutes) you can do this activity comfortably on a low-pain day, then on a high-pain day.

Low-pain day: _____

High-pain day: _____

Step 4. Calculate the average by adding these times together, then dividing the total by two.

Low pain _____ + high pain _____ = _____ (total)

Total _____ ÷ 2 = _____ (average)

Step 5. Once you have an average amount of time you can do that activity, subtract a few minutes to give yourself a cushion. This will be your daily baseline.

Average _____ – 2 minutes = _____ (daily baseline)

Step 6. Determine your weekly activity increase. Add five or more minutes to your activity each week until you reach your ultimate goal.

Your weekly activity increase: _____ minutes

Academic Pacing

Just as activity pacing can help you get moving again, *academic pacing* is a great strategy for increasing your ability to focus, think, and concentrate. If you haven't been able to do much academic work, use this pacing plan to warm up your great brain! As with activity pacing, start by setting a specific, measurable goal. Then track the length of time you can comfortably read, write, or go to class on easy and tough days. Establish your daily baseline, and start pacing. Here's how Dena paced:

> *Dena had chronic daily migraines that made her feel dizzy and foggy, making it hard to concentrate. She stopped going to school and couldn't do academic activities at home. She had piles of makeup work, and just thinking about it made her head feel worse. She decided to try academic pacing with the support*

of her parents, who agreed to reward her for each step she took toward resuming schoolwork.

Dena's ultimate goal was to complete all daily assigned reading. The amount of time she could read on a high-pain day was ten minutes. On a low-pain day, she could comfortably read for forty minutes. She completed her pacing worksheet and calculated a baseline reading time of twenty-three minutes.

Because difficult academic work triggered stress and made pain worse, Dena decided to start pacing using the Harry Potter series—pleasurable books she enjoyed. Each day, Dena set aside twenty-three minutes to read her fun, relaxing book. Every day she read, her parents rewarded her with points. They agreed that if she had ten or more points by the end of the week, she'd earn a gift card.

The first week, it was hard for Dena to get herself to read when she was in pain. But she was motivated by the gift card because she really wanted new audio speakers! Dena added ten minutes of reading each week, even though some days were really hard. By the month's end, she was reading two hours a day, taking hot-chocolate breaks as needed, and felt really proud. She slowly transitioned from pleasure reading to academic work, and within a month she was catching up in school.

Use this space to create your own academic pacing plan:

Step 1. Pick an academic activity you'd like to resume.

_____

Step 2. State your ultimate goal for this activity using specific measurements like time, duration, and frequency.

_____

_____

Step 3. Measure the length of time (in minutes) you can do this activity comfortably on a low-pain day, then on a high-pain day.

Low-pain day: _____

High-pain day: _____

Step 4. Calculate the average by adding these times together, then dividing the total by two.

Low pain _____ + high pain _____ = _____ (total)

Total _____ ÷ 2 = _____ (average)

Step 5. Once you have an average amount of time you can do this activity, subtract a few minutes to give yourself a cushion. This will be your daily baseline.

Average _____ − 2 minutes = _____ (daily baseline)

Reminder to do this academic activity every day—whether it's a high- or low-pain day. Make sure to take breaks: drink tea, go for a walk, pet your parrot!

Step 6. Each week, add five or more minutes to your activity until you reach your goal.

Your weekly activity increase: _____ minutes

Pacing to Resume School

If you've stopped attending school, you can pace to return. Find a point person at school, like a counselor or teacher, willing to help you coordinate a *school reentry plan*. To adjust to academic and social stimulation—and give yourself time to get used to people, activity, and mental exercise—pick one class that's a good starting point; for example, science, which starts at 12:00 p.m. and lasts for one hour. Make sure to identify a place where you can take short breaks and use coping skills, like the library or nurse's office. Your brain will start to adjust, because your brain is awesome. In a week or two, add in another class. Keep adding in classes until you're back full time! Here's how Charlie did it:

Charlie was in eighth grade when he was diagnosed with pancreatitis. It caused abdominal pain, vomiting, and nausea that prevented him from attending school. Even though medical treatment and dietary changes helped, he still experienced nausea and pain. After missing most of the year, he decided to try a school pacing plan. He felt nervous about going back—What if he was behind? What if his friends no longer wanted to hang out with him? What if his symptoms flared up in class?— but decided to try anyway.

His CBT therapist coordinated with his guidance counselor, and together they established a plan for Charlie's gradual return. To start, Charlie attended one class a day. It was English, his favorite, and he really liked the teacher. His CBT therapist taught him relaxation and imagery exercises to use in the mornings, which helped him feel calmer, eased his stomachaches, and turned down his pain dial. His grandpa gave him a stopwatch to hold in his pocket at all times to remind him that his family was always with him.

When Charlie returned to school, his friends immediately welcomed him back. No one teased him, and his teachers greeted him warmly. His stomach hurt, but he'd made a plan with the school nurse so he was able to rest in her office during flare-ups. By the second week, his body started adjusting and his abdominal pain was more manageable. He still hurt, but the breathing exercises and stopwatch helped. After a few weeks, Charlie felt confident enough to add in another class. School was stressful, but much less stressful than missing all of eighth grade!

YOU CAN DO IT!

Use Distractions to Lower Pain Volume

When you're absorbed in something fun, interesting, or distracting, you can some-times "forget" about your pain. Describe a time this happened to you:

_____

_____

_____

_____

_____

Developing Distraction Strategies

Distraction strategies manage pain by shifting attention away from it and onto something else. When you're distracted, your prefrontal cortex (the foremost part of your brain) sends a message to your pain dial, lowering pain volume. Distractions can be *cognitive* (for the mind, like brain teasers), *physical* (activities, tasks, sensations, movement), or *emotional*. Like Jax, you can combine various types of distraction strategies to manage your pain.

> *Jax struggled with Lyme disease. One Saturday, her friends got together to watch movies—but Jax was stuck in bed with a flare-up. Her friends texted her repeatedly to invite her over. She finally agreed, but became nervous in the car: What if her symptoms got worse after she left home? What if she was miserable and had to leave?*
>
> *Once Jax arrived and saw her friends' smiling faces, she felt more at ease. They lay on the floor together watching funny movies, laughing, and eating popcorn and M&Ms. When the movie ended, Jax realized she'd been so distracted by fun activities (movie watching, being with friends), enjoyable sensations (lying on the fuzzy carpet, crunching popcorn, melting chocolate on her tongue), and pleasant emotions (happiness, pleasure) that she hadn't thought about her symptoms for hours!*

DISTRACT USING ACTIVITIES

Make a list of favorite activities and pick one: go for a walk, create art, bounce a ball, cook a meal, play a game, go shopping, do something nice for someone (make a card for your mom or dad, call a grandparent!). What activities distract you?

_____

_____

_____

DISTRACT USING EMOTIONS

Read, watch, and listen to anything that generates pleasant emotions. If you're upset, watch a funny movie, listen to a comedian, or read a comic book. If you're bored, read an interesting magazine. If you're stressed, listen to calming music. Notice how your mood changes when you change the situation! How can you distract using emotions?

_____

_____

_____

DISTRACT USING BRAIN TEASERS

Engage your brain with tasks that take your mind off pain. Try Sudoku or a crossword puzzle. Solve a book of riddles. Count backward from two hundred by sevens, list the presidents, name the constellations in the starry sky. Work on a complicated math problem or jigsaw puzzle. What mental exercises distract you?

_____

_____

_____

DISTRACT USING YOUR FIVE SENSES

Use your five senses (sight, sound, taste, touch, and smell) to generate distracting sensations. Try cold or hot: apply ice to the back of your neck or give your feet a cold soak. Take a hot bath, light scented candles, listen to music, drink something cool and soothing. Go for a walk outside at dusk. Get a massage. Which senses can you use to distract?

_____

_____

_____

Distraction Brainstorm

Here's a list of distraction strategies assembled by teens coping with pain and illness, just like you. Think of activities like the ones below that don't center on screens (See: A Note About Screens). Check them off, cross them out, add your own! In chapter 4, you'll find descriptions for some you may not be familiar with—for example, diaphragmatic breathing, guided meditation, and body scans.

Take photos using a film camera.

Get fuzz therapy: scratch your cat or dog.

Do a crossword puzzle.

Cook or bake.

Read.

Draw.

Write a story and act it out.

Practice diaphragmatic breathing.

Walk or bike around the block.

Go to the library and borrow books.

Hike in nature.

Head to a destination: the pharmacy, library, or corner mailbox to mail a letter.

Get a donut from the corner café.

See how many push-ups and sit-ups you can do.

Listen to a guided meditation.

Try Sudoku.

Play a board game.

Build something: a house made of Legos, a pillow fort, a model airplane.

Write a letter to a grandparent, friend, or famous person.

Draw your family tree.

Make a list of the best Halloween costumes you've ever seen, and plan yours.

Video-chat with faraway family members.

Go to a dog park and befriend someone else's dog.

List goals you want to achieve someday.

Listen to an audiobook.

Organize one corner of your room.

Run an errand.

Do laundry to enjoy the feeling of warm clothes fresh out of the dryer.

Try a biofeedback app.

Taste a fruit or vegetable you've never heard of before. (What's a kumquat?)

Take a warm bath or cold shower.

Practice the body scan.

Try five-senses mindfulness.

Identify species of flowers, birds, and butterflies outside using nature guides.

Make leaf rubbings.

Learn all about primates like the slow loris.

Bounce a tennis ball against a wall.

Soak your feet in a bucket of ice water.

Try self-soothing.

Ask your parents how they met.

Look up after-school activities that sound interesting.

Color in a coloring book.

Research five places you'd like to visit.

Polish your nails (fingers and toes) or someone else's.

List animals that start with every letter of the alphabet (aardvark, bobcat, crocodile …).

Think of all the types of (1) dogs, (2) cars, (3) TV shows, (4) sports, or (5) movies you can come up with.

Make a list of favorites: color, animal, season, food, time of day, TV show, movie, author, athlete, book, actor, ice cream.…

Look up your favorite recipe, write out the ingredients, then make it.

Try guided imagery.

Stretch your muscles, one at a time.

Copy the words to a song, quote, or poem that make you feel good and tape it to your wall.

Make up a dance.

Learn to sew.

List things you're looking forward to this week.

Offer to do the dishes in exchange for chocolate.

Invite friends over for karaoke.

Make enough Rice Krispie treats to share with your neighbors.

Add your own ideas here:

_____

_____

_____

_____

A Note About Screens

Screens can be useful tools for pain management. However, too much screen time can be harmful. Screens keep you sedentary and still, which prevents you from effectively desensitizing your pain system. Brains needs exposure to real-life stimuli like people, activity, and sunlight to heal!

Screens are also bad for sleep: Their blue light reduces the amount of *melatonin* (a sleep hormone) your brain produces. This delays feelings of sleepiness, makes it hard to fall asleep, and disrupts your natural sleep cycle. Screens also stimulate your brain, providing sensory overload during a time when you should be helping your brain slow down. Lastly, screens activate—rather than quiet—your nervous system, causing excitation rather than calm. (See the section titled "Sleep Better to Feel Better.")

This doesn't mean you should avoid screens altogether; movies, TV, and video games can occasionally be great distractions. Limit screen time to two to three hours a day, and brainstorm other, nonscreen activities that also reduce pain volume, like those on your distraction list!

Soothe Your Senses

Another great pain coping strategy is *self-soothing*. When you self-soothe, you comfort, take care of, and are kind to yourself, and teach your brain that your body is safe. This turns down the volume on pain. A great way to do this is to consider how to soothe each of your five senses: sight, sound, taste, touch, smell. Combine these to make a self-soothing plan for tough days.

Sight: Walk in nature—the woods, the beach, a nearby park. Notice everything around you. Paint. Draw. Print pictures of the ocean and hang them on your wall. Pick flowers for your room. Sit in a garden and watch butterflies. Watch your favorite movie. Drive to a lookout and admire the view. What are your favorite things to look at?

_____

_____

Sound: Listen to calm, soothing music. Listen to nature sounds, like rain, a water-fall, or your cat purring. Download a white-noise app. Listen to an orchestra and pick out the instruments. What are your favorite sounds?

_____

_____

Smell: Notice different smells around you. Light a scented candle or incense. Take showers with fragrant soap. Take walks in the woods, breathing the smells of nature. Smell dinner cooking and identify each scent. Visit a cosmetics store and sample perfumes. Bake cookies! What are the most soothing smells?

_____

_____

Taste: Make "comfort food" or a favorite meal, and notice how it soothes you. Eat slowly, savoring each bite. Notice temperature and textures. Drink a mug of hot tea. Crunch on ice, drink a cold glass of lemonade. What are the most soothing things to taste?

_____

_____

Touch: Notice textures and temperatures on your skin. Take warm bubble baths. Pet your dog or cat for fuzz therapy. Hold someone's hand. Pop bubble wrap. Put on your favorite pajamas or your dad's sweatshirt. Wrap yourself in fuzzy blankets. What are the most comforting things to touch?

_____

_____

Put all these together to make a self-soothing plan for tough pain days. A good self-soothing plan, like Juliana's, incorporates all five of your senses to maximally soothe your brain and body.

Juliana was having a tough pain day, and her whole body hurt. To soothe, she made a plan using each of her five senses. She ran hot water for a bath (touch). She used a "bath bomb," which releases a scent, bubbles, fizzes, and turns the water pink (smell, sight). She gathered colorful magazines with pictures and distracting stories (sight). She poured a tall glass of iced tea because she liked contrasting hot water on her skin with a cold drink (taste, touch). She played her favorite playlist (sound). As Juliana sank into the bath, she focused on her soothed senses. For the entire hour she was in the bath, she felt relaxed and peaceful. When she got out, Juliana said to her mom, "I feel like a new person!"

Write your own five-senses self-soothing plan here:

_____

_____

_____

_____

_____

_____

Improve Your Mood with Pleasurable Activities

Living with pain or illness can mean giving up things you love, like fun hobbies and activities. But this only makes you feel worse, because you experience less pleasure. When you have pain, it's even *more* important to schedule activities that give you joy! Every minute you're engaged in a pleasurable activity is a minute you're less stressed, sad, and focused on pain. Pleasurable activities raise your mood to turn the volume down on pain.

What are some activities that give you pleasure? (Circle any that apply and add your own.)

cooking	drawing	playing drums
karate	going out with friends	camping
kite flying	designing clothes	going to concerts
singing	acting in plays	hoverboarding
shoe shopping	ballroom dance	horseback riding
going to the zoo	tennis	_____
fishing	swimming	_____
bubble baths	making pottery	_____
volleyball	baking bread	_____

Integrate pleasurable activities into daily life so that you make sure to do something enjoyable every single day! This is *especially* important on days you have pain.

Schedule one pleasurable activity every day this week:

Monday: _____

Tuesday: _____

Wednesday: _____

Thursday: _____

Friday: _____

Saturday: _____

Sunday: _____

Conclusion

Pain and illness can keep you sedentary and miserable. One way to fight back is to set goals, work backward, and pace to resume doing things you love. Coping strategies help turn down pain volume by distracting and soothing your (always connected!) brain and body. In this next chapter, you'll learn mind-body skills like mindfulness, biofeedback, and relaxation strategies to help manage your symptoms.

Chapter 4

Mind-Body Skills

Your Head Is Connected to Your Body!

There's no getting around it: your brain and body are connected 100 percent of the time. Pain and illness trigger stress. Stress activates your sympathetic nervous system (SNS), sensitizes your nervous system, turns up the pain dial, and causes more pain. *Mind-body techniques* teach you to use the power of your mind to turn off your SNS and take charge of pain. Research shows that these strategies, which include biofeedback, mindfulness, relaxation, and imagery, can decrease pain frequency and intensity, increase control over physical symptoms, reduce negative emotions like sadness and anxiety, and increase quality of life. Mind-body techniques help you alter major bodily functions, like heart rate, muscle tension, respiration, skin temperature, immune functioning, and pain. Imagine the power you'd possess if you could control your body with your mind!

Biofeedback: Hand Warming

As evidence that your mind affects body processes, biofeedback can teach you to make fireballs with your hands! *Biofeedback* is a scientifically supported pain-management technique in which we use feedback from our biological systems to modify formerly unconscious processes like heart rate, muscle tension, skin temperature, and pain.

We don't normally think of body temperature as something we control: if we're cold, we raise the thermostat or put on a sweater. But not after today! *Hand warming* is a biofeedback technique in which you use your mind to control your temperature. The science is this: Pain triggers stress, which triggers the fight-or-flight response. This response pulls blood away from extremities (hands, feet) and into your body's core. Typically, the more stressed you are, the cooler your extremities. The more relaxed you are, the warmer your extremities. Relaxation turns off fight-or-flight, increasing blood flow to your hands. And guess what blood carries? Blood carries heat. Congratulations, you're about to make fireballs with your hands!

How to do it:

Set aside ten to fifteen minutes for this activity. You can download a recording of this exercise at http://www.newharbinger.com/33522 or have someone read this to you.

For this activity, you'll need a "stress thermometer" to hold between your thumb and pointer finger to provide feedback about skin temperature. This is different from a fever thermometer. You can get one on Amazon, bio-medical.com, or stress-stop.com.

Before starting, hold the thermometer between your thumb and pointer finger to measure baseline (starting) finger temperature.

Record that here: _____

Now check in with your body and emotions:

Stress or anxiety rating (0 = none, 5 = moderate, 10 = extreme): _____

Pain rating (0 = none, 5 = moderate, 10 = severe): _____

Find a quiet place where you won't be disturbed. Turn off your screens or put them away. Lie or sit somewhere comfortable and quiet, like a couch or floor. Uncross your arms and legs, and close your eyes. Let your hands hang down by your sides. Hold the thermometer between your thumb and index finger throughout this exercise.

Take several deep breaths into your belly: inhale and feel your belly rise as it fills with air. Exhale and feel your body relax.

Clench your fists and pull them toward your shoulders, squeezing your biceps. Squeeze tightly for a slow count of ten. Let your arms hang loose, and let your body relax. Next squeeze your legs, thighs, calves, and ankles together for a count of ten...squeeze harder... then let your body relax.

Bring your attention to the top of your head. Sense into your face and let your facial muscles relax. Release your jaw and let it hang open.

Sense into your chest, heart, and lungs. Let your breath be slooow. Notice your pulse; feel your heart pumping blood around your body. Slow your heart rate by repeating to yourself, My heart is slow and regular. Sense into your neck and shoulders. Let your shoulders drop as if gravity is pulling them down. Let your arms be limp, loose, warm, and relaxed.

Imagine hollow tubes inside your arms, connecting the tops of your shoulders to the tips of your fingers. Imagine hot air flowing inside these tubes from the tops of your shoulders, past your elbows, into your forearms, your wrists, into the palms of your hands. Feel the hot air pooling in the tips of your fingers. Feel your fingers getting warmer and warmer. Imagine they're getting red and hot. Each time you exhale, imagine hot air flowing down into your hands.

Now imagine hot soup flowing inside your arms. Imagine this steaming hot soup flowing down from your shoulders, past your elbows, into your forearms, the palms of your hands, into the tips of your fingers. Feel your fingertips getting hotter and hotter as they fill with hot soup. Imagine the capillaries and blood vessels in your fingers expanding as your hands get hotter and hotter. Repeat to yourself, My arms are heavy and warm...my hands are heavy and warm. Let the blood flow into your hands. Feel the heat in your fingertips. Feel your hands throbbing and tingling as they get warmer and warmer.

Now imagine holding your hands over a campfire. Picture the fire's orange flames, the smell of burning wood. Hold your hands over the fire and feel the heat. As your hands and finger-tips get hotter and hotter, feel them tingle and throb. Notice your palms sweating. Feel the flame on your hands until they seem to be red, glowing with heat.

When you're ready, slowly bring your attention back to the room around you, open your eyes, and look at the thermometer. Look at the insides of your hands and press them to your face. Notice if they're warmer, redder, and sweatier than usual.

Your check-in:

Record your new finger temperature here: _____

Check in with your body and emotions:

New stress or anxiety rating (0 = none, 5 = moderate, 10 = extreme): _____

New pain rating (0 = none, 5 = moderate, 10 = severe): _____

What did you notice and how did you feel? Include any temperature changes.

_____

_____

_____

Behold the power of your mind! If your mind can heat your hands, what could it do to your pain?

_____

_____

_____

If you don't notice a significant change the first few times, fear not; like any skill, hand warming takes time and persistence. Try it every day and see how hot you can make your hands!

Mindfulness

Mindfulness is the quality or state of being present, attuned, and self-aware. Mindfulness techniques have become an integral part of many pain treatments. For example, mindfulness-based stress reduction (MBSR) is a scientifically supported treatment for chronic pain that uses mindfulness and relaxation strategies to calm the mind, relax the body, and lower pain volume. Research shows that regular mindfulness practice also improves concentration and sleep, decreases distress and disability, increases ability to manage and cope with pain, and can improve quality of life.

When we are mindful, we use our "attention muscle" to focus on what's happening inside us and around us in the present moment without judging anything as "good" or "bad." Mindfulness emphasizes noticing things exactly as they are, without trying to push them away or change them. Consider this: Our minds tend to drift backward into the past: *I shouldn't have done that!* Or, *Why'd I say that? That was so stupid!* Thinking about the past is stressful, because these things have already happened and we can't do much about them. Our minds also tend to shoot forward into the future: *What's going to happen to me? What if I never get better? Will I get into college?* Thinking about the future is anxiety provoking because we can't predict or control it, no matter how hard we try. This stress only makes us feel worse.

Mindfulness is the muscle we use to pull our attention from the past (what's behind us) and from the future (what's in front of us) back into the present moment. *Just right here.* Because chances are, you can handle Just Right Here. Here you are, sitting in a chair, reading this book. And you are okay!

In this chapter, you'll learn a variety of mindfulness and relaxation strategies, including watching the breath, belly breathing, body scan, and five-senses mindfulness to help rewire your pain system and lower pain volume. You'll check on stress and pain levels before and after each exercise. If the levels don't change right away, don't worry—change comes with time, repetition, and practice!

Watching the Breath

One effective way to pull your mind from the past and future into the present moment is to focus on your breath. Your breath is always with you. It is constant and calming, like waves in the sea. Focusing on your breath pulls your attention into your body, so that you can focus on the here and now.

How to do it:

Set aside five minutes for this activity. You can download a recording of this mindfulness exercise at http://www.newharbinger.com/33522 or have someone read it to you.

Before you start, check in with your body and emotions:

Stress or anxiety rating (0 = none, 5 = moderate, 10 = extreme): _____

Pain rating (0 = none, 5 = moderate, 10 = severe): _____

Find a quiet place where you won't be disturbed. Turn off your screens or put them away. Lie or sit somewhere comfortable and quiet, like a couch or floor. Uncross your arms and legs, close your eyes, and listen.

Imagine that your attention is a spotlight and you can control where it shines.

Shine that spotlight on your breath as it comes in through your nose.

Examine this in-breath with curiosity, as if you've never noticed how air feels before.

Without any judgment, feel the air tickle the inside of your nose.

Notice whether the air is warm or cool.

On your next in-breath, notice how the air feels traveling down into your lungs.

Feel your lungs expand and stretch as air comes into your body. Notice how your chest rises.

Hold your breath for a moment, noticing how it feels.

Notice the urge to release your breath.

Now slooowly exhale, feeling your lungs relax and your chest fall gently as the air leaves your body.

Notice the sound of your out-breath.

Notice the muscles in your body relax as you exhale.

Feel the air exit your nose; notice how it tickles the inside of your nose.

Notice whether the air is warm or cool.

No need to do or change anything: just notice how your body feels when you breathe.

Now bring that spotlight of attention to your ears.

Notice, in this quiet moment, what sounds you can hear. Try not to judge sounds as good or bad—just observe and report, like a forecaster reporting the weather.

If your mind starts to wander, that's okay. Simply bring that spotlight of attention back to your breath.

That's it! You did it! By paying attention to your breath and body in this moment, you practiced mindfulness.

Check in with your body and emotions:

New stress or anxiety rating (0 = none, 5 = moderate, 10 = extreme): _____

New pain rating (0 = none, 5 = moderate, 10 = severe): _____

What did you notice and how did you feel (emotionally and physically)?

_____

_____

_____

_____

_____

When and where can you practice mindfulness at school? At home?

(Example: *At school I can practice in the nurse's office at lunch; at home I can practice in my living room after dinner.*)

_____

_____

_____

While mindfulness is something we *do,* it also affects how we *feel* and *think,* which can break the pain cycle. The mindfulness muscle gets bigger and stronger the more you use it. Try exercising it once a day and see how skilled you get!

Five-Senses Mindfulness

Another way to practice mindfulness is to use your five senses to tune in to the present moment. This exercise increases joy and pleasure, alters attention, decreases stress and frustration, and promotes relaxation.

How to do it:

Set aside ten minutes for this activity.

Check in with your body and emotions:

Stress or anxiety level (0 = none, 5 = moderate, 10 = extreme): _____

Pain rating (0 = none, 5 = moderate, 10 = severe): _____

Select a piece of fruit from your kitchen (you'll need it for "taste") and go outside. Find a spot in your yard or a park where you won't be disturbed. Leave your screens inside or turn them off.

Focus on the nature around you. Let your breathing be slow and calm.

See: *Use your eyes to scan your surroundings. Notice shapes, shadows, and textures. Notice colors: green, white, yellow. How many different flowers and trees do you see? Look up at the sky and describe its color; notice the clouds. Where is the sun? Without any judgment, describe everything you see.*

_____

_____

Listen: *Close your eyes, tune in to your ears, and notice everything you hear. Tune in to the sound of the wind in the trees, the birds singing. Notice cars in the distance, dogs barking, and children playing. What can you hear?*

_____

_____

Touch: *Rub your fingers along different surfaces and textures. Touch a leaf, flower petal, tree trunk, park bench. Try to find different textures—smooth, rough, bumpy, cold, warm— and describe them. Feel the sun on your skin and breeze in your hair. Take a step and notice your feet in your shoes. What do you feel?*

_____

_____

Smell: *Breathe deeply. Notice everything you smell. Find a fragrant plant or tree, smell a flower. Rub a blade of grass between your fingers. Tune in to a scent you didn't notice before. What can you smell?*

_____

_____

Taste: *Examine the fruit you took outside. Imagine you're a space alien eating fruit for the first time. Before chewing, notice what it looks like, smells like, and feels like on your tongue. Is it cool, smooth, bumpy? Feel your mouth start to salivate. Slowly bite down, noticing the pressure of your teeth on the fruit. Taste it on your tongue, feel the texture in your mouth. Focus all your attention just on your senses. What can you taste?*

_____

_____

Check in with your body and emotions:

New stress or anxiety level (0 = none, 5 = moderate, 10 = extreme): _____

New pain rating (0 = none, 5 = moderate, 10 = severe): _____

What did you notice and how did you feel (emotionally and physically)?

_____

_____

_____

Anytime you are feeling stressed or having a flare-up, tune into your five senses to distract, calm, be mindful, and turn down pain volume!

Relaxation Strategies

Even if you don't feel stressed right now, pain and illness place tremendous stress on your body. *Relaxation strategies*, central to CBT and MBSR, teach you to slow your heart; decrease muscle tension; increase blood flow for faster healing; help you feel more in control of your body; and lower the pain dial to quiet pain signals. They also give you greater capacity to cope with pain.

Belly Breathing

Relaxation strategies often start with *diaphragmatic*, or *belly*, *breathing*. Your *diaphragm* is a muscle just below your ribs that contracts and expands when you breathe. Most of us tend to chest breathe, especially when we're sick or in pain. This stressed, shallow chest breathing provides less oxygen to your brain and can make you dizzy, light-headed, or faint. Test to see if you're chest breathing by putting a hand on your chest and see if it rises when you inhale.

In contrast, relaxed belly breathing uses your diaphragm and stomach muscles. When you belly breathe, you train your breath to go lower and slower, which increases your blood oxygen level, improves circulation to facilitate healing, turns off your SNS to calm your body, and helps reduce pain volume.

How to do it:

Set aside five minutes for this activity. You can download a recording of this exercise at http://www.newharbinger.com/33522 or ask someone to read it to you.

Check in with your body and emotions:

Stress or anxiety level (0 = none, 5 = moderate, 10 = extreme): _____

Pain rating (0 = none, 5 = moderate, 10 = severe): _____

Find a quiet place where you won't be disturbed. Turn off your screens or put them away. Set an alarm for five minutes. Lie or sit somewhere comfortable and quiet, like a couch or the floor. Uncross your arms and legs, and close your eyes. Place one hand on your belly and the other hand on your chest.

Focus the spotlight of attention on your breath.

Remind yourself that, in this moment, you have nowhere else to be and nothing else to do.

Take a slow, deep breath in.

Notice how the air feels at your nose. Notice whether it's warm or cool, and how it feels going down into your lungs.

On your next inhale, send the breath down into your belly. If the hand on your chest moves, send the air lower, into your belly.

As you breathe in, feel your belly expand as if it's a balloon. Feel the hand on your belly rise.

Hold your breath for a moment, and notice your belly, full of air. Notice the urge to exhale.

Then release the breath slooowly. As you exhale, let your shoulders drop and your back relax. Feel your stomach muscles relax. Notice your hand lowering as the air leaves your belly. Feel the air exit your nose and notice whether it's warm or cool.

Take another breath in. Focus all your attention just on your breath. Let your breathing be low and slow.

With each in-breath, send the air all the way down into your belly. With each out-breath, say "relax" to yourself and imagine all the tension draining out of your body.

Do this until the timer rings. If your mind wanders, simply bring the spotlight of attention back to your breath.

Check in with your body and emotions:

New stress or anxiety rating (0 = none, 5 = moderate, 10 = extreme): _____

New pain rating (0 = none, 5 = moderate, 10 = severe): _____

What did you notice about your body? Your emotions?

_____

_____

_____

Body Scan

The body scan is another pain-control technique that combines mindfulness, relaxation, and *somatic* (body) awareness to help you manage pain. It helps redirect attention, tunes you in to physical and emotional stress, and releases any tension you might be holding.

How to do it:

This activity takes only a few minutes, and you can make it as long or short as you like. You can download a recording of this exercise at http://www.newharbinger. com/33522 or have someone read it to you.

Check in with your body and emotions:

Stress or anxiety level (0 = none, 5 = moderate, 10 = extreme): _____

Pain rating (0 = none, 5 = moderate, 10 = severe): _____

Find a quiet place where you won't be disturbed. Turn off your screens or put them away. Set an alarm for five to ten minutes. Lie somewhere comfortable and quiet, like a couch or the floor. Use a blanket to keep your body warm. Uncross your arms and legs, and close your eyes.

Place one hand on your chest and the other on your belly.

Take in a slow, deep belly breath.

Focus your spotlight of attention on the air as it travels through your nose.

Notice whether the air is warm or cool, how it tickles the inside of your nose.

Send the air down into your belly. Feel your belly expand like a balloon; feel the hand on your belly rise. Hold the breath for a moment. When you exhale, release the breath slooowly. Feel the air at your nose as you breathe out, and notice whether it's warm or cool. Focus all your attention on your belly breaths.

Now send your attention down to your feet. Without moving them, feel your feet in your shoes. Notice the fabric of your socks on your skin. Feel your heels touching the couch or floor. Notice whether your feet are warm or cool. If there's any tension in your feet, let that tension go.

Sense up into your ankles, shins, and calf muscles. Feel the backs of your calves on the couch or floor. Feel the fabric of your pants on your skin. Notice whether your shins are warm or cool. If there's any tension in your lower legs, shins, or calves, let that tension go.

Sense into your upper legs, thighs, quads, and hamstrings. Feel the fabric of your pants on your legs. Notice the backs of your thighs on the couch or floor. Notice whether your upper legs are warm or cool. If there's any tension in your thighs, quads, or hamstrings, let that tension go. Let your legs be heavy…limp…loose…and relaxed. Imagine they're melting into the floor.

Sense into your hips and up into your belly. Feel your hand resting on your belly, and notice warmth there. Feel your belly fill with air as you breathe in…feel your stomach muscles relax as you slowly breathe out. Sense into your stomach and notice whether you're hungry or full, if your stomach is making any sounds. Without judgment, observe your belly. If there's any tension in your stomach or intestines, see if you can let that tension go. Allow your stomach and intestines to completely relax and unwind.

Sense into your chest, heart, and lungs. Notice your pulse as your heart pumps blood around your body. Feel your warm hand on your chest. Notice your lungs expand when you breathe in, and relax when you breathe out. If there's any tension in your chest, heart, or lungs, see if you can let that tension go.

Send your attention to your shoulders. Let your shoulders slump, as if gravity is pulling them down. Sense into your arms, noticing whether they're warm or cool. Feel the fabric of your shirt on your skin. Let relaxation flow from the top of your shoulders, through your elbows, into your forearms, wrists, hands, all the way into your palms and fingertips. Feel your warm hands on your chest and belly. If there's any tension in your shoulders, arms, hands, or fingers, let that tension go. Let your arms be heavy…limp…loose…and relaxed.

Sense into your back. Notice your upper back, middle back, lower back. Feel the fabric of your shirt on your skin. Feel the couch or floor against your back, noticing how you're supported. Notice whether your back is warm or cool. If there's any tension in your upper, middle, or lower back, let that tension go. Let the muscles in your back just relax.

Send your attention up your neck and around to the back of your head. Feel your head supported by the couch or floor. Notice where your head touches the pillow; feel your hair on your neck and scalp. Notice whether your neck and head are warm or cool. If there's any tension in your neck or head, let that tension go. Allow your neck and head to feel heavy and relaxed.

Send your attention to the muscles of your face. Notice your facial expression. Sense into your forehead, temples, eyebrows. Feel your eyes behind your eyelids. Sense into your cheeks and jaw muscles, and let your jaw hang open as it relaxes. Sense into your mouth and notice your tongue. If there's any tension anywhere in your face, let that tension go. Let all the muscles be limp, loose, and relaxed.

Sense into your ears and notice everything you can hear. Silently list the sounds in your environment without any judgment. What can you hear? If you start thinking about other things, gently bring your attention back to your ears.

Now do a full scan of your body, from the top of your head, down to your neck, chest and back, down your shoulders and arms, your stomach and hips, your legs, past your knees, all the way down to your toes. Let your whole body be heavy, warm, loose, and relaxed. Notice how safe you feel. This is your safe, relaxed place. You can come back here whenever you choose.

Now, with eyes still closed, picture the room you're in. Wiggle your fingers and toes, and when you're ready, slowly open your eyes.

Check in with your body and emotions:

New stress or anxiety rating (0 = none, 5 = moderate, 10 = extreme): _____

New pain rating (0 = none, 5 = moderate, 10 = severe): _____

What did you notice (physically and emotionally)? Were there any surprising sensations or sounds? Where did you discover tension?

_____

_____

_____

Pocket Relaxation

Now that you know how to relax both mind and body, here's a one-minute "pocket" relaxation to take with you wherever you go. Carry it in your pocket to use in class, the nurse's office, the dentist's chair, when you're stuck in traffic, or anytime you have a pain flare-up. No one needs to know you're doing it. It will help you catch stress, pain, and tension before they get too intense, and takes only a minute to do.

How to do it:

Find a place for a private time-out, or simply stay where you are. Close your eyes if that feels comfortable, and put one hand on your belly. Take a deep belly breath. Hold it for a few seconds, feel it in your body. Now slooowly exhale, and say "relax" to yourself. Let your whole body relax: the top of your head…face…neck and shoulders…arms…hands…back… around to your chest and stomach…hips and legs…knees…all the way down to your toes. Let your body get limp, heavy, and loose, like a wet noodle. Imagine stress and pain draining out of your body like a liquid, flowing out your feet and down into the ground. Hold that relaxed feeling, and slowly count to twenty. When you are feeling calm, slowly open your eyes.

Remember—the more you use this skill, the better you get at it! Try it a few times a day and see how you feel.

Here's David's story:

David has a painful dermatological condition that follows him around all day. Sometimes he's so uncomfortable at school that he can't sit in his chair. When David has a flare-up, his teacher gives him permission to go to the nurse's office. He brings along headphones so he can listen to relaxation and mindfulness apps to turn down pain volume. Some days, he needs to use pain-control techniques in the classroom. When this happens, David closes his eyes and uses his mind to scan his whole body, head to toe, and relax any tense muscles. He imagines stress flowing out of his body like black ink, sinking down into the ground. This helps him soothe, feel more in control of pain, and brings his attention back to class.

Write down your own ideas for using pocket relaxation:

(Examples: *At my brother's hockey game; before a test; while watching TV*)

_____

_____

Imagery

Another great mind-body technique is called *imagery*. Imagery allows you to use mental images to see, smell, hear, feel, and taste things that exist only in your mind—as with dreams and memories. In fact, every time you've daydreamed in a boring class, had a scary nightmare, or fantasized about what prom might be like, you've used imagery!

Amazingly, research shows that you use the same parts of your brain when *imagining* pain as you do when actually experiencing pain. If your brain believes you need protection—even if the danger is imagined—it will produce pain. Mental images also control physiological responses, so if you remember or imagine a stressful or painful event, your body will initiate a stress response. For example, vividly imagining or remembering a terrifying car crash triggers an emergency response: adrenaline pours into your bloodstream, your muscles contract, your heart rate increases, and your pupils dilate. If you remember or imagine pain, you may even feel physical pain.

On the other hand, if you imagine feeling safe, content and calm, and let your body relax, pain volume will decrease. In the exercises that follow, you'll use images to control your pain dial.

Safe-Place Imagery

Have you ever noticed that certain environments (like the dentist's office) make you feel stressed, while other environments (like a beautiful beach) make you feel calm? Well, you don't need to go to the beach to achieve calm: your brain can transport you to peaceful environments just by using imagery. In this exercise, you'll use your five senses to help your mind travel to a safe, relaxing place. This technique teaches your brain that your body is safe and facilitates relaxation to turn the volume down on pain.

How to do it:

Set aside ten to fifteen minutes for this activity. You can download a recording to listen to at http://www.newharbinger.com/33522 or have someone read it to you.

Check in with your body and emotions:

Stress or anxiety level (0 = none, 5 = moderate, 10 = extreme): _____

Pain rating (0 = none, 5 = moderate, 10 = severe): _____

Find a quiet place to sit or lie down. Turn off your screens or put them away, and close your eyes.

Take a few slow, deep, belly breaths. Imagine a safe, relaxing place, preferably in nature, that you've visited or made up. This safe place can be a beach, a trail in the woods, a mountain cabin, even your grandma's house—as long as it makes you feel safe and relaxed. Picture this place and use your five senses to complete the imagery activity below. Use the example to guide you.

Dr. Z's example:

My safe, relaxing place is a beautiful beach in Mexico.

Sight: I'm standing on a beautiful stretch of beach in Mexico. As I look around, I see colorful beach umbrellas, twinkling seashells, and the ocean stretching as far as the eye can see. The water is a peaceful, dark blue and the sand is golden-white. Waves lap gently at my feet, which are buried in the warm sand. Green palm trees with clusters of coconuts line the shore. The sun is setting, and the sky is filled with brilliant colors—orange, purple, magenta—as seagulls circle overhead.

Sound: I close my eyes and hear the sounds of wind and water. I hear boats rocking, kids splashing, waves crashing, people laughing. I notice seagulls calling and palm trees rustling in the warm breeze.

Smell: I inhale the scents of the beach. I smell salt water, seaweed, warm sand, and the faint scent of sunblock on my skin.

Touch: I notice the warm, wet sand between my toes and the cool ocean water lapping against my ankles. I feel the sun warming my skin and the breeze in my hair. I notice the feeling of my clothes on my skin—my wet bathing suit, my dry sundress.

Taste: I taste the saltiness of seawater. I imagine drinking a cold glass of lemonade on this hot, relaxing day, and feel the cool liquid going down my throat.

Your example:

Your safe, relaxing place is: _____

Look around your safe place. Notice the shapes, colors, textures. Describe the time of day, and who is there with you. Notice the sky and clouds. Is the sun setting or is it morning? Describe everything you see:

_____

_____

_____

_____

Describe everything you hear:

_____

_____

_____

_____

What can you smell?

_____

_____

_____

What can you feel? Notice textures, temperatures and touch:

_____

_____

_____

_____

What can you taste?

_____

_____

_____

_____

After describing this safe place, let yourself really be here. Completely relax into the scene. If thoughts drift into your head, that's okay—just bring your attention back to this place. You carry this relaxing place with you wherever you go. You can come back anytime you choose, whether at school or in the doctor's office!

When you have completed this activity, slowly bring your attention back to the room you're in. Check in again with your body and emotions, and notice any changes:

New stress or anxiety level (0 = none, 5 = moderate, 10 = extreme): _____

New pain rating (0 = none, 5 = moderate, 10 = severe): _____

What did you notice as you did this activity?

_____

_____

_____

This is a great activity to use if you're having trouble falling asleep. Sleeping is always easier when you feel safe and relaxed!

Self-Healing Imagery

Just as your brain can transform environments outside your body using imagery—from a boring bedroom to a Mexican beach—it can also transform the environment inside your body. Have you ever woken up panting and sweaty from a nightmare, your heart pounding? It was just your imagination, but your body reacted with genuine fear, as if the threat was real. An effective mind-body technique to change your pain response is called *self-healing imagery*, which uses the power of your imagination.

Try this: *Imagine holding a grapefruit. Feel the cool, round shape of the fruit in your palm. Imagine cutting it in half and inhaling the citrus scent. Squeeze the tart, pink juice into a glass and raise it to your mouth. Take a big mouthful of grapefruit juice. Inhale the smell, feel the tangy taste and texture on your tongue, feel the bittersweet juice in your mouth as you swallow.*

Is your mouth watering as if the experience is real? This happens because of the powerful connection between your imagination (your mind) and your body. Your body responds to the thoughts and images in your head. If you frequently imagine or remember pain, medical procedures, and other stressful events, your nervous system will prepare for an emergency by keeping you in a perpetual state of fight-or-flight. This turns *up* the pain dial, boosting pain volume. However, taking control of the images in your brain, and creating safe, calming images, lowers your stress—and turns the pain dial *down*.

How to do it:

This next imagery technique requires some assistance and creativity. It can be incredibly effective if you're willing to play along. To transform your pain, first read Glenn's examples that follow each step—as well as Karen's and Erik's, which follow immediately after the activity—so that you understand how this technique works. Then ask someone you trust to read the steps to you and ask you the questions listed.

Set aside fifteen minutes for this activity. You can download this exercise at http://www.newharbinger.com/33522 .

Lie down in a quiet place where you won't be interrupted. Turn off your screens or put them away, and close your eyes.

Take a few deep belly breaths, then slowly exhale. Belly breathe for a few minutes until your body starts to relax.

Step 1. *Travel inside your body now, into the place where you hurt, and focus all your attention on the pain. Notice the color, size, shape, and texture of the pain. Notice if it's dark or bright, heavy or light, hot or cool, thick or thin, solid or liquid, static or moving. Try to describe everything you notice about your pain.*

Glenn's pain image: Glenn's pain covers an extensive area of his leg. The most intense area of pain is his knee. This pain is in the shape of a pointy spear tip. It is hot, orange-red, and sharp. When Glenn closes his eyes and senses into his leg, the pain feels like a hot orange liquid, like lava from a volcano oozing outwards in a circle.

What does your pain look like? Describe its color, temperature, size, shape, texture, and movement.

_____

_____

_____

_____

This is your *pain image.*

Step 2. *Now imagine this part of your body without any pain. When this part of you is pain-free, what does it look like? What color, temperature, size, shape, weight and texture is it? Is it moving or static?*

Glenn's pain-free image: Without any pain, Glenn imagines that his knee is a cool wintry blue and smooth. The skin around the spearhead is cool and pale. It is solid and doesn't move. The circle of pain in his leg is shrunken and small.

Your pain-free image:

_____

_____

_____

_____

Step 3. *Imagine you can use magic to transform your pain. What magical process does your body need to transform the pain image into the pain-free image? Whatever you need to do to change your pain, imagine you can do it! This process can involve a change in color, temperature, size, shape, weight, speed, substance, or texture. You can imagine doing anything to your pain: turn it from orange to blue; cool, heat, or melt it; shrink or grow it; give it a blast of warm sunlight, icy wind, a deep massage, or a gentle touch; slow it down or speed it up; melt it or harden it; shave off parts or change its shape; change the texture or give it padding.*

Glenn's transformational process: To transform his pain from one state to the other, Glenn sends an icy cold waterfall down the inside of his knee. He imagines bathing his fiery orange pain in cascade of soothing, icy-blue water until he can feel his circle of pain shrinking and cooling. Since his pain image is sharp and pointed, he imagines the water wearing down the spear until it softens and smooths.

Your transformational process:

_____

_____

_____

_____

With your eyes still closed, imagine this self-healing process is actually working. Send the part of your body that hurts this magical healing process, and picture the pain changing. Imagine you are transforming your pain.

Slowly bring your attention back to the room. Before sitting up, do a check in: What did you notice changing as you did this activity (color, temperature, size, pain intensity)? How did your body feel?

_____

_____

_____

_____

Check in with your body and emotions:

New stress or anxiety level (0 = none, 5 = moderate, 10 = extreme): _____

New pain rating (0 = none, 5 = moderate, 10 = severe): _____

Try this imagery technique anew each time you have a pain episode. Pain is always changing! Try not to rely on old pain images or memories to inform your current experience—instead look inside each time.

Karen's example: *Karen's pain is a migraine. The pain is a thick, black, oozing fluid that clogs her head between her eyes and makes it throb at the temples. This painful metallic fluid is filled with sharp barbs that prick the inside of her skull.*

When Karen imagines her head pain-free, it is shiny, white, and clear, like an empty glass without any fluid. The texture is smooth and has no barbs. Her head feels light rather than heavy.

To transform her pain, Karen vividly imagines two holes magically opening in her temples. They are exit holes where the thick, black fluid drains out of her head and drips onto the ground. As the heavy metallic fluid flows out of her skull, it washes away the sharp barbs at her temples. She imagines her head feels lighter and that pain lessens as her head becomes weightless smooth, sparkling white, and clear as glass.

Erik's example: *Erik's has chronic pain in his stomach and intestines below his belly button. He describes his pain as a dark-green knot in his guts that is tight, twisted, hot, swollen, and lumpy.*

In his pain-free image, his stomach and intestines are untangled tubes: long, light pink, and healthy. The temperature is cool, and the texture is smooth without any lumps or tangles.

To transform the image from pain to pain-free, Erik imagines his intestines relaxing, untangling, loosening, and elongating. He sends his intestines a minty cool blue-green breeze to reduce heat and swelling. The cool, wintry tingling of the mint permeates his belly. As this happens, his stomach changes from dark green to light pink. He belly breathes, his stomach relaxes, and his pain changes. With everything stretching out, there is more space in his stomach and intestines, and pain becomes less intense.

Conclusion

Mind-body skills like biofeedback, mindfulness, relaxation strategies, and imagery are powerful tools to manage and cope with pain and physical symptoms. In the next chapter, we'll look at how your thoughts can change pain.

Chapter 5

Thoughts Affect Pain

Connect the Thoughts in Your Head with the Sensations in Your Body

Have you ever noticed that thoughts like *I'll never get better!* make you feel worse, while telling yourself *It's going to be okay!* can make you feel a little better? Research shows that stressful, negative thoughts—like the ones we have when we're sick—can exacerbate and even *cause* health problems and pain. For example, as you learned in chapter 2, negative thoughts and feelings activate stress hormones that can trigger headaches, stomachaches, and muscle pain. They can also trigger the release of chemicals called *cytokines* that can exaggerate or suppress the body's immune response. This means that negative thoughts aren't just in your head—they can also affect your physical health.

The good news is that there is also a connection between calming, positive thoughts and health. Positive thoughts that inspire relaxation, happiness, gratitude, self-compassion, and optimism facilitate improved immune functioning, lower risk of disease, and better overall health. They can also turn down your pain dial, lowering the volume on pain. This means that…drumroll, please…changing your thoughts can change your pain!

There are many ways to transform negative, harmful thoughts into helpful, healing thoughts. These thought-changing techniques are called *cognitive strategies*. In fact, the *C* in CBT stands for *cognitive*, a fancy word for thoughts. Mindfulness techniques also focus on noticing thoughts and shifting attention. These cognitive strategies help you tune in to, identify, and change the negative thoughts associated with pain and illness that keep you feeling miserable, low, and distressed. In this chapter, you'll learn strategies to change your thoughts to reduce stress and anxiety, lift your mood, and shift your attention away from pain. Give them all a try and see which work best for you!

Negative Self-Talk

We all engage in *self-talk*, or the things we say to ourselves when we think. Teens with pain and illness often experience *negative self-talk*, or negative thoughts about themselves, life, or pain, that brings them down and makes them feel worse. The first step to changing these thoughts is to pay careful attention: if you listen closely, you just might be able to hear what Pain Voice, or Sick Voice, is telling you.

Pain Voice

Pain Voice is your inner bully, the voice in your head that tells you awful, worrisome things. She's pessimistic, critical, and negative. You can recognize Pain Voice because she's very loud! She yells into a megaphone, drowning out all other thoughts—especially calm, logical ones. What she tells you sounds like the truth, but when you test these thoughts, you discover they're false. Pain Voice pretends she can predict the future and says it's going to be terrible. She says: "You'll never get better. Nothing will ever help you." But since she can't predict the future (who can?), Pain Voice is a liar!

Pain Voice is also very bossy about what you can and can't do: "You can't see your friends this week," or "You can't go for a bike ride, and you definitely can't have any fun." Basically, Pain Voice makes you miserable.

$$Pain\ Voice = \begin{matrix} Exaggerated \\ Negative \\ Critical \\ Untrue \end{matrix}\ thoughts$$

Picture your Pain Voice. Notice she's not you—she's just a bully in your head who thinks she's in charge. I picture my Pain Voice as a bossy blonde girl with a ponytail and plaid skirt. She has mean, bulging eyes, V-shaped eyebrows, and yells into a megaphone. I call her Beasley. My bully, Beasley, is a major *pain*.

Picture your Pain Voice. What does this voice look like?

_____

_____

_____

_____

_____

_____

Name your Pain Voice. _____

Tune in to your Pain Voice and really listen hard. You've heard her a million times before. What kinds of negative, critical, scary, self-defeating, mean things does she say to you? The next page lists some common Pain Voice thoughts. Circle the ones that are familiar, and add your own:

I'm broken.

My life is always going to be like this.

*I can't do anything on days
I'm sick or in pain.*

*There's no point trying this treatment
because nothing has helped so far.*

Nothing will ever help me.

*Nobody understands what
I'm going through.*

I'm in this alone.

I'll never get better.

*When I hurt, this means my
body is in danger of harm.*

*My friends have all
moved on without me.*

*Things are harder for me
than for everyone else.*

I'm being punished.

My life sucks.

*I'm so far behind in school
that I'll never catch up.*

Everyone thinks I'm faking.

Pain is ruining my life.

Pain is ruining my future.

*I'll never get into a good college
because I've missed too much school.*

Bad things always happen to me.

*I'll never be in shape like
I was before.*

My body hates me.

Tomorrow is going to be as bad as today.

_____

_____

_____

_____

The Voice of Wellness: Wise Voice

Fear not, brave friend—because you have another voice inside you, your *Wise Voice*. She is logical, calm, and smart. She helps you feel *better* instead of worse. You can recognize her encouraging, compassionate, and kind messages. As someone who loves you a whole lot, she sounds like your parents or best friend. Since Wise Voice is soft-spoken, loud Pain Voice usually drowns her out.

$$Wise\ Voice = \begin{matrix} Logical \\ Encouraging \\ Compassionate \\ True \end{matrix}\ thoughts$$

Picture your Wise Voice and bring her to life. My Wise Voice is an older woman with gray hair in a bun. She sits peacefully smiling with legs crossed, eyes closed. She is wise, calm, and confident. I call her Clara because she is clear and bright.

Picture your Wise Voice. What does this voice look like?

_____

_____

_____

_____

_____

_____

_____

Name your Wise Voice. _____

To help heal from pain and illness, we need to quiet Pain Voice and replace her with Wise Voice. But how?

Prove Pain Voice Wrong in Three Steps

Your bossy Pain Voice loves to be right. In order to shut her down, you must first catch negative thoughts (Beasley, is that you?) and thoughtfully determine, or check, whether or not what she's saying is true. What if the thought isn't a fact? What if the only purpose of the thought is to bully, squish, and fill you with self-doubt?

Because negative thoughts increase pain, make sure you don't thoughtlessly, automatically believe them. As soon as you recognize Pain Voice (It *is* you, you beastly bully!), you gain the power to change negative thoughts into more helpful, Clara-clear, Wise Voice thoughts.

Here's an overview of the three steps to shift from Pain Voice to Wise Voice. We'll use the rest of this chapter to become experts in steps 1 and 2. You'll learn how to change thoughts (step 3) in chapter 6.

- **Step 1:** Catch it.

  Get familiar with your recurring Pain Voice thoughts so you can recognize them the instant they happen. Slow them down so they're no longer automatic. Remember your *triggers* from chapter 1—what situations and emotions activate negative thoughts?

- **Step 2:** Check it.

  Once you've caught Pain Voice, question her to determine whether that negative thought is true. Gather logical evidence against it. Then challenge thoughts that are harmful, exaggerated, or flat-out untrue.

- **Step 3:** Change it.

  Use the evidence you gather to replace Pain Voice with the voice of wellness, your Wise Voice. At first, you may not hear Wise Voice very often, but she's even more powerful than Pain Voice. When you start noticing her kind, compassionate messages, she'll get even stronger.

Step 1: *Catch Pain Voice Using Thinking Traps*

It's normal to have a loud, negative Pain Voice when you're sick or in pain. These negative thoughts sound like the truth (*My life sucks!*) and trap you into believing them, but they're stressful, exaggerated, and untrue. Pain Voice thoughts are called *thinking traps*—distorted, negative thoughts that bring down mood, spike stress and anxiety, and lead to unhealthy behaviors like avoiding exercise, school, people, and activities. Thinking traps are dangerous because they *feel* true even if they're not *factually* true.

So how do you distinguish thinking traps from the truth? Well, you become a thought detective, capturing thoughts and examining evidence. One way to recognize a trap is to notice how a thought makes you feel. It is a *helpful* thought, or is it *harmful*? Check the list of Pain Voice thoughts you circled earlier—do they make you feel hopeful and inspired, or discouraged and miserable? Traps make you feel worried, sad, hopeless, or angry. Go through the following thinking traps and identify familiar thoughts.

BLACK-OR-WHITE THOUGHTS

When things seem black or white, all or nothing—if something isn't perfect, you see it as a total failure. *If I don't get an A on this exam, I'm a failure.* Or *I can only be happy if I don't have pain.*

Do thoughts like these sound familiar?   Y   N

Name one of your black-or-white thoughts:

_____

Is this thought *helpful* or *harmful*? (Circle one.)

This thought is a trap because the world doesn't exist in extremes. It's rare that you're at one extreme or the other, either the tippy-top of your class earning the highest grades on every test (black) or the other extreme, at the very bottom getting all Fs (white). Most of the time, you're somewhere in the middle (gray!). When you notice yourself going "black or white," remind yourself to "go gray" and imagine possibilities in the middle.

OVERGENERALIZATION

You believe that a single negative event, like a bad grade or a hard day, is an enduring, lifelong pattern. You use words like "always," "never," "everybody," "nobody," "all" and "nothing." *I don't have friends, nobody will ever like me.* Or *I can never do anything when I'm sick or in pain* or *My (whole) life sucks!*

Do thoughts like these sound familiar?   Y   N

Name one of your overgeneralizations:

_____

Is this thought *helpful* or *harmful*? (Circle one.)

This thought is a trap because one negative event isn't representative of all events. Does *everything* about your life suck because you had one bad day? Is it true *nobody* likes you or will *ever* like you? I call these *warning words* because they're dangerous exaggerations and rarely true, and they indicate that you've fallen into a thinking trap. Replace warning words with balanced words like "some" and "sometimes"; for example, *Today wasn't a great day, but not everything was bad. Good things happened, too.*

FILTERING

You focus on negative information and ignore the positive; for example, when you accept criticism and negativity, but reject compliments and kindnesses. *You get many positive comments on an Instagram post, but one person is critical. You obsess about this negative comment for days and ignore the positive feedback.*

Do thoughts like these sound familiar?   Y   N

Name a time you filtered:

_____

Is this thought *helpful* or *harmful*? (Circle one.)

This thought is a trap because your brain selectively, erroneously focuses on negative information and ignores the good. Why does one bad comment count more than a good one? You may dismiss a compliment by thinking *She's just being nice because she's my friend*, but what if she means it? It's easy to accept criticism over compliments, but if you only accept negative information, your mood and self-esteem will crash.

MISINTERPRETING

You believe an innocent body signal means something dangerous or harmful. Common examples include interpreting symptoms of anxiety, like a racing heart or chest pain, as a sign you're having a heart attack; interpreting stress-based stomachaches as an illness; or deciding that tingling in your arms or legs means you're having a stroke rather than panicking. You might also believe that all pain indicates that your condition is worsening when that may not be true.

Do thoughts like these sound familiar?   Y   N

When have you misinterpreted body signals?

_____

Is this thought *helpful* or *harmful*? (Circle one.)

This thought is a trap because misinterpreting body signals leads to anxiety, panic, and worried thoughts like: *What's happening to me?* Before you jump to conclusions, try listing likely alternatives. Is it more likely you're having a heart attack or that you're nervous about an upcoming test or medical procedure? And that stomachache may be the effects of stress on your gut's enteric nervous system, one of your body's emotion centers! It's possible that physical sensations don't indicate something medically dangerous.

MIND READING

You believe people are thinking negative things about you without even asking them. You "know" what's in other people's minds even though you have no evidence. *Those girls don't like me.* Or, *they all think I'm faking.*

Do thoughts like these sound familiar?   Y   N

When have you read minds?

_____

Is this thought *helpful* or *harmful*? (Circle one.)

This thought is a trap because while it would be amazing to read minds, chances are you don't have that superpower (sorry!). Want to test it out? Ask someone to think of a number between zero and one hundred and try to guess it on the first try. If you can't do it, this means you *can't actually read minds.* Assuming other people are thinking bad things about you is a surefire way to feel anxious, angry, and upset.

FORTUNE-TELLING

You believe you can see into the future and predict that things are going to be bad. Before a test you think, *I'm going to fail.* If you're sick or in pain, you think, *This treatment won't work.* Or, *I can't go on like this.*

Do thoughts like these sound familiar? Y N

When have you tried to predict the future?

_____

Is this thought *helpful* or *harmful*? (Circle one.)

This thought is a trap because…*Wait!* You can predict the future? Wow, we're gonna be rich! Quick, what are next week's winning lottery numbers? … Wait, what? You don't know? [Sigh.] Well, I guess that means you can't predict the future. If you're sick or in pain, predicting a negative, pain-filled future can make you feel terrified, depressed, and hopeless.

CATASTROPHIZING

You believe that the worst thing that *can* happen is *going* to happen. You wake up with a stomachache and think, *If I go on the class trip, I'm going to vomit and need to go home.* Or, *I've had pain for three days; that means I'm getting worse!*

Do thoughts like these sound familiar? Y N

What's one of your catastrophic thoughts?

_____

Is this thought *helpful* or *harmful*? (Circle one.)

This thought is a trap because instead of just predicting the future, you're predicting the *worst possible version* of it! When you predict catastrophes, you become anxious and upset, and avoid the things you're worried about. But since you can't predict the future, this is a trap! (If you *can* predict the future, please call me.)

HURT = HARM

You believe that all pain is an indication of bodily harm. *When I move my back, it hurts; therefore moving must be bad.* Or, *Going for a walk with a headache will make my condition worse.*

Do thoughts like these sound familiar?   Y   N

When have you assumed that hurt = harm?

_____

Is this thought *helpful* or *harmful*? (Circle one.)

This thought is a trap because things that *hurt* don't necessarily mean your body is being *harmed*, as you learned in chapter 1. Of course, there are times when pain indicates bodily harm and you need rest. But sometimes pain is a false alarm due to your overly sensitive pain system. In fact, movement and exercise are critically important components of chronic pain treatment! Activity and stimulation desensitize your brain and help you cope with pain.

LABELING

You call yourself a negative name or give yourself a label. Instead of saying *I made a mistake*, you think to yourself, *I'm an idiot.* Teens with pain or illness sometimes think, *I'm broken.*

Do thoughts like these sound familiar?   Y   N

Write one label or name you've called yourself:

_____

Is this thought *helpful* or *harmful*? (Circle one.)

This thought is a trap because calling yourself names only makes you feel bad about yourself. Self-esteem crashes, mood worsens, anxiety spikes, and pain volume intensifies. Be kind to yourself instead…being sick and in pain is hard enough as it is!

PERMANENCE

You believe things are permanent, and that the way things are right now is the way they will always be—forever. *My pain will never go away.* Or, *I'll never get better.*

Do thoughts like these sound familiar?   Y   N

What thoughts of permanence have you had?

_____

Is this thought *helpful* or *harmful*? (Circle one.)

This thought is a trap because teenagers are great at believing that now = forever! The only thing certain about life is that things constantly change. Pain changes all the time, so it could change for the better. Believing a rough patch is permanent can lead to depression and anxiety. Remember: you can't predict the future!

Step 2. *Check Pain Voice Using Detective Questions*

Once you've caught a negative thought, how do you determine whether it's true? It's time to *check* Pain Voice! If you continue to accept these thoughts as facts, pain volume will remain high. Assess truthfulness using the following detective questions. These logical, fact-based questions help you access your Wise Voice—the kind, calm voice that knows the truth. The moment you recognize that a thought is a thinking trap, you gain the power to change it. Here's how Cam applied detective questions to catch and check Pain Voice:

After a concussion kept Cam out of school most of junior year, she worried about her academic performance. She still had headaches, her balance was off, and she still occasionally missed school. Diagnosed with post-concussion syndrome, she grew increasingly concerned about how this would impact her future. Cam felt overwhelmed about grades and sometimes panicked before tests.

Cam learned cognitive strategies to help manage her pain. After writing down Pain Voice thoughts, she began recognizing them. Her Pain Voice was a snotty girl she called Pam. Pam the Pain Voice dressed in tight black clothes, had a short bob, wore lots of makeup, and constantly criticized Cam.

Cam noticed that her negative thoughts were frequently about her future. Sometimes she believed these thoughts and got trapped by them. The thinking trap that bothered her most was I missed so much school that I'll never get into college. *This thought sounded true, even though it was harmful and made her feel terrible. But this fortune-telling prediction was just Pain Voice Pam making her anxious and miserable. Because she could catch it, she was able to check it.*

Cam used the following detective questions to determine whether this prediction was the truth or a trap.

Thought: I missed so much school that I'll never get into college.

Is it a fact? (Note: a *fact* means it is unquestionably, absolutely, certainly true.)

No, it isn't a fact that I won't get into college.

Are you predicting bad things?

Yes. I'm predicting that, because I missed junior year and it affected my grades, I'm not going to get into college. But since I can't predict the future, this fortune-telling thought is a trap.

Are you using a *warning word*? (all/nothing, everyone/no one, always/never/ forever, best/worst...)

If I'm thinking I'll never get into college, this thought is a trap.

What evidence do you have that this might *not* be true?

Last year, my friend Benji got a concussion playing hockey and missed two months of school—and he got into college. I know students who didn't have stellar grades and they got into college. My sister's grades were worse than mine, and she went to community college and then transferred. I could do that, too. Maybe my prediction is wrong.

What has happened in the past?

Since this is my first time applying to college, this question doesn't apply.

What's the likelihood this bad thing will actually happen? (Try to give a percentage; for example, 1 percent = 1/100.)

If I applied to a hundred schools, some safeties and some reaches, I'd certainly get into one of them! The likelihood that I won't get in anywhere is probably zero percent.

What else—neutral or positive—might happen in this situation other than what you're predicting?

Neutral: I could apply to schools with my average grades and get rejected by a few and get accepted by a few, just like most other students.

Positive: Because of what I've been through, I could write my college essay about post-concussion syndrome and maybe even earn a scholarship!

What's the worst-case scenario? Could you handle it?

Worst-case scenario would be rejection from all schools. I'd be devastated…but it wouldn't destroy me. I'd survive. I'd attend a local community college and could always transfer. Or I could take a gap year and volunteer at the zoo, like I've always wanted to do. So yes—I could handle it.

What would you say to your best friend or a family member who expressed this concern to you?

I would say: "It makes sense you're worried about getting into college after what happened. Your concussion and its aftermath have been terrible. I know it's been hard going from A-grades to being so dizzy and headachy that you miss tests and your grades crash. But this injury hasn't changed who you are: you're still smart, competent, and capable! If you want to go to college, you will. Your worry is reasonable, but it's not factual. Don't let Pam the Pain Voice get you down!"

Now it's your turn. Pick a thinking trap or Pain Voice thought and write it in the space below. Challenge this thought using the detective questions. Determine why this thought is flawed, and see if you can prove why it's a trap and not the truth!

Your negative thought: _____

Is it a fact? (Note: a *fact* means it is unquestionably, absolutely, certainly true.)

_____

Are you predicting bad things?

_____

_____

Are you using a warning word? (all/nothing, everyone/no one, always/never/ forever, best/worst...)

_____

What evidence do you have that this might *not* be true?

_____

_____

_____

_____

What has happened in the past?

_____

_____

_____

_____

What's the likelihood this bad thing will actually happen? Try to give a percentage. (Reminder: 1 percent = 1/100. What this means is that out of every hundred instances, the terrible consequence you're predicting happened once. For example, if you predict there's a 1 percent chance your airplane will crash, this means that out of every hundred planes that take off globally each day, one crashes.)

What else—neutral or positive—might happen in this situation other than what you're predicting?

What's the worst-case scenario? Could you handle it?

What would you say to your best friend or a family member who expressed this concern to you?

Conclusion

Now that you've learned to check and challenge Pain Voice, it's time to take her power away—and strengthen and empower Wise Voice. But how? In the next chapter, you'll learn Step 3: how to transform pain by transforming your thoughts.

Chapter 6

Transform Thoughts to Transform Pain

Change Pain Voice

In the last chapter, you learned how thoughts affect pain. You caught Pain Voice (step 1) and learned to check, challenge, and prove her wrong using detective questions (step 2). The next step, step 3, is to *change* Pain Voice and start talking back to her. This chapter will teach you to create factual, helpful Wise Voice responses to Pain Voice, and apply coping thoughts to fight back so that these thoughts can't hurt you. Never get bossed around again!

Thought Tracking

To bust Pain Voice, start tracking your thoughts. You can download a copy of this tracker at http://www.newharbinger.com/33522.

First, list your Pain Voice thoughts. Notice if they're helpful or harmful, whether they're the truth or a trap. Next, write out the answers to the detective questions—these are your Wise Voice responses. Your Wise Voice responses should include *evidence* as to why Pain Voice is wrong. At the end of this activity, you'll have a Wise Voice response ready for combat—so that every time you hear Pain Voice from now on, you'll be prepared to retaliate. Your Wise Voice grows stronger every time you use her!

Your Thought Tracker

Situation	Pain Voice	Helpful or harmful?	Trap or truth?	Wise Voice
Need to go to school after missing 3 weeks	If I go back to school, I'll be so far behind that I won't understand anything the teacher is talking about.	Harmful	Trap	This negative prediction is not a fact. I'll probably understand *some* things. I'm smart and competent. Last time I was behind, I made up the work and everything was fine.
Pain flare-up	I can't handle this!	Harmful	Trap	This negative prediction is not a fact. I've had 82 pain flare-ups this year, and I handled all of them. I've proven that I'm strong and resilient. There is a 0% chance I can't handle this.

Going Gray

Pain Voice and Sick Voice love speaking in black-or-white thinking traps. For example, it's easy to think that having pain or being sick means you can do *nothing*, while being pain-free means you can do *everything*. These exaggerated, extreme thoughts limit your ability to cope with pain and live your life.

One method for tackling these thoughts is to consider: what happens when you mix black (nothing) and white (everything) together? You get *gray*. When you notice yourself thinking in extremes, try to "go gray" and imagine possibilities in the middle. If high-pain days mean zero activity and low-pain days mean lots of activity, what options exist in the middle on days with some pain? Here's an example of how this works.

Black Thought: When I have pain, I can't do *anything*.
No school
Stop cello
No hiking
Don't see any friends

White Thought: When I don't have pain, I can do *everything*.
School daily
Cello after school every day
Hike every weekend
See friends daily

Gray Thought: On a day with *some* pain, I can do *some* things.
School for half day
Play cello at home for 10 minutes
Hike for 15 minutes on Sunday
Invite one friend over this weekend to watch a zombie movie

Here is how Marjorie went "gray":

Marjorie was a dancer who stopped entering dance competitions when she was diagnosed with a neuromuscular disease. After months of treatment with medication and physical therapy, her balance and coordination improved enough that her doctor cleared her to gradually start dancing again. But Marjorie was scared and believed she needed to keep resting. She hadn't gone to practice or seen her dance team since her diagnosis because it was too hard to watch them compete without her. On bad days, she curled on the couch with her cat and watched hours of TV. She felt miserable. The longer this went on, the less energy and motivation she had.

When Marjorie learned about "going gray," she realized Pain Voice was saying she'd never dance again and should quit the team. Her black-and-white thought was: When I'm symptomatic I can't dance at all, but when I'm symptom-free I can dance daily. *She developed a plan to try dancing for ten minutes on days with some symptoms.*

On Monday, she woke with fatigue, pain, and fear. She considered skipping dance as usual but reminded herself that a day with some symptoms meant she could do some things. She put on her dance clothes and did ten minutes of warm-up exercises, holding on to a bar for support. She was out of shape, but it felt good to put on dance shoes, great to stretch and move her body, and miraculous to discover that she didn't need to give up her love of dancing entirely just because she had neuromuscular disease!

You can practice going gray using the following table. Enter your black-and-white thoughts and corresponding activity levels. Then consider: how can you go gray on a day with some symptoms? Think of different categories like school, social, hobbies, after-school activities, and exercise. Use units of time and other measurements to make activity goals realistic, specific and achievable: for example, fifteen minutes of skateboarding three times this week at 5:00 p.m.

Black	Gray	White
If I have pain, I can't do anything.	If I have some pain, I can do some things.	If I don't have pain, I can do everything.
If I'm in pain this week, I can't skateboard.	If I have some pain this week, I'll skateboard for 15 mins three days after school (M, W, F).	If I have no pain this week, I'll skateboard for as long as I want.

Coping Thoughts

Just as negative thoughts discourage you and make symptoms feel worse, *coping thoughts* help you feel better. Coping thoughts are soothing, calming thoughts that encourage you and reduce worry about pain. They help you get through your day, accomplish goals, and manage pain so that you can function. They come from your kind, compassionate Wise Voice, and remind your brain that your body is safe.

Coping thoughts are handy when Pain Voice gets loud, like when you have a doctor's appointment, pain flare-up, or an exam. As soon as you feel stressed, anxious, or angry—and hear your negative, pessimistic Pain Voice—pause, take a breath, tell yourself to *stop*! Then use a coping thought instead. Coping thoughts sound like this:

- This episode will pass.

- I've had eighty-two pain flare-ups in my life and I survived *all* of them. I'll survive this one, too.

- I know how to cope with this.

- I'll distract myself with a game (puppy, TV show, friend) for fifteen minutes and see if it helps.

- I'm going to be okay.

- If I start having pain, I'll use relaxation strategies to lower pain volume.

- I'm working on getting better every day.

- I can use my self-soothing plan.

- I am strong!

- I'm not alone. I have love and support to help me get through this.

- Just breathe.

What are five kind, compassionate, calming things you can say to yourself when you're anxious or symptomatic, or hear Pain Voice? You can use any of these coping thoughts, or imagine the sweet, soothing things you'd say to friends or family members.

1. _____

2. _____

3. _____

4. _____

5. _____

Put a copy of these coping thoughts in your backpack, on your wall, and on your fridge. Practice coping thoughts daily so they become as familiar as your worried thoughts. Just as Pain Voice got strong with a lot of use, Wise Voice needs a chance to grow strong, too. The more you use her, the stronger she'll get—until she's loud enough to drown out Pain Voice!

Language Matters: Your Brain Hears Everything Your Mouth Says

You may think the things you say aren't very important. However, *your brain hears everything your mouth says*. The words you say aloud are transmitted from your mouth, to your ears, and relayed up to your brain for processing. So every time you say things like, "I'll never get better," or "*If* I ever play sports again" (instead of when), your brain hears this and *it believes you!* For this reason, it's very important to choose your words carefully.

Some common words that describe chronic pain or illness reflect powerlessness and low self-reliance. Circle any words that sound familiar:

sick	damaged	powerless
ill	disabled	
weak	broken	

When you say these words, do they make you feel good—like you can do anything—or bad, like you'd rather crawl under a blanket? Words focusing on pain and powerlessness keep you scared and miserable. Instead, flip that language upside down. Start using words that make you feel strong and empowered instead, like these:

resilient	competent	powerful
healthy	confident	
strong	capable	

If it feels hard to tap into your power right now, that's normal. Pain takes away power! But you can *take power back* by using powerful words, even if you have to fake it 'til you make it. Read the examples, then complete the following sentences:

I am *resilient* because:

(I never stop trying and always get back up when I get knocked down.)

_____

I feel *healthy* when I:

(go swimming at the YMCA.)

_____

I feel *strong* when I:

(walked up to the drama director and asked if I could act the lead role.)

_____

I am *confident* about (physical attributes, skills, accomplishments):

(my ability to spell complicated words.)

_____

I am *capable* because I can do the following things on my own:

(repair computers, get myself to and from school.)

_____

I feel *powerful* when I:

(go backpacking with Mom.)

_____

Ten Good Things

This activity regulates pain by inspiring feelings of happiness and gratitude. Noticing the good things in your life, no matter how small, helps you focus on things for which you're grateful, lifting your mood and shifting attention away from pain to things that inspire joy. This trains your brain to notice people and experiences that generate feelings of happiness, inspiration, safety, and love. It also tunes you into things that make life worth living!

Research shows that gratitude practices and positive thoughts improve overall mood; increase your sense of meaning and purpose; reduce frustration, anger, and irritability; reduce loneliness; promote immune functioning; increase ability to cope with pain; reduce symptoms of illness; and improve overall physical health. In fact, a regular gratitude practice like this one can actually change your brain pathways!

Positive thoughts and gratitude also increases production of *serotonin* and *dopamine*, chemical messengers in your brain called *neurotransmitters* that regulate mood, sleep, appetite…and pain. For these reasons, the Ten Good Things activity can be a powerful pain management technique.

How to do it:

Find a quiet place to sit where you won't be disturbed for ten minutes. Turn off your screens or put them away. Make a list of ten things you are grateful for or that make you feel happy. These can be memories, kind things people have done for you, kind things you have done for others, a list of favorites (foods, movies, books, animals, vacations), activities you're looking forward to, people you admire, and any good things that have happened in your life. They don't have to be big things—they can be as ordinary as your cat purring or a gooey slice of pizza. It could be something that happened this week or many years ago. Here are some examples:

1. My wonderful friends

2. Hiking in the wilderness to find owls

3. The name Marjorie

4. Holding doors open for strangers

5. Learning about the brain

6. Bioluminescent jellyfish that make their own light

7. Freshly baked New York bagels

8. Tortoiseshell butterflies

9. Bookstores, especially ones with a secret door disguised as a bookshelf

10. Swimming in cool lakes in summertime

Yadira learned how to focus on the good things this way:

Yadira was miserable. Her chronic illness, despite being better than before, still caused her pain. She stressed about schoolwork, running the school newspaper, and captaining the golf team. She'd been fighting with her sister, which got so bad that last week her sister pushed her. On top of that, Yadira's boyfriend was leaving for college. These situational and emotional triggers made her body feel worse. On a scale of one to ten, her pain was an eleven.

She was irritable and moody, thinking things like There's nothing good in my life. *When Yadira learned the Ten Good Things activity, she started paying attention to the small things in her life that made her less miserable, even if only briefly—like pancakes for dinner and laundry warm from the dryer. For the next week, she listed ten things every day that made her grateful and happy. When she did this, Yadira noticed that her mood lifted and attention shifted, and she could focus on the good things in her life.*

After two weeks, Yadira framed her top twenty things, decorated the frame, and hung it next to her bed. She loved looking at it, and noticed that, on the days she wrote good things, her pain was easier to bear!

To generate ten good things, finish the following sentences.

I feel grateful for…

_____

_____

_____

Something kind I did for someone (or someone did for me) was...

_____

Something that made me happy recently was...

_____

Write your ten good things here:

1. _____

2. _____

3. _____

4. _____

5. _____

6. _____

7. _____

8. _____

9. _____

10. _____

Imagine a Miracle

Another cognitive strategy for coping with pain is to *imagine a miracle*. Use your powerful brain to imagine a future free of struggle with pain and illness, in which you are living a good life. This exercise helps you overcome hopelessness by looking beyond obstacles that keep you stuck, and inspires you to think about goals and how you'll achieve them. Giving yourself permission to imagine a miracle can be transformative...it can also be a road map to health and healing!

How to do it:

Sit somewhere calm and quiet where you don't be disturbed. Turn off your screens or put them away.

Imagine yourself five years from now. Imagine that a miracle has occurred, and you've overcome pain and illness. You are happy, active, and fulfilled. You are wherever you dream of being, doing whatever you dream of doing: at your ideal school or job, living your ideal life. You are healthy, strong, and have achieved your dreams. After envisioning this miracle, answer the following questions, as Henry did here.

You wake up without any pain or illness. What's the first thing you do?

When I realize I have no pain, I jump out of bed and toss my crutches. My dog and I run to my best friend's house. We go to the ice cream shop (for breakfast!) and I run the whole way there.

_____

_____

_____

How does it feel to be without pain or illness?

It feels amazing. I feel lighter. I walk and run whenever I want. I smile a lot.

_____

_____

What do you do for school or work?

I live in Mexico and teach English to children. I have a big community of family and friends and speak fluent Spanish. I love teaching and never miss a day of work.

_____

_____

_____

What do you do for fun, and who do you spend time with?

I started a local softball team. I'm the fastest runner and always steal bases. I also listen to music and bake banana bread! I spend time with the other teachers, the kids I teach, and new friends.

_____

_____

_____

_____

Five years ago, you were struggling with pain and illness. What are the steps you took to get from there to here?

Five years ago, I had CRPS and couldn't walk. I was frustrated because I wanted to spend a summer volunteering in Mexico, but the program wouldn't admit me. I set a goal to get strong enough to walk with just one crutch by March. I went to physical therapy, did pacing and desensitization exercises, and learned CBT skills to manage pain. When my mood started improving, I had more motivation and energy. By March, I was strong enough to walk with one crutch; then without any by June. Since the Mexico program demanded I be able to run, I used pacing to start jogging. It took some time, but eventually I was able to run again! I went to Mexico to teach and it changed my life. This is my calling. Now I am fit, active, doing what I love, and I feel amazing!

_____

_____

_____

_____

_____

_____

What qualities do you have that enabled you to take these steps?

Tenacity, resilience, patience, and persistence

What helped the most?

Picking an end goal and a starting point. End goal = walk without crutches by summer so that I can go to Mexico. Starting point = go to PT daily and CBT weekly. Every successful baby step gave me momentum to continue toward the next small goal.

What obstacles did you face as you healed, and how did you overcome them?

At first I was scared to walk with pain. CRPS treatment required me to use my painful leg—but that hurt, so I avoided it. I also didn't have much motivation at first, but when I identified the meaningful goal of going to Mexico to teach, my motivation increased. I was determined to prove I could do it, and I did!

Conclusion

Pain Voice is powerful, but not more powerful than you. Wise Voice and coping thoughts—filled with compassion and good things—can help you take your power back. In chapter 7, you'll learn how sleep, nutrition, exercise, and friends can also be medicinal.

Chapter 7

Lifestyle Affects Pain

Brains Love Balance

Why do doctors ask about lifestyle decisions like sleep, nutrition, and exercise? Because your body craves *homeostasis*, or balance. When your body is out of balance, you're more prone to sickness and pain. Your body is happiest when you drink enough water, keep your blood sugar steady, sleep consistently every night, get sunlight, use your muscles, and aren't too sedentary. Not too little of anything, and not too much.

Your brain helps you balance by sending signals that something isn't right. For example, hunger pangs and headaches are signals that you're low on fuel and need to eat. Drowsiness and irritability can be signals that you need more sleep. When a room gets too hot, your body instructs you to shed that sweatshirt! Your brain has many ways of telling you that something's off balance—including physical symptoms like pain.

Being off-balance is a trigger for pain.

To prevent and cope with episodes of pain and illness, make a homeostasis plan:

- Eat three healthy meals + snacks each day.
- Set regular sleep and wake times to get eight to ten hours of sleep nightly.
- Drink water throughout the day.
- Exercise and move daily to keep bones and muscles strong.
- Go outside, be in nature, get sunlight.

In this chapter, we'll talk about important lifestyle decisions. We'll start with sleep since you do it every night!

Sleep Better to Feel Better

Sleep plays an important role in pain and illness. Pain can trigger various sleep issues: irregular sleep patterns, trouble falling asleep, nighttime awakenings, and poor sleep quality. This then triggers stress and anxiety about being unable to sleep, which turns up your pain dial. Lack of sleep is also associated with increased pain and worsening symptoms.

Human beings are *diurnal*, which means our brains are programmed to be alert and awake when the sun is shining, and to shut down and sleep at night. This is distinct from *nocturnal* animals, like owls and bats, whose brains are programmed to sleep during the day and wake at night.

Your sleep cycle is regulated by a brain structure called the *suprachiasmatic nucleus* (SCN). The SCN is your built-in alarm clock (how cool is that?). It influences your body's twenty-four-hour rhythms—when you get hungry, feel alert and active, and crash and need sleep. The SCN is programmed by sunlight, which means that you can "set" your SCN like you set your alarm at night. This is in part due to a brain chemical called *melatonin*, which regulates your sleep-wake cycle. This cycle allows your body to repair and refresh, and keeps you in sync with the sun and outside world.

However, when you're feeling sick and in pain, your sleep cycle is easily thrown off balance and homeostasis is disrupted. Poor sleep at night leads to sleeping late or napping in the afternoons. Daytime sleep makes it even harder to sleep at night. Lying in bed awake for hours triggers frustration and worry about your inability to sleep, making it even *harder* to sleep. This leads to yet another night of poor rest and sleep catch-up the next day...and around and around the cycle goes.

Sleep Tracking

Let's peek at your typical sleep habits. This will help determine what sleep strategies will be most helpful. Track your sleep habits for a week and record them here, or download a copy of this chart at http://www.newharbinger.com/33522.

Your Sleep Tracker

	Example	Mon.	Tues.	Wed.	Thurs.	Fri.	Sat.	Sun.
Bedtime	11pm							
Wake time	7am							
Number of naps	1 nap							
Insomnia?	No							
Night awakenings?	Yes, 2							

Sleep Hygiene

To treat sleep issues common to chronic pain and illness, use *sleep hygiene* to recover from pain-related sleep deprivation and establish healthy sleep practices. These tips improve sleep by reducing insomnia, night awakenings, and other sleep issues. If you use all these tips, you may still have challenges, but sleep won't be one of them!

- Get into bed only when sleepy.

  "Tired" and "sleepy" are not the same. You may feel fatigued and tired after a long day but still not be sleepy enough to fall asleep. Getting in bed before you're sleepy leads to lying there, frustrated and awake.

- Create a comfortable sleep environment.

  Make your room dark, cool, and quiet. Use curtains so sunlight won't wake you before wake time. Temperature is also important; have you noticed how hard it is to fall asleep on hot summer nights? Our bodies sleep better in cool rooms. Use a white-noise machine or fan to keep your bedroom quiet and peaceful.

- Use your bed only for sleep.

  Find another comfortable place to watch TV, read, or text. Let your brain associate bed *exclusively* with sleep. Why? Your brain quickly learns relationships between things. If you lie in bed awake, your brain will associate "bed" with "wakefulness." If you use your bed only for sleep, your brain will learn that "bed" = "unconscious and drooling"!

- Get out of bed after twenty minutes.

  If you can't fall asleep, don't lie in bed worrying. Get out of bed after approximately twenty minutes and do something calming: read a book on the couch, listen to relaxing music in a comfy chair. Get back into bed when you're sleepy. Why? The longer you lie in bed stressed about not sleeping, the higher anxiety gets. The higher anxiety gets, the less likely you are to sleep! Lying awake in bed for long periods also teaches your brain to associate bed with anxious wakefulness, rather than relaxed sleepiness.

- Have calming, soothing activities ready.

  When you can't sleep, don't search for something to do. Keep a coloring book, magazine, or headphones in a place that's comfortable and accessible, like next to your couch. Make sure to choose activities that are relaxing— like drawing or reading—rather than activating, like playing videogames or watching murder mysteries.

- Set a sleep time and wake time.

  Brains love routine. Waking up and falling asleep at the same time every day sets your SCN (biological clock). Consistent sleep and wake times are crucial, *especially* if you're not attending school—otherwise your clock will have no rhythm. The earlier you wake up, the earlier you'll be able to fall asleep! Why? Because your body craves balance, your brain is happiest when it has a routine—so turn it "off" and "on" at the same time every day. Regular sleep-wake times decrease sleep difficulties.

- Get exposure to sunlight.

  First thing in the morning, open your curtains and get sunlight. Your SCN, which triggers the release of "sleep" chemicals in the dark, breaks these down to signal "wake" in the light. This sets your biological clock, and reminds your brain that light = wake, dark = sleep.

- Don't take naps.

  Restrict sleep to nighttime only. As tempting as naps are, especially when you're in pain, teach your brain that "sleep" happens at night, and "awake" happens during the day. Napping partially satisfies sleep needs, which lessens your need to sleep at night.

- Don't check the time.

  Watching the clock only increases stress and anxiety: *It's 2 a.m.; I won't be able to function tomorrow!* The more anxious you get, the *less* likely you are to fall asleep—so cover your clocks and flip your phone.

- Have a relaxing pre-bedtime routine.

  Before bed, take a hot bath, read, do relaxation exercises or meditations. Avoid homework, screens, stimulating activities, and anything stressful immediately before bed. Make a list of relaxing, pre-bedtime activities you can try.

- Don't take your problems to bed.

  Do you ever lie in bed thinking through problems or worrying about things you need to do? Bedtime is a bad time to worry and problem solve. Pick a "worry time" a few hours before bed to write down concerns and to-dos.

- Exercise.

  Exercise regulates brain chemistry and helps your body feel tired. It also eats up stress hormones, like adrenaline, that your body produces during the day. Exercise earlier in the day and avoid exercising in the evening.

- Avoid caffeine and alcohol.

  These substances interfere with natural sleep-wake signals. If you're already having trouble sleeping, they will only get in the way of tuning in to your natural sleep signals.

- Avoid sugar and big meals before bed.

  Sugar and food are fuel that prepare your body for action! Teach your brain that nighttime is for slowing down, not revving up.

- Avoid sleeping in more than two hours on weekends.

  It's lovely to catch up on sleep, but what happens when your body gets used to staying up 'til one and sleeping until noon on Saturday and Sunday? By Sunday night, you can't fall asleep until late, so Monday morning feels miserable. This pattern leads to sleep deprivation, difficulty attending school, and increased pain. Limit extra weekend sleep to a few hours max.

- Avoid sleeping with pets.

  But they're so cute and fuzzy! True, but they also snore, kick, lick your face, and climb in and out of bed—which disturbs your sleep. No wonder you're so tired in the morning!

- No screens before bed.

  Limit screen time to two to three hours per day. Turn off screens an hour or two before bed and do something else (read, draw) instead. Remove screens from your bedroom at night; they're too tempting. Leave them in a basket in the kitchen or give them to your parents. Why? Blue light from screens suppresses melatonin, the brain chemical that regulates sleep. Low melatonin = less likely to fall asleep. Screens also stimulate your brain, providing sensory overload during a time when you should be helping your brain shut down. Lastly, screens turn on your SNS—and adrenaline is just no good for sleep. Brainstorm calming activities that don't involve screens, like the ones in this book!

Your Sleep Hygiene Plan

Sleep hygiene works best if you use all these tips, but if you need a place to start, pick two or three. Changing habits is hard and doesn't happen overnight. It's like building a muscle—it takes practice and time. Try a few and see how it goes!

Three sleep hygiene strategies you'll try this week:

1. _____

2. _____

3. _____

Daily bedtime this week: _____ p.m.

Daily wake time: _____ a.m.

Three relaxing, nonscreen activities for your pre-bedtime routine *(take a hot bath, read a magazine, listen to a body scan)*:

1. _____

2. _____

3. _____

Where you'll go if you can't fall asleep and need to get out of bed *(pillow pile in the corner of your room; living room couch)*:

_____

Relaxing activities you'll have ready in case you can't sleep *(headphones + music, coloring book)*:

_____

_____

Ideas for not looking at clocks *(turn bedside clock around, put phone facedown)*:

_____

Where you'll store screens before bed *(kitchen drawer, Mom's room)*:

_____

Exercise and the Brain

Why are people always telling me to exercise?

It can be annoying to hear doctor after doctor tell you to exercise—especially if you're in pain. As frustrating as it is, here's why they insist: Studies show that exercise increases energy and reduces fatigue among people with chronic pain and illness; stimulates muscles and bone repair; improves joint function; reduces risk of developing chronic illnesses; improves sleep; and can reduce pain. There's more: Exercise helps your blood circulate, which provides your body with oxygen to support tissue repair, facilitates healing, and boosts immune functioning. It also bolsters self-esteem, decreases and prevents stress and anxiety, and lifts mood to reduce depression. Whew! That's a lot of stuff!

On the flip side, lack of movement leads to reduced immune functioning, stiffness and muscle tension, feeling weak and lethargic, decreased motivation, and increased, prolonged pain. Because of this, being sedentary—not exercising—is one of the biggest risk factors for developing lifelong chronic pain and illness. (All this research makes me want to go for a walk.)

In addition to healing your body, exercise changes…wait for it…your brain. (Surprise!) Exercise rewires your sensitive brain, stimulating the production of neurotransmitters that are part of the pain relief response, including:

Serotonin—regulates mood and other functions. When serotonin goes up, mood goes up, and pain volume is turned down. Most commonly prescribed antidepressant and antianxiety medications and some pain medications target serotonin.

Dopamine—transmits feelings of pleasure and reward to turn down your pain dial.

Endorphins—natural painkillers that muffle pain. Pain medications actually imitate the effects of endorphins! (Isn't it cool that your body created them first?)

Exercise regulates these neurotransmitters. It also eats up stress hormones, like adrenaline and cortisol, released during fight-or-flight to promote relaxation and healing. It may seem counterintuitive, but if you're sick or in pain, it's *especially* important to exercise.

If you've been inactive for weeks or months, remember to resume exercise slowly. Use your pacing plan (See chapter 3)! Go to physical therapy. Take a daily walk or try yoga, which combines stretching, strength-training, and mindful body awareness.

Sunlight and Nature Are Medicines

Pain and illness try to keep you stuck indoors without activity, exercise, friends, or sunlight. But there are reasons to fight back: Exposure to sunlight is critical for health. Sunshine regulates your sleep and wake cycles, increases serotonin to improve mood, and stimulates production of Vitamin D—which is critical for physical strength and healthy functioning. Sunlight may also provide protection against illnesses such as rheumatoid arthritis, asthma, and infectious diseases. Research suggests that nature can also positively impact mood, memory, attention, concentration, and ability to cope with pain. So whenever you schedule activities or practice coping exercises, consider doing them outside. *Sunlight and nature are medicines!*

Nutrition and Health

Food is your body's fuel source, like gas in a car. But food doesn't just give you energy: adequate nutrition is crucial for good health. Food contains nutrients like vitamins and minerals that help your body run smoothly, like a machine. For example, calcium, a mineral found in dairy products, helps strengthen and repair bones. It facilitates your immune system, helps blood clot, and allows brain cells to communicate. Without calcium, your brain and body simply wouldn't function.

Sometimes teens in pain eat less, skip meals, or develop unhealthy eating habits. This can cause exhaustion, fatigue, headaches, body aches, and pain. It can also lead to vitamin or mineral deficiencies, meaning your body is getting fewer nutrients than it needs. When you are deficient, your body is less able to manage pain. Deficiencies also prevent your immune system from functioning, increasing susceptibility to illness and making it harder for your body to fight off infections. *Being vitamin- and mineral-deficient can not only make you sick but also prevent you from getting well.*

Food, or lack of it, can also affect mood. Have you ever been hangry—so hungry you became irritable and angry? This is your body telling you that you're out of balance and need food! But not all foods are created equal: Some foods are health-ier, while others are less helpful. For example, processed foods high in sugar and preservatives, like fast food, soda, and sugar cereals, can exacerbate inflammation and trigger headaches. This doesn't mean you should stop eating all your favorite foods—it just means that you need to find a good balance. What you put into your body determines what you get out of your body.

Nutrition for Pain

When you're sick or in pain, it's important to eat a variety of fresh whole foods, including fruit, vegetables, whole grains, dairy products, lean proteins, and healthy fats. Here are some healthy foods that promote healing. Optimize your body's ability to fight pain and circle a few you're willing to try!

- Fruit: red grapes, blueberries, strawberries, apples, oranges, pears, cherries, bananas

- Vegetables: leafy greens, carrots, avocados, beets, broccoli, brussels sprouts, cabbage, cauliflower, kale

- Nuts: walnuts, almonds, pecans, peanuts

- Seeds: pumpkin, sunflower

- Whole grains: brown rice, lentils, oatmeal, quinoa, couscous, whole-wheat bread, pasta, popcorn

- Black beans

- Eggs

- Dairy: milk, yogurt, cheese

- Fish: salmon, tuna, trout, mackerel, herring

- Chicken soup (ask Grandma for her recipe!)

- Antioxidant tea: green tea, ginger tea

- Olive oil

Your Nutrition Plan

Three healthy foods you'll add to your diet this week:

1. _____

2. _____

3. _____

One unhealthy food you'll eat less of:

_____

Your plan to ensure three healthy meals a day *(Set a "meal alarm," tell your parents your nutrition plan, go shopping for groceries on the list)*:

_____

_____

_____

Ideas for integrating healthy foods into meals *(Add fruit to breakfast, switch to whole-grain bread for lunch, add a vegetable at dinner, snack on nuts instead of cookies)*:

_____

_____

_____

Social Support: Friends Are Medicine

Social support plays an important role in pain: it's one-third of the biopsychosocial model. Consider this: What punishment is worse than prison? It isn't homework (but good guess). If you misbehave in prison, you're put in solitary confinement—isolated in a room by yourself, with no contact or communication with anyone.

What does it say about humans that the worst punishment you can give us is isolation from others?

Humans are biologically programmed to be social, and healthy functioning depends on it. To survive in the wilderness when we were hunters and gatherers, we needed to collaborate, cooperate, and care for one another. Having more people around provided safety from predators and protected the tribe, and being alone for too long was dangerous. In fact, social behavior is so critical that your brain evolved a system to reward you for it: when you're social, your brain releases oxytocin, serotonin, and dopamine, chemicals that transmit feelings of happiness, connectedness, reward, and pleasure.

When teens are in pain, they're often cut off from friends and peers, and feel left out or left behind. When we're socially isolated, we become anxious, lonely, and depressed—negative emotions that increase pain volume. Social isolation also triggers the stress hormone cortisol, weakening your immune system. It's even thought that the pain of isolation and rejection is neurologically similar to physical pain. It's therefore important for your *physical* health to take care of your *social* health!

When you're sick or in pain, social support is more important than ever. Tap into your trusted support system—family, friends, teams, religious group—and spend time with people who adore you. If you don't have a ready-made support group, find activities that reduce isolation. How can you increase social support?

Here's what Sohita did:

> *Sohita had a maxillofacial condition that caused facial pain and drooping on the left side of her face. She felt embarrassed by how she looked and worried that people would be horrified by her appearance. As a result, she had trouble leaving the safe confines of her house. She was isolated and lonely, and felt sad and forgotten.*
>
> *Sohita loved playing board games, so her dad offered to take her to the game store to buy one. She wanted to go but was nervous she'd bump into someone from school. Her dad suggested going during school hours, when her peers were occupied, so she agreed. When Sohita stepped outside, no one stared. In the parking lot, no one ran away screaming. At the game store, no one pointed.*

The shop owners invited customers to sit down and try a new game. Sohita sat next to a girl her age, who smiled and said hi. Sohita started playing the game and talking to her new friend. It felt amazing. An hour later, her dad wanted to go home, but Sohita felt so good that she didn't want to leave. She and her new friend signed up for regular Wednesday game nights so they could see each other once a week. This experience reminded Sohita that her medical condition didn't have to control who she did or didn't talk to, and it didn't define her life. She felt so much more confident that she reached out to school friends and organized a game night at her house. Having friends helped her feel...normal!

To come up with your friends-are-medicine plan, circle any that might work and then add your own ideas.

- Text or call a friend.

- Find an online support group for teens with your same condition.

- Go to the local dog park and befriend dogs and their owners.

- Invite a friend over to watch a horror movie.

- Go to the local game store for game night.

- Start your own book club.

- Join a choir (even if you can't sing!).

- Sit on your front stoop and make friends with a neighbor.

- Invite a classmate out for ice cream.

- Ask your doctor to connect you with other teens with your condition, or to help you start a group/listserv.

- Start a garage band.

- Join your sports team for an outing, even if you can't play.

- Start a cupcake-baking company with friends.

- Join your local gym and take a class (yoga, spinning, Pilates).

- Get a group together to go to the movies.

- Take an art or computer-programming class.

- Join a lunchtime school club.

- Ask the barista at the café how her day is going.

- Sign up for a teen group at your local library.

Your ideas:

_____

_____

_____

_____

_____

_____

Conclusion

You're almost there, rock star! Now that you're armed with ways to improve your health by improving sleep, exercise, nutrition, and social support, let's put everything together. In the next chapter, we'll combine the different parts of this book to create a pain plan and some daily structure. This will help you stay motivated, organized, and on track. You got this!

Chapter 8

Putting It All Together

Bring It Home

We get better at the things we practice. For example, to get strong arms, lift weights at the gym every day, and soon you'll develop big muscles! If you want to be a "mathlete," practice math every day to become a math star. When you practice something, the brain pathways dedicated to that skill get bigger and stronger. This learning is the reason why the skills we practice become easier and more automatic.

If you want to break your pain cycle, rewire your pain system by establishing a *home-practice routine* and use coping skills—Every. Single. Day. To do this, pick a time and place to practice these skills, even if it's for just ten minutes. It takes a few days to establish a routine, but once you're in the habit of practicing daily, it's easier to keep it up! The most important time to practice is *when pain is low, medium, or absent*—that way, when you have an intense flare-up, your skills will be learned and automatic, and you'll be able to quickly and effectively tackle pain.

Victor's example:

Skill: Mindfulness

Daily practice time: 7:30 p.m. (after dinner but before homework)

Practice location: On the couch in the den

How you'll remember: Set phone alarm, practice with Marie-Helene

Your home practice:

Skill: _____

Daily practice time: _____

Practice location: _____

How you'll remember: _____

Five-Things Plan

You now have a boatload of strategies to improve your health by changing thoughts, emotions, coping strategies, sleep habits, nutrition, exercise, and social and school choices. One great way of putting this all together is to create a Five-Things Plan. Starting today, your mission is to do five things every day to help yourself feel better. Your five things can include any pain coping skill or activity that lowers pain volume and helps get your life back. These are the only guidelines: one thing needs to be *outdoors*, and one thing should be *physical* (you can combine these by exercising outside!). If you're trying to get back to school, pick one academic thing (reading, writing).

Step 1: Make your own personalized Five-Things menu.

Using strategies in this book combined with your own personal goals, make your own menu. For each skill, you can include multiple options for practicing that strategy, as seen on Amanda's menu on the next page. It's okay if some activities fit into two categories; for example, if riding your bike counts as pacing and also a pleasurable activity, you can list it as an option in both categories!

Amanda's Five-Things Menu

Skill	Options
Triggers and emotions	Track triggers, tea-kettle, complete pain recipe worksheet
Activity pacing	Complete pacing worksheet, walk around the block, ride stationary bike for 20 minutes, kick soccer ball outside for 30 minutes
Academic pacing	Attend one class at school daily, read a fun book at home for 20 minutes, do 15 minutes of math homework
Distraction	Complete distraction worksheet, pet puppies at pet store, return book at library, watch movie, draw
Pleasurable activity	Dance every day for 10 minutes, garden outside for 15 minutes, play catch with my dog for 20 minutes daily, paint, ride bike outside for 20 minutes
Biofeedback	Hand-warming
Relaxation, mindfulness	Mindfulness app, belly breathing, body scan, yoga, five-senses mindfulness
Imagery	Safe place imagery (imagine a beach), self-healing imagery
Catch and check thoughts	Thought tracking, thinking traps, detective questions
Change thoughts	Wise Voice, coping thoughts, gratitudes, ten good things, gray thoughts, imagine a miracle
Sleep hygiene	Bed at 11pm and wake at 7am daily, cover clocks, get out of bed after 20 minutes if anxious or not asleep
Nutrition	Eat one fruit or vegetable with each meal, replace cookies with nuts for snack
Social connection	Invite one friend over Friday for game night, swim with Sophia this weekend, call one friend

You can download a blank copy of this menu at http://www.newharbinger.com /33522.

Your Five-Things Menu

Skill	Options
Triggers and emotions	
Activity pacing	
Academic pacing	
Distraction	
Pleasurable activity	
Biofeedback	
Relaxation, mindfulness	
Imagery	
Catch and check thoughts	
Change thoughts	
Sleep hygiene	
Nutrition	
Social connection	
Other ideas	1. 2. 3.

Step 2: Establish a reward plan.

Ask your parents to participate in your plan by rewarding you for using five healthy coping skills each day (hopefully they'll say yes!). Rewards help motivate you and make things more fun. Brainstorm rewards you'd like to earn, from small to big, and make a "reward menu" that looks like a birthday wish-list. You can earn a small daily reward for doing five things (like extra screen time), or add up points after seven successful days to earn a larger reward at the end of the week (a trip, clothing).

Amanda's Reward Menu

1. 20 extra minutes of screen time

2. Slumber party

3. Red Velcro sneakers

4. Swim lessons

5. Trip to Yosemite with Dad

Your Reward Menu:

1. _____

2. _____

3. _____

4. _____

5. _____

Step 3: Select five skills to practice each day this week.

Put these in the chart below, along with the time and place you'll complete these skills. Put the chart somewhere visible—your wall, the fridge—as a daily reminder. Commit to using these skills every day for one week. Use the chart below to track daily progress. You can adjust your Five Things the following week or keep the same ones, as long as one thing is exercise and one is outdoors! Then select a reward from the reward menu. For this example, Amanda and her dad decide she'll earn one point daily toward a Yosemite trip, worth a total of seven points. If she does Five Things every day for seven days, she earns the trip (1 point x 7 days = 7 points). Remember: rewards are only granted for doing *Five Things each day*. If you earned a reward today, log this in the bottom row. Next week, you can adjust your Five Things or keep the same ones. Amanda's Sunday chart below earned a point:

Amanda's Five Things for Sunday 8/16

Skill	Goal	Completed?
1. Activity pacing	Walk around the block at 9am for 20 minutes (exercise + outdoors)	Y
2. Relaxation, mindfulness	Mindfulness app: body scan at 8pm	Y
3. Cognitive	Write out Wise Voice coping thoughts at noon	Y
4. Nutrition	Eat one fruit or vegetable with each meal: grapes with breakfast, apple with lunch, carrots with dinner	Y
5. Social connection	Invite one friend over for game night on Friday	Y
Reward: 1 point toward Yosemite trip!		

You can download a blank copy of this chart at http://www.newharbinger.com/33522.

Your Five Things for (date) _____

Skill	Goal	Completed?
1.		
2.		
3.		
4.		
5.		
Reward:		

Step 4. Track weekly progress.

Use the table below to track weekly progress and rewards. For example, after one week, Amanda is close to earning her Yosemite trip, but isn't quite there because she used coping strategies only four days out of seven.

Amanda's Weekly Tracker

	Five things completed? (Y/N)	Reward (points or items)
Monday	Y	1 point
Tuesday	N	-
Wednesday	Y	1 point
Thursday	Y	1 point
Friday	N	-
Saturday	N	-
Sunday	Y	1 point
Total	**4 days**	**4 points**
Reward?	**N**	**(Almost there!)**

Your Weekly Tracker

	Five things completed? (Y/N)	Reward (points or items)
Monday		
Tuesday		
Wednesday		
Thursday		
Friday		
Saturday		
Sunday		
Total		
Reward?		

Make a Pain Plan

When you feel calm and confident in the face of pain, a flare-up is much less scary. One way to feel prepared is to create a Pain Plan. A Pain Plan is your plan for a tough day that includes effective coping strategies that work for you. This will give you, your parents, doctors, and teachers a road map for how to handle a hard day. Make a plan for home and one for school.

Write out your plan with markers and colorful pen. Tape it to your fridge, put it in your backpack, give your parents a copy, and give one to your teacher or school nurse. This way, if you start feeling bad, everyone will calmly and confidently know exactly what to do—especially *you*.

Eli's pain plan for migraines looks like this:

Home	School
1. Hydrate, eat something	1. Hydrate, eat a granola bar
2. Lie down on the couch for twenty minutes	2. Lie down in nurse's office for twenty minutes
3. Cold pack on head	3. Cold pack on head
4. Relax: listen to guided workbook audio, use mindfulness apps, belly breathe, body scan	4. Relax: bring headphones to listen to mindfulness apps, belly breathe, body scan
5. Distract: hang out with the dog, finish puzzle, bake bread	5. Distract: listen to podcast, bring colored pencils to school and draw
6. Self-talk: "I've had 42 migraines in my life, I know I can get through this one. This won't last forever."	6. Self-talk: "I've had 42 migraines in my life, I know I can get through this one. This won't last forever."
7. Rescue meds for quick relief	7. Rescue meds for quick relief

You can download a blank pain plan at http://www.newharbinger.com/33522.

Your Pain Plan

Home	School

What to Do If You Can't Get Out of Bed

Sometimes teens with pain or illness feel stuck: stuck in bed, stuck at home, just stuck. It's too painful to get up, let alone go outside or go to school. To overcome this hurdle, use the Five-Step Bed Plan.

Step 1. Think about getting out of bed. Use *imagery*. Visualize yourself successfully standing up and walking around your room. Imagine the feeling of your feet on the floor.

Belly breathe: Take three slow, deep belly breaths.

Use self-talk. Notice *Pain Voice*. Listen for *thinking traps*. Talk back: state why they're not true. Tune into *Wise Voice* and use *hurt vs. harm*: "I've gotten out of bed a million times before. Standing up and moving will not harm my body. Moving is the first step toward helping my pain."

Step 2. Move: Sit up. Get blood flowing to your legs by tensing and releasing your calf and thigh muscles. Press your legs and heels into the mattress, then squeeze them together. "Bicycle" your legs in the air while lying on your back.

Self-talk: "This is just my sensitive pain system giving me a false alarm. Moving hurts, but it won't harm me!"

Think of a reward you'll give yourself for getting out of bed: eating a delicious breakfast, watching a show, or cuddling the kitten. This is hard work!

Step 3. Hang your legs over the side of the bed. Let your feet touch floor. Notice how you feel (nervous, excited, overwhelmed) and what's happening in your head. What are you thinking?

Self-talk: Use encouraging, motivating *coping statements*: "I can do this! Just one small step at a time. Pain has been in control for too long. I'm taking control back."

Belly breathe: Take three slow, deep *belly breaths*.

Step 4. Stand up slowly. Hold on to something if you feel unsteady. Walk toward your reward! Scratch the cat, drink hot chocolate, get a hug from your mom. If you're tracking Five Things, make "get out of bed" a thing and give yourself points.

Step 5. Feel proud of yourself for fighting back against Pain Voice, who tells you "you can't." *You can!*

Pain Identity: Who Are You, Really?

It's easy for a teen's life to revolve around pain and illness. In fact, pain can consume your identity. Pain is the reason you don't see friends, stop playing sports, miss school, and lose touch with your community. It's the thing you think about most, the task demanding so much of your energy. Pain can take charge of everything—including who you are. As one teen said: "I'm the girl who spends weekends in the hospital, who's constantly trying new meds, who has to leave school early for doctor's appointments. I'm the girl who's always sick and can't go to parties or on school trips. Sickness has overtaken every aspect of my life. *I am my illness.*"

But now that you've read this book, you know that pain isn't in charge—*you are.* Pain no longer gets to dominate your identity or define who you are. You're about so much more! It's time to take your power back. Let's brainstorm what really defines you, who you *actually* are underneath that pain.

My identity:

People who are most important to me:

_____

_____

_____

Three things I love most in the whole world:

1. _____

2. _____

3. _____

What I like best about myself:

_____

_____

_____

My hobbies:

_____

_____

_____

Subject(s) I like to study most:

_____

_____

_____

Favorite movies:

_____

_____

_____

Favorite books:

_____

_____

_____

Favorite foods:

_____

_____

_____

People I feel most like myself around:

_____

_____

_____

Three things that make me laugh:

1. _____

2. _____

3. _____

I'm really good at:

_____

_____

_____

My favorite memory:

_____

_____

_____

I'm an interesting person because:

_____

_____

_____

When I get older, I'd like to be (list as many ideas as you have!):

_____

_____

_____

You are so much more than your pain!

The Beginning

Ha! I bet you thought this was going to say "conclusion." Well, guess what: you've arrived at the beginning. True, it's the end of the workbook—congratulations, you are officially one step closer to a less stressful, less painful life! You hung in there, you did the work, and I am so proud of you. But though this book may be ending… *the rest of your life is just beginning.* You now carry these strategies with you wherever you go. Take them out into the world and use them, so that *you* are in charge of your pain!

Acknowledgments

Profound gratitude for Drs. Lorimer Moseley, international pain expert, author, and name-abbreviator, for his generous feedback; Elliot Krane for his insightful foreword; and Matt McKay for believing in this book. A special thanks to Drs. Victor Yalom, Jay Schulz-Heik, Cristina Benki, Erik Peper, Amy Gelfand, and David Becker for their friendship, consultation, and collaboration; and to Tesilya Hanauer, Jennifer Holder, and Karen Schader for their invaluable edits. And, finally—to Dr. Glenn Rosenbluth, who inadvertently set me on the path that would change my life.

Apps and Websites to Lower Pain Volume

Practicing pain-control techniques is even easier when you have support and guidance. Here are some great resources that include guided audio for belly breathing, body scans, and other mindfulness and relaxation practices. These apps and websites are (currently) free. Try them all and see which ones you like!

Websites

Dr. Z's guided audio for this book: http://www.newharbinger.com/33522

Comfort-Ability, relaxation and mindfulness audio: https://www.thecomfortability.com/blogs/guided-exercises-mindfulness

Dr. Tonya Palermo's guided audio exercises for pain: http://www.seattle childrens.org/research/child-health-behavior-and-development/pediatric-pain -and-sleep-innovations-lab/selected-recent-publications/

Dr. Dawn Buse's audio (under the "relaxation" tab): http://dawnbuse.com /relaxation.htm

Guided mindfulness-based stress reduction (MBSR) exercises (left side under "practices"): https://palousemindfulness.com/

UCLA's guided meditations: http://marc.ucla.edu/mindful-meditations

Dr. Z's website: http://www.zoffness.com

Apps

Stop Breathe Think: guided relaxation and meditations, plus an "emotional check-in." Exercises range from 3–15 minutes.

Headspace: relaxation and mindfulness audio.

Relax Melodies: guided meditations with music and nature sounds. Includes audio for sleep.

Breathe2Relax: teaches diaphragmatic breathing. Change "breath settings" to extend your exhale and facilitate greater relaxation.

Rain Rain: relaxing soundscapes for studying, relaxing and sleeping.

BellyBio Interactive Breathing: teaches and monitors belly breathing.

Lists of awesome apps: https://www.painbc.ca/recommended-apps-help-manage-persistent-pain and https://paindoctor.com/pain-diary-apps/

Additional Resources

American Pain Society: list of pediatric chronic pain programs (under "Additional Resources," http://americanpainsociety.org/get-involved/shared-interest-groups/pediatric-adolescent-pain)

Stopchildhoodpain.org: information on pain conditions and treatments

CarePath: apps and resources for understanding and managing pain (https://www.mycarepath.ca)

Coping Club: coping ideas for youths with pain and illness (http://copingclub.com)

Pain Bytes: pain management ideas for youths (https://www.aci.health.nsw.gov.au/chronic-pain/painbytes)

Child Kind: library of resources on pediatric pain (http://library.childkindinternational.org)

Rachel Zoffness, PhD, is a clinical psychologist, medical consultant, educator, and author specializing in chronic pain, medical illness, and injury. She provides cognitive behavioral therapy (CBT) to teens and adults, provides lectures and trainings, and serves as a consultant to hospitals and health professionals. Zoffness—also known as 'Dr. Z'—teaches at the University of California, San Francisco (UCSF) School of Medicine, providing pain neuroscience education to medical residents and interns. She was trained at Brown; Columbia; the University of California, San Diego; San Diego State University; the New York University Child Study Center; Mount Sinai West; and the Mindful Center.

Zoffness taught undergraduate psychology courses at San Diego State University, supervised therapists-in-training at the Wright Institute Berkeley Cognitive Behavioral Therapy Clinic, and has published extensively on evidence-based therapies. She serves on the steering committee of the American Association of Pain Psychology (AAPP), founded AAPP's pediatric division, and is a member of the East Bay Pediatrician's Journal Club. She collaborates with UCSF's Pediatric Brain Center, and Pain and Palliative Care Clinic; Stanford's Pediatric Pain Management Clinic; the Osher Center for Integrative Medicine; and consults on the development of international pain programs. When not seeing patients, Rachel can typically be found hiking and chasing butterflies.

Foreword writer **Elliot J. Krane, MD**, is a graduate of the University of Arizona College of Medicine, and completed his medical training in pediatrics and anesthesiology at Massachusetts General Hospital, and Boston Children's Hospital. He has held faculty positions at the University of Washington and Seattle Children's Hospital, where he and his colleague Donald C. Tyler, MD, started the first pain clinic for children in the US.

More ⏱ Instant Help Books for Teens

An Imprint of New Harbinger Publications

**THE INSOMNIA WORKBOOK
FOR TEENS**

Skills to Help You Stop Stressing &
Start Sleeping Better

978-1684031245 / US $17.95

**THE ANXIETY
WORKBOOK FOR TEENS**

Activities to Help You Deal with
Anxiety & Worry

978-1572246034 / US $15.95

**THE RESILIENCE
WORKBOOK FOR TEENS**

Activities to Help You Gain
Confidence, Manage Stress &
Cultivate a Growth Mindset

978-1684032921 / US $16.95

PUT YOUR WORRIES HERE

A Creative Journal for Teens
with Anxiety

978-1684032143 / US $16.95

**CONQUER NEGATIVE
THINKING FOR TEENS**

A Workbook to Break the
Nine Thought Habits That Are
Holding You Back

978-1626258891 / US $16.95

**EATING MINDFULLY
FOR TEENS**

A Workbook to Help You Make
Healthy Choices, End Emotional
Eating & Feel Great

978-1684030033 / US $16.95

newharbingerpublications
1-800-748-6273 / newharbinger.com

(VISA, MC, AMEX / prices subject to change without notice)

Follow Us

Don't miss out on new books in the subjects that interest you.
Sign up for our **Book Alerts** at **newharbinger.com/bookalerts**

Register your **new harbinger** titles for additional benefits!

When you register your **new harbinger** title— purchased in any format, from any source—you get access to benefits like the following:

- Downloadable accessories like printable worksheets and extra content

- Instructional videos and audio files

- Information about updates, corrections, and new editions

Not every title has accessories, but we're adding new material all the time.

Access free accessories in 3 easy steps:

1. Sign in at NewHarbinger.com (or **register** to create an account).

2. Click on **register a book**. Search for your title and click the **register** button when it appears.

3. Click on the **book cover or title** to go to its details page. Click on **accessories** to view and access files.

That's all there is to it!

If you need help, visit:

NewHarbinger.com/accessories

new harbinger
CELEBRATING
40 YEARS

Also by Robin Kirman

Bradstreet Gate

The End of

Getting Lost

a novel

Robin Kirman

Simon & Schuster

new york   london   toronto   sydney   new delhi

Simon & Schuster
1230 Avenue of the Americas
New York, NY 10020

This book is a work of fiction. Any references to historical events, real people,
or real places are used fictitiously. Other names, characters, places, and events
are products of the author's imagination, and any resemblance to actual
events or places or persons, living or dead, is entirely coincidental.

Copyright © 2022 by Robin Kirman

First Simon & Schuster hardcover edition January 2022

SIMON & SCHUSTER and colophon are registered trademarks of Simon & Schuster, Inc.

For information about special discounts for bulk purchases,
please contact Simon & Schuster Special Sales
at 1-866-506-1949 or business@simonandschuster.com.

The Simon & Schuster Speakers Bureau can bring authors to your live event.
For more information or to book an event, contact the
Simon & Schuster Speakers Bureau at 1-866-248-3049 or
visit our website at www.simonspeakers.com.

Interior design by Ruth Lee-Mui

Manufactured in the United States of America

1   3   5   7   9   10   8   6   4   2

Library of Congress Cataloging-in-Publication Data is available.

ISBN 978-1-9821-5985-6
ISBN 978-1-9821-5987-0 (ebook)

For Emmanuelle

The End of

Getting Lost

One

Gina // Lake Walen

June 1996

It was the end of getting lost—a moment when travel could still feel like taking leave of the familiar, before there were ten different means for a person to be reached in almost any corner of the world in which she might be standing, when letters and postcards would still follow slowly on the heels of a young couple moving across Europe, and two people in love could escape their old reality a little, experiencing the world before them like a shared dream.

The year was 1996, the month June, when Gina and Duncan arrived at the Walensee, a lake less than an hour's drive from the clinic near Zurich where she had spent the past two weeks. She'd come there to recuperate from a head injury she'd suffered from a bad fall in Berlin. The injury hadn't been a small one, rehabilitation was required, but now that Gina was well enough to do without doctors and nurses, she and Duncan had escaped to the Swiss countryside. The scenery around Lake Walen was possibly the loveliest and most peaceful that she had ever seen: small villages

1

of white, red-roofed houses, lush fields of wildflowers and, across the still, blue water, green mountains topped with milky clouds. They'd spent three days there in a small guesthouse, hiking and biking among the villages, or boating on the lake. Duncan didn't usually swim, and the lake water was cold, but Gina liked to jump in anyway in the hours when the sun was strongest. After she'd tired herself with laps, and as the light began to weaken, she'd leave the water to go inside and dress, and then they'd bring their chairs down to the grassy banks to take in the sky and lake, lit pink and gold by the setting sun.

During this quiet hour, Duncan, who was a classical composer, listened to music with headphones on his Discman, and, beside him, Gina read—Fitzgerald's *Tender Is the Night*, which Duncan had bought her that week as a gift. He'd been aware a Zurich clinic featured in the story, otherwise under the impression that it was a romance about a glamorous American couple traveling in Europe. The day after Duncan gave Gina the book, her doctor at the clinic had remarked on the Swiss sanatorium, and Gina had been forced to tell Duncan that it wasn't a happy story, that the wife in the novel was mentally ill.

"Oh God, forget it, then," Duncan had pleaded, but she'd made clear that reading it didn't upset her. On the contrary, it soothed her to return to a novel that she'd read before and remembered—in better detail than she possessed regarding her own recent life.

In the last weeks, Gina had often felt like she was crazy—though the doctors in the hospital in West Berlin and at the Zurich clinic had made clear that what she'd experienced was entirely a physical trauma. She'd suffered a concussion and intracranial swelling, and no one could predict what sort of recovery she'd make. The consensus by the end was that she'd been lucky. Her sight and hearing were normal and she had no speech difficulties, no aphasia. Her mind was sharp, her reasoning was good, and her moods were stable. Her dizzy spells were now gone, her balance and motor coordination perfectly restored. In fact, only two weeks after her injury, she was taking runs through the Swiss woods.

The only significant loss in functioning involved her memory. She couldn't recall anything of the accident or of the months leading up to her trip. Beyond that, there were stretches of experience that remained missing, which she didn't know she missed—her dance performances that year, the departure from New York of their two close friends—until Duncan would refer to these and nothing would come to mind.

At the same time, there were also many things that she did remember that before she'd forgotten. It was as if her mind had been shaken during the impact, and material that had been buried cast up to the top again. Scenes from her childhood, for instance, a trip she'd taken with her parents to Italy when her mother was still healthy. Gina could see her mother quite clearly, as she'd looked on that visit—in a white dress walking barefoot on the beach, her dark curls to her shoulders, her smile wide and bright as the pale sand—looking, Gina realized with a pang, very much the way she herself looked now.

Her recent brush with death had brought her closer to her late mother, and closer too to Duncan, who had hardly left her side since the accident, except to see that she received the best possible care. Unimpressed with the medical standard in Berlin, where she'd been hospitalized first, he'd proposed moving her to the clinic just outside of Zurich, where the techniques for physical rehabilitation were more advanced. Gina was a dancer, he let the doctor know, and therefore required special treatment.

The Swiss clinic had been state of the art, and during her stay there, Gina often wondered how all this would be paid for. She had a hefty inheritance from her mother, but Duncan had always refused to touch it and insisted she keep it in an account separate from him. He preferred to live frugally from what they earned, though in this case he insisted on sparing no expense.

"I'd pay any amount to have you back as you were again."

She'd grasped then how much the prospect of losing her had undone him. In some ways, her accident had been even more frightening for Duncan, as the only one who could recall it.

She'd asked him, once, to describe that day for her: They'd been in Berlin almost a week when Gina set off for a morning walk around the city. Duncan would have joined her, but that morning he'd been struck with musical inspiration he wanted to get down onto paper. As Duncan worked, morning turned to afternoon, and Gina still hadn't returned. He was beginning to grow nervous when the phone rang in his room. A hotel receptionist was calling to relay a message from a local hospital. Gina had suffered an accident.

Duncan had rushed over to the address that he'd been given: the Charité Hospital on Luisenstrasse. There, the doctor presiding over Gina's case told him what had happened, that Gina had been found at a construction site at Potsdamer Platz. It seemed she'd gone poking around one of the sections that was off-limits and that she'd slipped along the way and hit her head on a piece of exposed pipe. Tourists had discovered her, unconscious, and called an ambulance. Inside her pocket was a hotel key with her room number, and this was how she'd been identified and

Duncan had been reached. Her prognosis was still uncertain then; the doctors didn't know what state she'd be in when she awoke.

"I thought I'd lost you," Duncan told her. "I lived it in that hospital that night, life without you. You were gone."

In moments when she caught him looking at her, she could see that this was true—he seemed not to trust that she was real, as though at any instant she might disappear.

"Still here," she'd tease him, smiling reassuringly, but hiding her private thoughts—she was mostly there, sure, but what parts of her were lost?

She'd asked Duncan to fill in any large events of the last year. He insisted her life had gone on much as before. She'd continued dancing with the same experimental company, and Duncan continued to play piano there to accompany rehearsals. They collaborated on their own work: Duncan composed music and she choreographed dances to go with it. The biggest change was that Duncan had landed his first significant commission, which enabled them to afford this trip, their belated honeymoon. She and Duncan had been married for over a year; they were the only couple that had married among their young friends. But since then, they hadn't been able to find the time or funds for such a frivolous excursion. And now, here they were.

Their travels, Duncan told her, were to last the whole summer, starting in Berlin and moving west. They'd planned on heading to either Munich or Vienna, but they'd changed their minds on the day that Gina was released from the clinic in Zurich, after they'd sat down in a café and she'd noticed a discarded *International Herald Tribune* left behind on a chair. America was gearing up for an election in the fall: Clinton against Dole. In Russia, the first presidential election was also underway, with Boris Yel-tsin struggling to maintain power. Also that spring, Bosnian war criminals were ordered by the UN to stand trial; a bombing by the IRA in Manchester had injured two hundred people, and, back in America, a man named Ted Kaczynski had been identified as the Unabomber and indicted. As Gina read, her heart started to thud—the sheer breadth of what she'd missed, the many events unfolding that she knew nothing about. After that, they'd agreed on stopping at Lake Walen: a place with no one around to prompt her thoughts besides a landlady who came to drop fresh daffodils inside their room, a place where it was easy to forget the larger world, and so forget what she'd forgotten.

Now, on their fourth and last day here, she and Duncan planned on renting the landlady's car to visit the Churfirsten mountains, where they would hike to the Paxmal, the famous monument to peace.

They left after breakfast and drove out to the bottom of the mountain to begin the long, steep hike. The way up was diffi-cult, and Gina found herself thinking of the man who'd made this trek on his own hundreds of times in order to construct the monument: a rectangular stone building with thick columns, a reflecting pool in front, and, along each side of the pool, stone walls decorated with mosaics. According to the guidebook, all this work had been accomplished by a single artist, and had taken him twenty-five years of grueling effort. The story moved Gina—the solitude in which this man maintained his vision. She wrapped her arms around Duncan and leaned into him, hold-ing him tight. She'd always longed for an artistic life, but feared its loneliness. What a gift to have Duncan, her husband and a composer, a man she could both love and create with, sharing in beauty together.

The hike down the mountain was quicker, but still, by the time she and Duncan returned to the guesthouse for lunch, it was quarter past two. The cook was upset over having to put out food so late, since lunch service, she reminded them, was officially meant to end at two.

"I guess it's not just a cliché," Duncan muttered under his breath, "the Swiss and time."

As a punishment, the cook brought out the same food she'd served for lunch the day before: reheated salmon and potatoes.

As Gina picked at a spongy bit of potato, Duncan pushed his plate away. "Forget this, we've got the car all night. Let's drive somewhere and get a real meal."

After the lunch, which the cook frowned to see they hadn't eaten, they stopped at the reception desk so that Duncan could tell the owner of the guesthouse, Ms. Arner, that they wouldn't be around for dinner.

"I think my wife and I could use a night out."

My wife. The description sounded alien to Gina; *wife* and *husband* were terms they'd used only in private, when they didn't need to hide how much those archaic, yet still fresh, titles thrilled them.

They returned to their room, where Gina pointed out that there was enough sun left for a swim. At the lake, Duncan splashed around up to his waist, while Gina jumped in with a shout and swam laps in the cold water for as long as she could stand it.

When she emerged, shivering in the last rays of sun, Duncan

was waiting for her with a towel. He wrapped himself around her, containing the warmth between them. When he spoke, chest pressed to her bare back, his words seemed to vibrate within her. "This might be the happiest that I've ever been."

Around six they started getting ready. Duncan whistled as he dressed in a yellow linen suit that he'd gotten before they left Zurich. He hadn't brought many clothes with him on the trip, preferring to travel light, picking up what he needed as they went. Gina put on a blue dress, then searched for the silk satchel that contained her jewelry.

Inside, there wasn't much: a pair of diamond earrings that she'd received from her grandparents at her high school graduation, an anklet she'd bought in college, on a trip into the city with her best friend, Violet. Her most cherished piece was a ring she'd been given by her mother, a yellow stone, not precious, but exotic: it had functioned as an engagement ring until Duncan could afford a proper one—what little money they had they'd spent on simple bands. Hers hung a little loosely on her finger, she'd noticed; apparently she'd lost some weight from the stress her injury had caused her.

Feeling around in the satchel for her mother's ring, she found a chain caught among some threads at the bottom. She pulled it out: a silver bracelet with a turquoise stone at the center. It must be from her father or other family in Santa Fe, she thought, but when she turned the piece over, she noticed an inscription on the back: *For My Love.*

"Did you give this to me?" she asked Duncan, thinking that he knew her taste too well to choose a piece that was so bland.

He laid the bracelet in his palm and took note of the

inscription. "It's from an aunt of yours. Some sort of family heirloom."

Could she have forgotten such a thing? She felt a moment of unease at her failure to recall, but told herself not to dwell on such details. Did she really need to know the story behind every small object in her possession—the countless bits of information that we all carry with us and let shape, in some cluttered and arbitrary way, our sense of who we are? There was something freeing in forgetting, she'd discovered, as if all these tiny accretions were like layers of clothing that kept you from feeling the air, the night, the life that was cloaked around you.

She looked over at Duncan, seeing him almost freshly then, with the years together stripped away, revealing the qualities she loved in him: his gentleness, his intelligence, his delicate dark features and the green eyes that always had a slightly distracted look about them, like he was listening to some inner song only he could hear.

He turned to take her arm then, and she stepped out into the cool Swiss evening, with the sounds of crickets and lapping water and a man beside her with a mild voice and smiling face who'd stood by her and loved her since she was nineteen.

The drive to the restaurant wasn't an easy one. The roads were dark and curving, the signs difficult to spot. She and Duncan had to pull over twice to consult a map before locating the simple stone building with a restaurant in the back. The room was rustic but elegant, with exposed wooden beams, red tablecloths, and candles.

Duncan pulled out Gina's seat for her and, as she thanked him, she almost called him by the wrong name. "Graham—" she began, and stopped herself, puzzling.

Before she could remark on it, Duncan rushed to speak. "Supposed to be classic Swiss cooking, this place."

"I don't think I know what that is."

"Well, the guidebook says we need to get the cholera."

"Like the disease?"

"Exactly." He described for her what he'd read: "During the epidemic, since people were afraid to leave their homes, they'd throw everything into a pie."

"Desperation casserole." She laughed, and she could see how much it pleased him, since the accident, to see her having fun.

They turned to study the menu and Gina noted the prices. "Duncan, it's too expensive."

"Oh, it's fine. One plate of cholera won't kill us."

"I'm serious. The way we've been spending, and we've still got months ahead—"

"We're fine," he insisted, and reached across for her hand, just as the waiter stepped up to pour their water and describe the evening's specials. Gina tried to listen, to let her concerns go, though she couldn't quite believe that Duncan, who'd worked sometimes for free as a composer, had suddenly been paid enough to afford all this. As she wondered, she became aware of another distraction: a man was watching her from across the room. She looked away, concentrating on her order, but when the waiter left, the man was still staring. He was heavyset, with receding white hair and a pink face.

Meanwhile, Duncan had begun to speak about their itinerary. "Plus, later in the summer it will be packed, which is another reason to start there."

"What's that?"

"The South of France."

"Sorry, I wasn't listening," she admitted, and, leaning forward, added more softly, "There's a man over there who keeps looking at me. Do we know him? In the corner, with the white hair."

Duncan turned in his chair to check, and Gina saw the man lower his eyes.

"Never seen him. But he looks pretty harmless to me."

After a moment, the man went back to staring, and Gina began to fidget in her seat. She'd been out in public so little since her accident, and some of the effects of her injury had made her self-conscious. She felt a sudden urge to study herself in a mirror, so she stood and told Duncan she was heading to the bathroom.

In the mirror above the sink, she confronted a woman of twenty-five, her curly auburn hair cut shorter than she recalled wearing it, which made her look younger than she was. Nothing showed of her injury but the remnants of a scrape across one cheekbone. She smiled, just to make sure her smile was even, as it had not been in the first days at the hospital. This small change, temporary as it proved to be, had terrified her. She'd found herself thinking of her mother—after her stroke, her smile had never been the one in the pictures from before.

When Gina stepped out into the dining room again, Duncan wasn't at their table. She spotted him in the corner, speaking with the man who'd been staring at her. Catching her eye, Duncan abruptly excused himself to meet her back at their table, settling into his seat just as she settled into hers.

"Did you find out who he is?" she asked him.

"A German tourist. He said he'd seen you performing in Vienna."

"*Really?*" She supposed it was possible: she had spent two

summers in Vienna, dancing for an international festival, though her parts hadn't been large ones. "I'm surprised anyone would notice a single dancer in a group."

"*I'd* have noticed you," said Duncan, smiling.

The food arrived. Gina had ordered the *pastetli*, a meat pie, which she no longer felt like eating. She was agitated, suddenly, restless in her chair. Her first Vienna tour, as magical as it had been, had also directly preceded her mother's death. She'd had the call from her father about her mother's final, fatal stroke a week before she was due to return home.

She felt a sudden pang—homesickness, she thought. Now and then she'd had the impulse to call her father, though Duncan had reminded her of the risks involved in that. Her father was bound to panic at the news of the accident. After his wife's stroke, Mr. Reinhold never remarried. Gina became his everything. It would terrify him to learn his only child, so far from home, had suffered a brain injury of all things, and, even if her not calling might cause him worry too, nothing could be worse than his reliving some version of her mother's decline, noting minor gaps in Gina's awareness, or some way in which she might fail to be the person that she'd been before.

"Are you all right?" Duncan asked, peering up from his plate.

"I'm fine." She saw no point in spoiling things with her grim thoughts. "Go on with what you were saying."

"Our itinerary." Duncan hesitated but, after a short pause, went on. "I'd been thinking France, I guess, along the Riviera. There are some quieter spots, and better to visit now than in July or August, when the whole region is packed. Plus I speak French, so we can navigate more easily. What do you think?"

She hadn't given much thought to their travels, though now that

Vienna had been mentioned, she felt she'd like to go there again. And she'd intended to drop in too on her friend Violet, in Prague.

"If we're heading west, doesn't it make sense to visit Vienna and Prague first? I'd like to visit Violet for a day or two at least."

Duncan raised his glass quickly, and wine spilled onto his upper lip. "You don't remember what happened with you two? That argument you had?"

No, she didn't have the slightest recollection of any fight with her best friend, though it wasn't inconceivable that it could happen. She and Violet both had strong opinions, about their work and about Duncan—whom Violet had never liked—and it was a function of their loyalty to one another that they hadn't butted heads more often. "When did we fight?"

"It was after she'd moved to Prague. Over the phone. I guess she'd been dismissive about a piece I'd written. Nothing new, but this time she'd gone too far and you were really shouting, said you'd had it, you were done with her."

Violet putting down Duncan was plausible enough, though Gina didn't see much point in staying angry when she'd forgotten why she was.

"In that case, I think I should definitely call her. Take the chance to repair things while I'm here."

Duncan took a bite of his casserole and chewed it before responding. "Right, sure you should. Though I don't see any reason to put yourself under pressure right away. Plus, Prague isn't a simple place to get around, so maybe better to start with Vienna?"

She pictured Vienna then, recalled the nights she'd spent there on her first visit. She and her fellow dancers had performed at the Volkstheater, a grand building on the corner of Arthur-Schnitzler-Platz, stretching out backward, like a crouching animal. There were two tiers of columns at the entrance, but the relative modesty of the exterior gave little hint of what lay inside: red velvet seats and curtains, crystal chandeliers, a fresco on the ceiling. Perhaps it was the sheer beauty of the place that caused her to put more into her dancing in Vienna than she ever had before. Her limbs felt more powerful, her instincts freer. She'd had the thought that this was her apotheosis, the moment when her talent as a dancer reached its peak, and she would look back on those nights, years later, and recall that fleeting bliss.

"Yes, right. I think Vienna would do me good."

"Great, then we're decided."

Duncan clinked his glass against hers and Gina took a sip of wine. Soon she began to relax, to enjoy the food, the cozy room—until the man who'd been staring at her before rose from his table. She watched him lay his napkin down, squeeze by another diner, and make his way toward her. For a moment, she thought the stranger might say something, but when she looked up he turned away, disappearing out the door into the darkness.

The next morning, a vision struck Gina as she woke from sleep. She was in a gallery, in a white and airy space, with paintings on the walls. She crossed the room and came to stand in front of a portrait of Duncan and herself. This was a painting her father had done of them for their wedding. She stood there, facing the portrait, in an atmosphere of sadness, and then a tall, sandy-haired man stepped up alongside her. He leaned over and whispered something in her ear that made her start.

She sat up sharply, there in the bed she shared with Duncan. He was awake, looking at her.

"A bad dream?" he asked her, rubbing her back.

"No, just a thought . . . nothing." She lay back down beside him and felt his hand stroke her thigh under the sheet.

He'd been especially hungry for sex since the accident, and she'd been too, maybe for the connection it gave her to him, or the grounding in her own body. She was young and healthy, alive, his touch reminded her, and she curled under him as he began to kiss her, her cheeks, her neck, lifting up her top to bare her stomach.

She looked down at him, at his smooth shoulders, that transfixed expression he always wore when he was aroused, moving in a daze but deliberately, a mood of sex he'd absorbed from her, years ago, but which had since become a state evolved together— their style of movement, their patient tangles. Arching up over her, he reached for the nightstand drawer. She drew him back to her.

He hesitated, about to say something, until she reached for him by the hips and drew him inside her. She looked him in the eyes so he could read her desire, then pulled him closer so that his face was at her ear and she could hear the sounds he made, deep and adult one moment and in the next just like the eager boy who'd been almost a virgin when she first led him to her bed.

"I love you," he told her after, dropping behind her and pressing her up against him so she could feel his heart going fast.

"I love you too."

They lay there like that, in the quiet morning light, until Duncan finally stood and announced he'd take a shower.

"Want to join me?"

She did, really; he looked sweetly boyish standing there, with his face flushed, naked before her. But then she recalled her

15

vision that morning and felt an urge to write it down. Had it been a dream? Or a flash of memory, like she sometimes had now? She wanted to collect these impressions that came to her, usually when she wasn't hoping to have them, when she wasn't trying to remember anything at all.

"You go ahead. I'll have a last dip in the lake before we go."

He nodded, disappointed, but she rose and kissed him again before he turned toward the bathroom and she moved to the desk. As the shower ran, she jotted down what parts of the image she could recall—*large gallery, Dad's show—Santa Fe? Stranger with blond hair.* She supposed she might ask her father to tell her if such a show had taken place, but these were just the sorts of questions that would make him worry. How frustrating it was not to be able to simply pick up the phone and have some answers.

Their room seemed smaller and more confining now. Crossing to the suitcase, she rummaged for her swimsuit. As she did, she came across the pad of stationery she'd brought with her, along with matching envelopes.

If she couldn't call her father, why not at least write him a letter? In a letter she could craft precisely what she wished to say. Crossing back to the desk and pulling out a fresh page, she began:

Dear Dad,

I'm writing to you from the countryside not too far from Zurich where Duncan and I have been resting up after Berlin. Berlin was thrilling and exhausting. I'm sure you'd be inspired by it. Everywhere the past is being smashed and rebuilt. Imagine a whole city intent on erasing history, reinventing itself according to new possibilities. It's like an art studio twenty miles wide.

She thought of other details she might invent—going to one of the nightclubs that had sprung up in old industrial sites, drinking with East Berliners and hearing their stories of childhoods filled with longings, disloyalties, and daily duplicities. Instead she caught herself, feeling guilty for enjoying the fiction a bit too much. Staying on course, she considered what else she should say. She ought to tell her father how to reach her, but the letter would take up to two weeks to arrive in Santa Fe, and then his reply would take as long to cross the ocean again. By that time she had no idea where she and Duncan might be.

Vienna will be next—Duncan and I leave today—though after that, nothing has been planned. I'll have to phone at some point when our itinerary is more solid, but in the meantime, I hope you're staying cool in the Santa Fe summer. Wear a hat—maybe I'll pick one up for you, something stylish from Paris or Rome. Miss you, Daddy, and love you.

Your girl,
Gina

She was signing the letter as Duncan stepped out from the bathroom in a towel. She folded up the paper and slid it inside an envelope. Duncan mentioned that they had stamps at reception. "I'll bring it down later with the luggage," he offered, bending to kiss her, brushing back the hair that clung wetly to his face.

Checkout wasn't until one, so Gina went to take her final swim while Duncan finished packing and settled the bill. Leaving out a change of clothes and putting on her bathing suit, she walked barefoot to the lakeside, which was grass nearly to the edge. She jumped into the water to avoid stepping on the pebbly bottom, and as she did another memory came to her—visiting Abiquiu Lake as a small girl. This was in the years before she could swim, before she was long and strong, when she would cling to her mother's warm body, lacking the courage to let go, the faith that, alone, she wouldn't just sink and sink and sink.

Now she swam hard, as if swimming against her own fear and confusion, the quiet terror that not knowing parts of her past still caused her. She swam for so long, in fact, that her lips began to quiver from the cold, and she worried that she'd be late to leave. Hurrying onto the grass, she raced up to the room to get changed.

Dressed again, she went to the reception room, spotting Duncan with his back to her. He was speaking into the desk phone.

"Yes, it all came through, thank you. I just wanted to add, I hope you know I never meant to hurt you."

She stopped herself, hearing these words. She'd assumed he was dealing with something practical, a reservation or an incorrect bill.

The landlady, Ms. Arner, called to her from across the desk and Duncan turned too, facing Gina with a casual expression in no way suited to the tone in which he'd just been speaking. Putting his hand over the receiver, he mouthed to her, "My mother."

"Ah, right."

She backed away, not to intrude. It was unfortunate how little interaction she and Duncan's mother had with one another, but she'd come to accept that this wasn't likely to change. Mrs. Lowy had been born a Jew in Alsace-Lorraine during the Second World War and, from the moment she'd heard Gina's last name was Reinhold, she'd regarded her with suspicion. Gina could only imagine what the woman would make of their visiting first Berlin and then Vienna.

"We'll need to talk about this another time, okay? I'm sorry. I promise I'll call again." Duncan hung up the line, shaking his head.

"Is everything all right?" Gina asked him.

He didn't answer right away. The call seemed to have unsteadied him. "Just had to check in, let her know we're okay."

"And apologize?"

"For leaving her behind, taking a trip, leading our own independent happy lives." He smiled, but Gina was still bothered.

"You didn't tell her we were headed to Austria?"

"No, God no. She thinks we're in London. She sent us letters there, apparently. I had to pretend we'd gotten them."

Regrettable as it was, she understood that lies like these couldn't be avoided. She and Duncan were both obliged to lie about this trip, in different ways, to protect their parents' feelings. She thought about the letter to her father, which she spotted atop a small pile of letters on the table behind the desk. Ms. Arner was standing by the table, copying something into a ledger.

"Thank you," Gina called to her. "For everything. It's been perfect here, really."

"Oh, it's been my pleasure," said Ms. Arner. "I wish all my guests could be this nice; I wish all couples could be so cheering as you both."

Gina smiled at the woman and then at Duncan, who was still watching the phone, distracted. When he noticed her looking at him, he quickly warmed, wrapping an arm around her waist. "There's a one o'clock train from Zurich to Vienna," he announced. "I've called a car to take us to the station."

Despite her unease that morning, she couldn't help but be excited that they were off to Vienna. Soon she'd be seeing that lovely city again: the fine, pale buildings tiled in bright orange or domed in verdigris; the rows of trees, the fountains and the statues, the monuments that peered out in the distance, extravagantly lit. She hadn't gotten to visit nearly enough of it during the rush of the festival, night after night spent dancing in that glittering theater, then spilling, drunk from motion and exhaustion, onto the vibrant streets. She'd made a mental list of all that she meant to see once the performances were done, but circumstance intervened, a dreadful call came from her father, and so those sights remained unreached: the Tiergarten, the Prater, the Hotel Sacher—all penetrated by a deeper yearning that made her wary of visiting without Duncan there too.

She leaned against him, thinking of how he'd held her after the flight home from Vienna—he'd arrived for her mother's funeral ahead of her, and was there to greet her when she stepped, in a daze, from the plane in New Mexico. Her Duncan. Her home, wherever in the world they might be.

Two

June 1996

*V*ienna was aglow. It was as elegant as Gina had described it after her first return, a time that had once felt far in the past, but which, in the last weeks, felt strangely near. It had been a shock to realize that time could be erased in this way—that Gina could suffer a fall and suddenly he was faced with the woman she was a year ago. He kept trying to imagine himself in Gina's place, waking up in a foreign country with no idea how he'd gotten there, and only one familiar face to rely on as a guide.

Now Gina was enjoying the chance to play guide for a change.

She sat beside him, rapturous at the taxi window, pointing to the buildings she still recognized.

"That's the Kunsthistorisches Museum," she said, "and there's the Hofburg Palace. And that one, over there, that's the Staatsoper." She pointed to a building in the distance, intricate and lit bright gold, like an immense filigreed treasure.

He forced himself to smile so as not to reveal his alarm: if she could recall the buildings in Vienna, what else might she soon recall?

They were approaching the Danube River now, the shining city reflected in the water, and Duncan did his best to relax into the ride. The car radio played and he focused on the music—he'd have preferred to hear classical while exploring this city, home to Strauss and Schubert, and the stomping ground for so many others of the world's greatest composers, Beethoven, Haydn, Mozart— but the taxi driver preferred to play American pop songs. "Don't Speak" came on, and Duncan hummed along, waiting to see if Gina did the same. All spring that song had played back in the States, and yet Gina didn't know it—he watched her to be sure, to see if the words didn't rise to her lips unbidden. Her silence calmed him. He exhaled and turned back to the window, relieved. No, she did not remember, not the faintest note.

The car crossed the bridge and headed up a wide road, Prater-strasse, on the way to their hotel. Together he and Gina had chosen a hotel not far from the train station and in the same area as the Prater, Vienna's famous amusement park. The room cost a third of what they'd pay in other parts of the city, both of them agreeing that the money they saved on the hotel could be spent elsewhere. He wondered if Gina regretted this decision now, leaving behind the charm of the other districts. In Praterstern, the main square was plain, with a few trees and a gangly-looking column. The streets were darker and more deserted. A cable car ambled behind them. He hoped she wasn't disappointed.

Their hotel on Walcherstrasse was even more dismal than Duncan feared. The lobby was old-fashioned, with a green carpet that looked mildewed, and a chandelier with many of the glass pieces missing. The man at the desk wore a suit with a bow tie;

his thinning hair was combed sideways and his lips were so red it seemed as if he were wearing makeup.

"*Willkommen.* The Lowys, yes?"

"That's right." Duncan came to the desk and he and Gina set down their bags.

"Your room is ready. I'll just need to see your passports." The man took Gina's passport first, then Duncan's, which he lingered over for some time, copying the details into his ledger, then pausing to study the picture.

"Could we just have those back, then?" Duncan reached to take them.

"All for you, Mr. Lowy." The man smiled. "That name, it's Jewish, is it?"

Duncan was at once unnerved and relieved—was that it, then? The man's curiosity was over the Jewish name? He hesitated, not sure how to take this, but the clerk rushed to reassure him.

"I like Jews very much!"

Gina pinched Duncan's arm, and they proceeded to the elevator, while the desk clerk lingered behind with their luggage. Once the elevator door had shut, Gina jumped onto her toes, her eyes wide with disbelief. "He likes Jews very much!"

"Right, we're his favorite after schnitzel."

Her laughter stopped; she was looking at him seriously. "Are you uncomfortable here?"

"Of course not." Though he had to wonder if it might be true; he was plenty on edge already.

His anxiety was twofold—compounded by guilt over how his mother would suffer to see him here. The farthest his mother had ever agreed to travel during his lifetime was to Florida, to visit a cousin in Miami Beach. Not once had she returned to her birthplace in Alsace, an oft-disputed part of France bordering on Germany. She'd survived during German occupation in the care of a Catholic family, while her parents fled across the Alps. What family was left after the war moved to the US, and Duncan's mother had never had a good word to say for Europe. Growing up, Duncan ate exclusively American meals, and when the only languages offered at his school were German and French, his mother harangued the principal for weeks. European music she wasn't able to renounce, but she did everything else she could to forget the Continent, which remained dangerous to her, treacherous, and would always be, no matter how much history elapsed between the present and those events that had shaped her earliest perceptions. As Duncan grew older, he'd sought to escape the confines of his mother's fearful judgment, but being here, in Hitler's native country, he couldn't help but feel the shame he already carried with him deepen.

Naturally, he could never tell his mother the details of this trip. As far as she knew, he was in London—that part of what he'd told Gina was the truth, though he hadn't relayed the rest of the story that he'd given his mother: that he was pursuing a professional opportunity through his college roommate, Blake. Such stories were nothing new. Duncan had survived his childhood by telling his parents what they wanted to hear. His father, mild and appeasing, could tolerate the truth, but not the pressure of hiding it from Duncan's mother, for whom the truth was mostly overwhelming. So from an early age, Duncan had learned to hide any aspects of reality that might distress those he loved. He supposed that a kind liar, the sort who omitted and elided to please others, was at least the better sort of liar to be.

"I'm very glad we're here," he said, as he and Gina headed down the dark hotel corridor. "No one who cares about music should miss Vienna. Plus, you love it here, and anything you love, I want to be a part of."

He stopped to kiss her just as the clerk from reception appeared behind them, carrying their luggage.

"Oh, excuse me," said the clerk, lowering his eyes.

"She's also crazy about Jews," said Duncan, and Gina had to stifle her laugher while the clerk opened the door, handed them the keys, and left.

Their room was dim and musty: dark lampshades choked the meager light and the walls were done in textured wallpaper that had faded unevenly. Though it was after ten and they were too tired to wander far, neither Gina nor Duncan felt like staying in. They hurried through the lobby to do some light exploring. There were restaurants by the train station, but these looked seedy, so they walked the other way and settled on a corner restaurant, where they ordered goulash and strudel and a carafe of wine. Gina was tipsier than Duncan when they got back to the room, and by the time he'd brushed his teeth, she was already curled up in bed, asleep.

Seizing this opportunity for privacy, he went down to the lobby and asked the desk clerk to point him to the nearest public phone.

"You might use ours here, sir."

"A little air would be nice," Duncan said.

The clerk looked disapproving. "There are phones by the train station. But at this hour, I warn you, you'll find all sorts."

"All sorts is perfect," said Duncan and, with a wave, he stepped outside.

The train station was well lit but mostly empty at this hour.

A few homeless people lay on blankets in one corner and, on the other side, where the buses came in, three young men with shaved heads were talking loudly, drunk. The scene was hardly different, Duncan thought, from the sort he encountered on his block back in the East Village. Once, in the first year he and Gina lived there, he'd nearly been mugged at the entrance to his walk-up, but what had scared off his assailant was a rat scurrying across the man's foot. The memory of this now distant life caused Duncan to shiver.

At last he found a working phone, and searched his wallet for the number of the answering service that he'd hired in Zurich—such were the methods for staying connected before cell phones were common. A service was safer, he'd decided, than messages on a machine that someone else might try to retrieve.

He dialed, and a woman soon informed him he had six new messages.

"You'd like to hear them?"

He wasn't sure he would, no. He couldn't imagine any of the news would be good. Still, he supposed that he'd better learn what he could about the mess accumulating in his absence. "Yes, please, thank you."

"Okay, then. Ms. Smyth from Carter Properties said that you're behind on rent. And there was a call too from your bank."

"I've been remiss with bills, since I've been traveling," he began and stopped. This stranger, he had to remind himself, wasn't owed an explanation. "Thank you, what else, then?"

"An Esther Lowy left a message too, wanting to know why she can't reach you in London. She says that she tried your friend Blake, but that he said you'd left. And then there was a message

26

from a Blake Flournoy asking why your mother thinks you're in London with him."

In the silence that followed, Duncan wondered if the woman was hoping he'd respond, if she'd begun to take an interest in the story, to become curious, herself, how the pieces fit together.

"Any other calls?" he pressed her.

"Yes, sir. Another message from a Frank Reinhold, saying he needs to speak to his daughter, and if you're with her, to please call him."

Gina's father—this message troubled Duncan most. Any parent whose child was out of contact would be worried, and Gina's father was especially possessive. For this reason, he'd never been in favor of her relationship with Duncan and had grown, over time, increasingly mistrustful of him. The man must be itching for a word with Gina, whom he typically called several times a week. Duncan ought to find some way to explain her silence and reassure him she was well—and quickly.

"Sir?" The woman on the line interrupted his thoughts. "You still have another message."

"Right, yes. Go ahead."

"From a Graham Bonafair. He says to tell you that—"

"That's fine." Duncan stopped her there. He was feeling suddenly that he couldn't handle any more.

"You don't want me to read the message?" The woman's voice was grave; she seemed concerned. "I think maybe you ought to hear it."

"No, no, that's fine. I'll look into it," he said, feeling he'd made a mistake letting a stranger in on his communications. "I think I won't be needing your services any longer."

"Is there a problem, sir?"

"Not any problem, no. You can redirect my calls back to my line. I'll just call into my machine from now on." He took a breath, minding his manners. "And thank you. I'm grateful for your help. I really am."

He hung up the phone and stood a moment, considering what he might do next. The drunken men were laughing. A cool wind blew, and Duncan hadn't worn a jacket. All he wanted was to get back upstairs to Gina, to put his worries behind him, but he knew he ought to deal with at least some of these messages while he had the chance. Since it was already eleven at night in London, whereas in New York it was only six, he chose to make his first call to Blake.

Blake Flournoy had been Duncan's college roommate since the start of freshman year. They'd been placed together randomly by the school—certainly Blake hadn't been the type that Duncan would have chosen to live alongside. He had a smug look about him, shrouded in polo shirts and an eternal tan, his dark blond hair effortlessly upright off his forehead, swept sideways, in the style that boys less suave were struggling at that time to achieve with mousse. He gave off a general impression of indifference, skated through his classes, and kept their room a mess; his voice had a deliberate flatness to it, as if nothing were worth placing strain on his vocal cords.

"Yup." Even in a single word, Blake's tone was unmistakable, the blunt voice that many others found rude, but which gave Duncan permission to be his less polite, less cautious self. It was something he'd gotten used to, becoming close friends with Blake during college and remaining so after, even once Blake had moved to London.

"Hey, it's me."

"Duncan, holy shit. I've been trying you. Where the hell are you?"

"And a holy shit also to you."

"Your mom called yesterday, you know that? I'm assuming you're calling because you know that."

"Yes, I know, and thanks for handling her." He had no doubt that Blake had dealt with his mother well. During college, on mornings when Duncan slept in, Blake was always there to make up a story for his mother when she called. More than anything, it was Blake's lying to his mother that had forged the trust between them. Before meeting Blake, Duncan had borne the weight of his lies in secret, guiltily, but Blake's laxer conscience had lightened Duncan's too.

"And I guess you also know," Blake continued, "that she thinks you're here with me, applying for a job."

The job bit he'd improvised at the last minute. As long as he was already lying to his mother, he figured he might as well tell her something she'd like to hear: like that he was finally reconciled to the idea of a regular, well-paid corporate job. "I'm sorry, I should have told you I was using you as an excuse. Honestly, I never thought she'd follow up. I'm not sure why she did."

"Well, I am," Blake announced, and then said nothing, waiting for Duncan to ask. In small ways, Blake often insisted on having the upper hand—a quality Duncan had overlooked until Gina pointed it out, with obvious distaste.

"You're going to clue me in or what?"

"Some guy called her, asking after you, which got her all nervous."

At this, Duncan's pulse jumped. He must calm himself: of

course there were several possible explanations. He didn't need to think the worst. "This guy give a name?"

"She didn't tell me. But she seemed concerned that you might have gotten yourself into trouble."

"Shit. Okay." He was thinking of his mother, of the anxiety that must be suffocating her. He could hear her voice, the voice from his childhood that met him at the door if he was even ten minutes late coming home from school: *Someone could have taken you! A car could have struck you! Do you know what agony you've put me through?*

What reaction would she have now that he was across an ocean, unreachable, while she received alarming phone calls from strangers—saying what? He cringed to think.

"Duncan?" Blake was speaking to him again. "*Are* you in some sort of trouble? Is it a money thing? You need to borrow?"

"It's . . . it's nothing you need to worry over. I should just call my mother, reassure her."

"But Duncan, where are you? How can I reach you?"

"I'm, uh, moving around between hotels."

"Which hotels? Where?"

"Thing is, I can't really predict."

"Christ, Duncan, just tell me where you are, man! City? Nation? Continent?"

He felt a sudden urge to give in, to confess everything to his old friend, but his better judgment intervened. If there was one area where Blake had failed him as a friend, it was in his attitude toward Gina. To cynical, pragmatic Blake, Gina was a deluded romantic, and a dangerous one at that. To Blake—and come to think of it, to his mother too—it was Gina who'd led Duncan astray in his life, her fault that he'd forgone financial success for artistic failure, and now, whatever trouble Duncan might be in, Blake would assume this must be her fault too. So Duncan resolved to admit nothing. "Gotta go, then, Blake. More soon."

He could hear an exasperated Blake shouting at him as he hung up the phone.

Before dialing again, Duncan paused a moment, hand on the receiver, head bowed, bracing himself for his mother's panic. She picked up on the first ring.

"Mom," he said casually.

"Duncan, thank goodness! You're alive!"

"Of course I'm alive." He was having that feeling he often did when phoning his mother—at once sorry that he hadn't called sooner, and sorry that he'd called at all. He could hear the TV in the background, the six o'clock local news, which his parents watched nightly, and which always seemed to enumerate the dangers lurking just outside.

"Where are you?" she demanded. "Blake told me you'd left London for Wales."

"Yes, right, on a brief visit. A small reward."

"Does that mean the interview went well?"

"Hard to say, really, just have to wait." He could hear, through her anxiety, a note of hope. He wasn't sure if he felt better or worse for having offered it to her, though if she was thinking about the job, he supposed this was a good sign—that whatever else she'd heard about him hadn't left her too distressed. "While I've got you, Blake did mention that you'd had a call from somebody asking about me."

"That's right. A friend of yours. He said he needed to get in touch with you and asked if I knew how to reach you. He said it was important."

"And did he give a name?"

"Graham Bonafair."

A sour feeling came over Duncan, though he could hardly call himself surprised. It was to be expected that Graham would reach out to anyone who might have contact with Duncan. At least it appeared that Graham hadn't told his mother much, had in fact shown great restraint. For now. But perhaps behind this call was a tacit threat, a way of making clear that Graham could always reach out to those Duncan was close to and tell them as much as he pleased. And what could Duncan say or do to protect his mother, or anybody, then? Nothing. All he had in his power to do was to cheer her in the moment, to offer his mother whatever empty promises she needed: yes, he'd call again in a few days; yes, he'd be on a flight home soon; yes, he was hopeful about the job, felt his luck was due to turn.

"I'll call you again soon, Mom. And I don't want you to worry about me. I love you. I'm okay. You can trust me."

Three

Gina // Vienna

June 1996

Their first morning in Vienna was a lovely one, the sky blue and the sun warm, and Gina suggested she and Duncan take the train to Stephansplatz to enjoy a long walk through the center of the city. They began at St. Stephen's Cathedral, a Gothic building with a roof of patterned multicolored tiles. The last time she'd seen this church, its roof had reminded her of a snake. She supposed it was a reflection of the guilty mood dogging her on that trip, of her unease recalling the company she'd been in.

She'd left Duncan behind in New York then, and during the two weeks she was in Vienna, she'd felt terrible for doing that— thinking of him stuck in the heat in their apartment with the air conditioner that sputtered only lukewarm air. Meanwhile, she was visiting this remarkable city and in a grander style than she'd ever enjoyed. The dancers were put up, just two girls to a room, in a very good hotel in the MuseumsQuartier, where nearly all of the festival was scheduled to take place. Throughout the week, she'd been entertained by supporters of the festival; she'd been escorted by a Viennese politician to the Rathaus; she'd visited the Schönbrunn Palace; and was invited to watch the horses perform at the Hofburg within the Spanish riding school. That afternoon, one of the festival's board members, a Frenchman with dark hair to his collar who smelled of cigarettes and cologne, had taken a special interest in Gina and had invited her to visit the Staatsoper for a performance of *Aida*. Later, the same Frenchman had taken her walking precisely here, to Stephansplatz. She said nothing of this to Duncan now, only suggested they move onward, which they did, stopping for a visit at the Hofburg Palace, then walking through the lovely, expansive park along the palace up to the opera house.

Today, Gina found the Staatsoper less dramatic than it had seemed, lit up at night, when she'd visited with the Frenchman, but here in the daylight with Duncan, she could appreciate the finer details: statues under the arches of the second level, the bronze horsemen charging on either end of the roof. A crowd had gathered around the corner to observe a group of street musicians: a man with a violin and a female singer. They were performing lieder, and Duncan was familiar with the song, one by Strauss, mournful and haunting. They stood listening, Duncan's arm around her shoulders, and she was calm again.

From the opera house, they wandered into the Hotel Sacher, Vienna's most famous hotel, a tan five-story building occupying the whole block. Gina wanted to have a look inside, though she assumed tourists were discouraged from doing so. The best way to avoid being asked to leave, Gina suggested to Duncan, was to appear as if they had a purpose, to look as if they were there to meet a guest.

"Therese said in the lobby, didn't she?" she said to Duncan loudly as they walked past a porter at the door. "Or was it the dining room? Maybe we should have a look in there?"

She was heading for the dining room when one of the bellhops approached her asking if he could help her. "We're meeting friends," she told him.

"Which friends are those, madam?"

"The woman is Therese," she said, and turned to Duncan. "Funny, I don't think she gave her last name. But she'll be down soon." She smiled now, at the bellhop. "We're expected."

"Perhaps if you would wait by the doors, then."

"Of course," she agreed, but, not to be thwarted, started off anyhow. "I'll just run to the bathroom first, if that's all right."

Gina hurried away, hoping she hadn't left Duncan in a rough spot, and that he, like her, could seize on an excuse to quickly tour around. Moving past the bathrooms, she peered into a dining hall—the walls, curtains, and carpets a rich forest green. There was a second dining room, done entirely in red, and then another room, a bar, whose walls and velvet chairs were all deep blue. When she returned to reception, Duncan was nowhere to be found. Possibly he'd been embarrassed and had moved outside. She was heading for the exit when the same bellhop who'd approached her before stepped up to her again. "Your husband found those friends of yours you were looking for."

"Did he?" She smiled, though she couldn't imagine what could be meant by this, how Duncan could have given that impression. The bellhop gestured ahead, and she followed the line of the man's sight over to a spot in the lobby next to a large painting of a ship at sea. Duncan was standing with a very distinguished older couple. They were chatting together, their behavior so jovial that she also would have assumed they knew one another. But the couple struck her as unfamiliar.

The man had a baggy face but a warm smile. He was dressed with flair, in a white blazer and white pants, a pale orange scarf around his neck. The woman beside him was tall and thin, with white-blond hair, a high forehead, and slightly bulbous eyes. She wore a long, high-collared dress and heeled boots that made her taller than the man. She studied Gina with not entirely friendly attention.

"And she's back," Duncan announced, as Gina came to stand beside him. "This is my wife, Gina."

The man took her hand and introduced first himself and then his partner. "Riccardo Bianchi and my fiancée, Astrid Du Bellay."

"Riccardo is the director of the Teatro alla Scala in Milan," Duncan explained. "And Astrid is one of the program directors for the Salzburg Festival. They're here in advance of that."

Gina shook hands with the couple, caught off guard to hear they were so prominent, and surprised too that Duncan would know them. She'd been the only one to visit Vienna, after all, the only one who'd received such introductions.

"And are you also in Vienna ahead of the festival?" Astrid addressed her with a thin smile. "You're a dancer, isn't that right?"

Gina was startled too to find the woman knew this. "I am, that's right. But I'm not dancing now."

"We're on vacation," Duncan put in. "A sort of belated honeymoon."

"Lovely," said the woman stiffly.

"And how do you happen to know each other?" Gina asked, unable to contain her curiosity.

"Duncan was friendly with my daughter," said Astrid.

"Actually," said Duncan, "Gina and Marina were closer friends."

Were they? Gina couldn't place the name, though for the sake of appearances, so as not to offend the girl's mother, she pretended to recall.

"It was a while ago," Duncan continued. "She and Gina met during Gina's first summer in Vienna. Marina said she was thinking of moving to New York."

"And how's Marina now?" Gina asked Astrid, searching for something to say to indicate her interest in her daughter.

"Still in New York. Still working on her film, but I assume you'd know that. She hasn't said much about that lately, but Marina doesn't tell me everything."

Duncan nodded, smiling. Gina noticed his jaw tightening.

He put out his hand. "It was so nice to run across you both. I think Gina and I should get moving. We've got a packed day."

Astrid seemed prepared to see them go, but Riccardo wasn't quite. "If you're staying in Vienna, we'd love you to join us for dinner. Some friends will be here at eight thirty. Festival people, mostly."

"Oh, no," Astrid shook her head, chastising him. "Don't put them on the spot. They don't want to attend some dinner with a bunch of dreary people with white hair." And then, a conspiratorial smile. "Young couples in love have better ways to spend their time."

"Ordinarily we'd be happy to," said Duncan. "But I'm afraid we can't."

Gina looked over at him, unsure of what was happening. Influential figures like these were the sort of people that Duncan ought to be scrambling to join for an evening. Why was he instead in a hurry to escape? But then, perhaps this interaction fell under the category of those made uneasy simply due to her lapse in memory. She held her tongue. Duncan thanked them for the invitation and stepped away, steering Gina through the lobby and outside.

"Why *not* join them later?" she asked him, once they were out in the open air. "They seemed like interesting people, people we know, apparently. And maybe helpful to you too."

"I don't think that's very likely."

"Why not?"

"I doubt Ms. Du Bellay's my biggest fan. Things got a little awkward with Marina."

"Awkward in what way?" She was trying to sound relaxed, and yet she felt a knot growing in her stomach.

"Artistic differences. Personal differences. She'd hired me to do the score for her film and it just didn't work out." He shrugged, clearly wishing for her to drop the subject, but his reluctance was only arousing her need to know more.

"Why are you acting so uncomfortable about it?"

Duncan halted where he stood, concentrating on his words. "You're right, I don't like to talk about it." He sighed, mussing his hair. "Marina came to New York a year after you'd met, saying she was in film school and working on a first feature. You introduced me and she hired me. I wasn't sure about the project, but the money she was offering and my knowing who her parents were made it hard to walk away. Anyway, in the end I never did finish the piece for her, and still she offered to pay me." He looked away as he continued. "I didn't deserve it, but I felt I needed the money. So I took it."

She was piecing it together: this story and the mysterious

commission Duncan had been reluctant to discuss. "Did you need it for this trip? Is Marina's money paying for this trip?"

He nodded, still looking off into the distance, sheepish.

Yet she relaxed. This was a story she could believe—he felt guilty for running into the mother of the girl whose money he was spending to be here, especially because in some way he'd failed Marina. "I get it. Though I don't think you should feel guilty for being compensated for your work. God knows you've done work you weren't paid for, so you're owed money for work you didn't do."

"Thank you." He leaned down and put his hands on her shoulders, his forehead to her forehead. "I felt ashamed to tell you. But it's a relief, really, that you know. I hate having secrets between us."

"How many more are there?" She smiled, trying to make a joke of her misgivings.

She wanted to believe that the issue had been settled, and yet a feeling had been roused in her that she couldn't place, but which she knew must be tied to events she'd forgotten. As she blinked, she pictured a woman roughly setting down a wineglass. It was only the glass Gina saw, not the woman or her surroundings, nothing else to provide a hint of what this could mean.

They'd begun walking again, leaving the Hotel Sacher behind as they proceeded along Kärtner Strasse. The sky was growing darker, and the lights were coming up inside the shops along the street. Gina had walked this street before, during her Vienna tour, and soon sharper memories crowded out the vaguer ones. Kärtner Strasse was a favorite destination with several of the dancers, who'd go peeking into the designer shops selling dresses or shoes or bracelets for thousands of shillings. The girls would go in, and soon an older gentleman with an interest in the arts would go in after them, and some minutes later, the girls would come skipping out again with their shopping bags. Gina had tried to be broad-minded, to not judge these girls, many of whom had almost no money, not enough to buy themselves a gift, not even enough to buy gifts for friends and family at the holidays. Her own money had spared her the temptation to exploit admirers, but she knew for others it was harder. She thought now of Duncan—of how much shame he must have felt over taking money from a girl with more cash than talent, to compromise himself this way, all so that he and Gina could have this trip together.

She took his hand as they walked on, feeling her suspicion dissipate. She knew how it pained Duncan to be reliant on what money she had, how much he must have wished to treat her for a change. Whatever had enabled them to travel, here they were, and she would try to be grateful for it. Turning from Kärtner Strasse, Duncan steered left, onto the Graben, another of Vienna's central streets: six-storied white buildings lined the way in neat, stately rows, and at its end stood the copper-domed St. Peter's Church.

After a visit to the church, the time was six and Gina was feeling hungry. She and Duncan hadn't given any thought to dinner, but she proposed they pick a place along the walk. The area was crowded and cheerful, with restaurant after restaurant open onto the wide street, their tables nestled under smooth square umbrellas, tan and red and green. They chose a spot not far from a large Gothic column topped with gold and ordered meat and dumplings and sauerkraut and beer. The beer was served in immense steins but, to her surprise, Duncan finished his when they were just halfway through the meal.

"Share another?" he asked her.

She consented, though she didn't much want to.

On the walk from the restaurant to Stephansplatz, Duncan's steps weaved a little, his arm hung around her shoulder, weighty. On the train, though, under the bright lights, he seemed to sober up, chatting about the places they might visit the next day. When the train pulled into Nestroyplatz, a man entered their car: pale with pockmarked cheeks and a scar over one eyebrow. He studied her and Duncan, and she supposed he must have identified them as Americans, because he soon began singing in an exaggerated American accent.

"For all those times you stood by me. . . ."

She didn't recognize the song, which the man continued crooning, in a mocking saccharine tone. *"For all the truth that you made me see. . . ."*

"Very good, thanks." Duncan tried to stop the man, but his singing only grew more strident. "We're the next stop," Duncan whispered to Gina, so she'd know she wouldn't have to endure this too much longer, and she felt relieved. The train pulled up to the platform, the doors opened, and a moment after they were through, the man behind them exited the train as well and caught up to them, still singing.

Finally, Duncan turned to address him. "Okay, thanks, show's over."

"If you like it," said the man, "then pay for it."

"So this is a shakedown, huh?" Duncan was still trying to be friendly, but a new toughness showed in his posture.

"It won't be costing much to help support a local singer."

Gina could smell the alcohol on the man's breath. "Go ahead," she urged Duncan, hoping to resolve this quickly.

Duncan reached for his wallet and offered the man a bill. "You have a good night, then."

Duncan took Gina's hand and turned to go. They stepped outside, under the darkening sky, and hurried away from the station, in the direction of their hotel, leaving behind the relative crowds for a deserted square. Gina hadn't dared to look behind and so hadn't realized, not until she felt Duncan's hand yanked from her grip, that the man had come racing toward them. He toppled Duncan and dropped him to the ground.

He was reaching for Duncan's pocket, for his passport and wallet, straddling Duncan, who was squirming beneath him. Alongside, Gina stood frozen, afraid to leave Duncan to get help, yet feeling useless for doing nothing.

She began shouting. "Robbery! Police! *Polizei!*" The man turned to look at her and screamed at her to shut up, offering Duncan just the chance he needed to buck the man off of him. On his feet, Duncan followed up with a hard kick to the man's stomach. Gina jumped back, shocked to see such fierceness in Duncan, in whom she'd never witnessed the least violence. While the man remained doubled over, Duncan kicked him again, this time on the side, knocking him down. He went to kick him a third time, but Gina pulled him back.

"Stop, stop, please. Let's just go."

Duncan stood, panting and patting himself down to be certain he'd lost nothing. He began backing away, afraid to turn and take his eyes off of the man. He walked that way, backward, until the crosswalk, and then he and Gina broke into a jog, dashing across the street, down the block, and into the lobby of their hotel.

"We need to lock the doors," Gina informed the man at the desk, the same clerk who'd checked them in the night before.

"What's happened, madam?"

"A man attacked my husband and we ran."

"Good God!" The clerk nervously hurried from behind the desk and turned a key in the front door. "I don't believe this is my city now. How awful. Are you hurt?"

"We're just shaken," she replied, while Duncan stood silent all the while, still panting, looking at the door.

"But you did see him?" the clerk asked, peering out also. "You can give a description to police?"

"No police," said Duncan gruffly, speaking up at last.

"If you're uncomfortable," said the clerk, "I can speak to the police for you."

"I said no."

The clerk looked up at him, startled by his roughness. Gina was taken aback too and recalled the way Duncan had kicked that man, and kicked again—with such mad determination, as if he were fighting not over a wallet, but for his very survival. What was it, this new desperation?

"You don't think we should at least report it?" Gina asked him gently.

"There's no point to it. Police won't get anywhere. That thief's long gone by now." Duncan exhaled, clearly mustering calm and trying to sound reasonable. "And on the off chance they do catch him and choose to try him, then we get held here or called back to Vienna from wherever we are, and spend what should have been our vacation in an Austrian courtroom, watching some lowlife get put in jail for five days. No, Gina. Not after everything we've done to get here." His tone softened and he wrapped an arm around her. "I'd rather that guy took my wallet than be robbed of this time with you."

43

Standing against him, she could feel his body heat and smell his sweat and the odor of this other man, which made her uneasy.

"What's the matter?" Duncan asked her, nervous.

"You smell like that thief."

"I'll go clean up," Duncan suggested, and started walking toward the elevator. "We'll revisit this tomorrow," he called over his shoulder to the clerk, who looked unhappy with the outcome but wasn't capable of contradicting the wishes of a guest. Together Gina and Duncan entered the elevator and rode up to their room.

Inside, Duncan yanked off his shirt and then went to take a shower. She waited for him to finish, still absorbing the shock of the evening, still unable to calm down. The image that had come to her earlier that evening returned: the woman lowering a wineglass. This time Gina saw her face: pale, with full lips and large, wide-set eyes.

Who could this woman be? What could this mean? Why, Gina wondered, was she so on edge? She had no rational basis for thinking Duncan had ever been unfaithful. She hadn't caught him in a lie, or in possession of secret pictures or letters, or sneaking off to make a private call. Or had she? Thinking back upon that last day in the Walensee, she remembered how he'd spoken softly to the person on the phone. His mother, he'd claimed, but the tone wasn't one he used with his mother. *I hope you know I never meant to hurt you.* No, no, that was a tone he might have used with Gina, with a lover.

When Duncan stepped out, clean, warm, wrapped in a towel, he came over and began to kiss her. She could feel that he was seeking relief from the incident, a way to overcome the strangeness between them, and yet, for her, that sense of strangeness did not pass.

"Duncan." She put her palms against his chest, holding him off.

He murmured inaudibly, still kissing her neck.

"That call you made, in the guesthouse at the Walensee, was that to Marina?"

He stopped kissing and looked up at her, surprised. "What? What are you asking me?"

"Before we left Lake Walen, you made a call. I heard you speaking."

"It was to my mother, like I said. Why would you doubt that?"

"I don't know. That couple today . . ."

"Today was unsettling. I got shaken up too." Gentle again, he took her in his arms and pulled her down onto the bed. He no longer kissed her, but simply held her, in a way she knew was meant to comfort her, but which made her feel too that he was trying to control her.

"I think maybe we need to just lie together and relax, okay? It will all be okay. We're safe. We've got each other," he said, now stroking her hair. "Right?"

Gina slept fitfully, hovering between thinking and dreaming—every so often she would remark the clock, time passing, and Duncan dozing beside her. At around four in the morning, she sat suddenly upright, struck by a scene, a memory involving the woman she had pictured. She and Duncan were at a party inside a town house, a fancy building with a hundred people crammed inside. An argument had broken out over a line that had formed outside the bathroom.

One of the guests was knocking aggressively on the bathroom door. "There are people out here. Quit fucking!"

Gina heard voices from inside, a woman shouting and giggling.

"One sec," said a man's voice, also from behind the door.

But the man in line had no intention of waiting. The lock must have been weak or the door improperly closed, because it swung open to reveal a thin blonde pulling up her skirt. Another person, a young man, was with her. When he heard the door open, he jumped and turned. It was Duncan.

Gina had spun and walked away and Duncan had come after her. Nothing had happened, nothing sexual, he promised. The blond girl had jumped into the bathroom and pulled him in and he hadn't known what to do.

"I didn't want to offend her. She's your friend. You'd wanted me to meet her."

And this was when it hit her, what she must have known instantly at the time, but had to reconfigure now, in Vienna, a year later—the girl in the bathroom was the same girl she'd met in Vienna the summer before, the same girl she'd asked Duncan to meet hoping she might get him work, and who would go on to pay Duncan the commission that was funding their trip now: Marina Du Bellay.

Gina looked around the dim room, too agitated to sleep. She had to move to rid herself of the irritation. At times it felt as though only through movement could she find the way to how she felt, whereas while lying down her feelings became knotted and illegible to her. So she walked, first circling the room and then out in the hall alone, letting her feet and thoughts move in one direction and then in another.

Was Duncan cheating? Having an affair with an aristocrat's

daughter? He could have been taken in by her flattery—he'd always quietly craved affirmation. And Marina had believed in him, had offered to help him, pay him, this young woman with her good taste and her connections. Had he been motivated by a combination of ambition and lust, the two together too much for him to resist?

For some time she was convinced by her own story, but then she'd as effectively dismissed it as what it was: a story. Probably Duncan had only allowed himself to encourage Marina's interest a little, knowing she might be of use to him, and knowing that her interest otherwise meant nothing to him. Was this any different than the young girls from her Vienna visit who allowed the older men to pay for their shopping trips? She didn't have any proof that Duncan had cheated on her, nor did she have any past experience leading her to think he would.

She returned to bed but found herself unable to lie still. After a time she was up again, pacing the room. He'd never made her doubt his loyalty to her. She knew she shouldn't be suspicious, but then again, she wasn't herself. Why not put her mind at ease, if she could?

She stepped up to the suitcase and opened the zippered pocket where Duncan kept his work folder. There was an understanding between them that she wouldn't look inside, wouldn't pry into what Duncan was writing, but await the time when he was ready to present it. Duncan's sensitivities even trained her to avert her eyes when he opened that folder. Yet, tonight, driven by this phantom sense of betrayal that wouldn't leave her, that was precisely what she chose to do.

She took a last look at Duncan, peacefully sleeping, before she carried the folder into the bathroom. There were pockets on each side. The left pocket was filled with sheet music, some of the pages blank, and a few with notation. Inside the right pocket were other documents Duncan had deemed important during travel—medical records, hospital bills—nothing inappropriate, so that for a moment she felt ashamed of what she'd done. She shut the folder and lifted it to return it to the other room, but as she did, something slipped out from between the sheets of music. An envelope. She picked it up from the floor and recognized the address, in her writing: *Frank Reinhold, 112 Sandoval Street, Santa Fe, New Mexico.*

The letter from Lake Walen. Might Duncan have simply forgotten to send it? Though she was almost sure she recalled seeing it on Ms. Arner's desk before they left the guesthouse. Perhaps there was some reasonable explanation for his holding on to it, and still the doubts this letter raised prompted her to continue searching. The next item she found was also nestled in the far back, behind the composition sheets. A postcard addressed to her closest friend, Violet, now living in Prague.

Violet Sharpe, care of the National Marionette Theater, Prague.

The card was dated, she noticed, the same day as her accident. She must have meant to send it then. She sat down at the edge of the tub, feeling dizzy.

According to Duncan, she and Violet had argued, experienced a rift, so that Gina had determined not to see her on this trip. The postcard, meanwhile, started off with a friendly announcement of her visit.

Dear Violet,

Good news. I'm planning to make the trip to Prague after next week!

Can't wait to see you. It feels like ages since we've met, so much happened after you left New York. That whole world collapsed for me. The worst is behind me, as you know, and I've been happier lately, and will be even happier to see you. I'm so excited to see what your life in Prague is like. Changes are a blessing—and so are those good friends we hold on to through them all.

Love,
Gina

Reading the note dismayed her further—not only was there no indication of any argument like Duncan had mentioned, but Duncan's description of the last year as uneventful seemed to be a lie as well. According to this note, her world in New York had *collapsed*.

She sat still, unsure what to do next, whether to awaken Duncan and demand answers to her many questions, or to put these things away and wait until her thoughts had time to settle and she could reach a steady judgment.

Why would Duncan choose to pretend she and Violet were at odds, why would he wish to keep her from her friend? She could only summon one explanation for it: he wished to prevent a visit with Violet because he had genuine cause to fear a meeting, because—Gina could only imagine—Violet knew something of their past that Duncan was frightened would come out.

What could he have done? How awful could it be?

She wanted to forget it all, put the folder back and return to loving Duncan the simple way she had before. The idea of not loving him, of not believing that he was truthful to her, was so unsteadying that the postcard fell from her shaking hands.

49

It was only then that Gina noticed the picture on the other side. The postcard was from her father's gallery, and the image was one she'd seen before, her vision: a photograph of her back as she stood before a portrait of Duncan and herself. Duncan's image was only half visible in the postcard because it was obscured by a figure, a man, tall, slim, blond, standing to Gina's right. He was standing so close their shoulders nearly brushed, and he was turning to her as if to whisper something in her ear.

She breathed. She gathered herself and went, wrapped in a sweater, wobbly-legged, to the hotel lobby. She'd brought the postcard with her to consult the return address where they'd been staying in Berlin: *Hotel de Rome, Behrenstrasse 37.*

The clerk sat at his desk in front of a miniature TV. A drama was playing: *The X-Files* in German. The clerk was absorbed by the show and startled by her sudden entrance. He hurried to lower the volume.

"Sorry to bother you," Gina said, "but I'd like to make a call. My husband is sleeping and I don't want to disturb him."

"You wish to call police, then?" the clerk asked her, hopeful.

"Not the police, no. I need to make a call to a hotel."

The man seemed disappointed, but obligingly pulled out a phone from behind the counter. With the clerk's help, she dialed information first and had him request, in German, the number. A woman picked up promptly. Gina spoke with her, explaining she'd been a guest at the hotel some weeks ago.

"Very good, Ms. Reinhold, and what can I do for you?"

She wasn't entirely sure herself what she was expecting, and yet a premonition drove her to inquire whether someone might have been trying to reach her. "I left abruptly and I'm wondering if maybe you have any messages for me?"

"Let me check, madam."

The woman placed her on hold, with music playing in the background, and the desk clerk slowly, after what he deemed an appropriate time, drifted back into his chair and resumed watching his program, with the volume low.

"Ms. Reinhold?"

"Yes, yes, I'm here."

"Sorry to have kept you, but, in fact, there is a message for you."

Her heart was beating fast; she closed her eyes before whatever words came next.

"It's from a Graham Bonafair. He says to please get in touch with him as soon as possible, wherever you might be. It's very important, he says, that he reach you."

Graham Bonafair. The name was familiar, and yet she couldn't place it.

"He's left a number for you, here in Berlin. If you have a pen, Ms. Reinhold, I'll give that to you now."

Her hand was trembling so much she struggled to write. She considered whether she might dial the number now. No, she'd settle herself first. Back in her room, she placed the paper with Graham's number in her purse, then returned to the bathroom to clean up the folder she'd left, in her impatience, lying on the floor. With everything straightened, back in its place, she lay down in bed beside Duncan.

For hours she lay awake, tormented by her doubts, watching him quietly breathing beside her. She'd resolved to spend her life with this man, she thought, believing there was no one with whom she shared a deeper understanding. Her Duncan. Possessed by her, known by her. Only now, in their dark room, he seemed all shadows, hidden. How much of the truth was he concealing? For how long? Was this Duncan who lay before her the man she believed him to be?

Four

His mother's moods were the weather of Duncan's childhood, the sky under which he'd moved. When she was better, he'd be able to forget about her a little, exist for days almost guiltless and free—hanging out after school with friends, walking home slowly with the neighbor's pretty daughter. But then, abruptly, without warning, his mother's fear would erupt and he'd come through the front door to find her crying, held by his frowning father, her pretty milk-white face grown contorted as she sobbed, *"How could you run off like that? How could you leave me to worry?"*

"I'm sorry, Mommy, I'll stay right here. Please don't cry."

Even at a young age he'd felt his inherent badness, overwhelmed to see his mother in such pain, and to know he'd caused it—so selfishly—in order to snatch some trivial pleasure. He'd feel thoroughly demonic and, for the weeks that followed, he'd strive to make it up to her, to do the things she wanted from him—listen to classical music with her or help her around the house. As he grew older, he began to recognize the extremity of his mother's demands, and how deeply he and his father were enslaved to them.

This insight might have relieved him, but at the same time he came to understand her history, and the horror of it made it impossible to blame her for anything she did. His mother's childhood in France had been a nightmare: for several years she'd wondered if her parents were alive or dead, if she would ever see them, if one day one of the kids in her town who knew she was a Jew would tell the Germans and she'd be picked up and killed. After the war, when she was reunited with her family, only half remained. Her father had died of pneumonia while in hiding, and her brother, sent to live with another family, had run away and had never been found. So Duncan's mother had come with his grandmother to the States, and, fifteen years later, married Duncan's father, the meek son of Polish immigrants who'd been crushed by the Depression.

Together, Duncan's parents had opened up a stationery store and set up a home in Toms River, New Jersey, that on the surface seemed as secure as any other. But inside, Duncan's home was different: darker and less hopeful. Fine for others to believe life was a playground, fine for them to go riding skateboards into town, or make out with girls behind the movie theater, but Duncan had to stay within his mother's sights.

Thus, he turned his energies to piano. His mother played well, and purchasing a piano for their home had been one of her few indulgences. From his perch at the bench, his eyes would wander from sheet music to the window and beyond, where other kids swatted badminton racquets or splashed around in inflatable pools.

He'd discovered music in much the way he supposed other lonely children had before him—to express all the feelings and curiosities he couldn't give voice to any other way. His mother seized on his interest and ability, and gave him lessons herself. Around the time he turned thirteen, though, his skill exceeded hers and she decided to spend the little extra cash they had on a piano teacher who came to the house two times a week. Her name was Lillian and she was pretty and kind and a little shy, with glasses and dark hair cut into bangs and a soft, singsong voice.

Duncan quickly came to adore her and not to mind so much the hours he was kept at home to practice. All week he'd prepare for when they met, hoping not only to amaze her with his playing, but to find other ways to impress this rare, beautiful interloper. He listened to all the classical music he could get his hands on and in the library found music criticism, which he could paraphrase to sound insightful. He also began to invent pieces of his own, modifications on those Lillian gave him to practice. None of these was especially original, but his first attempts astonished Lillian more than he'd thought possible.

"Duncan, that's beautiful," she'd said, her small, pale hand on her chest. "Can you play it for me again?"

Of course he would! There were no words he craved hearing as much as that she'd liked something he'd done and wanted more. As he played, he couldn't keep himself from smiling, or peeking over to see her close her eyes, or lean her head back, exposing her pale, perfect neck. It felt like magic to be able to elicit such responses from a grown and lovely woman. As if he'd stopped being a shy thirteen-year-old, someone beneath her interest, and become the master of her feelings. Powerful. A man.

He began to fixate on a future where he'd be a successful composer, admired by his peers, adored by some delicate, romantic woman like his teacher. Soon, nothing else interested him as much as sitting home and writing music. No type of frivolous play with neighborhood boys and girls compared to having Lillian declare that he was special, in possession of a gift—something that his mother, too anxious to admit to any goodness, never did.

If only that gift had stayed their secret, he and Lillian could have continued that way for much longer, but eventually she got the notion that Duncan needed more than she could give him, and felt compelled to tell his mother her opinion. She believed Duncan to be a musical prodigy who, with the right instruction and support, had a chance of becoming a very talented composer.

"And have you told him this?" his mother asked, Duncan listening in from the next room. "Have you given him these ideas about himself?"

"I've tried to encourage him, if that's what you mean."

"You weren't hired to do that," said his mother, in the stern tone that made her Alsatian accent even more pronounced.

Duncan realized that he'd made a terrible mistake in not preventing Lillian from speaking with his mother. He was immediately angry at himself for failing to predict her reaction. Lillian couldn't have guessed—why would she assume that any mother wouldn't be overjoyed at the thought of her child being a prodigy? She didn't know what sort of woman Esther Lowy was. Playing music was a hobby in his mother's mind, part of becoming a cultivated person, but it shouldn't be permitted to interfere with schoolwork or plans for a legitimate career. Neither she nor Duncan's father had been able to attend college, and even by the modest standards of most Toms River residents, they lived frugally. Any savings they amassed was put in an account for Duncan's college education. Like many immigrant parents in America, his mother maintained the view that she was denying herself luxury so that Duncan would be able to afford it later. In turn, her expectation for him was that he'd eventually pursue a secure and lucrative field like finance or law, to repay their sacrifices. Music—the piano—was a distraction, a fantasy of his artistic greatness that only threatened to divert him.

Still, Lillian hoped to convince her, and soon the women stepped out from the kitchen and Duncan was asked to perform the pieces he'd composed.

His fingers stiffened as he played, as if his mother's judgment penetrated skin and joints. The melodies he'd been so proud of when Lillian heard them now sounded like lifeless imitations. One piece was simply a variation on the main theme from Schubert's Unfinished Symphony, another sounded like the second movement of Mendelssohn's First Cello Sonata, and a third was a modified étude by Chopin.

"He has an ear, all right," his mother began, "and some technical dexterity. But I don't see any evidence of much musical imagination. Nothing like the genius you're leading him to think he has."

He was devastated. Anger sounded in him like a song. He wanted to summon his defiance right then and there, to say in forceful sound what his mother's fragility prevented him from ever expressing in words. He heard the beginning of the piece already, haunted, full of the gloom his mother cast upon him, moving between frustration and sadness—only then did he recognize how much his musical idea recalled a melody in Prokofiev's "Alexander Nevsky," and he felt more furious still. Could it be that his mother was right? That all he could do was ape the masters and fool a young woman into thinking he was capable of more?

Lillian never came back to the house after that.

Duncan's mother didn't abandon lessons altogether, but she replaced this gentle woman who believed in him with a bitter older man who cringed beside him at the smallest fault in his playing. Duncan resented his new teacher and dared to risk, for the first time, feeling resentment toward his mother. Bad enough that she'd isolated him from his classmates and made him an oddity, stuck at home alone; then she'd taken away the one person who'd lifted him out of his loneliness and made him believe in his talent. No matter the motives his mother might give—that she was only concerned with what was best for him, for his future success—he now saw her efforts at protecting him for what they truly were: a deliberate campaign to trap him with her in her misery. A change took root in him. He began to cultivate a private freedom, to keep his motives secret, to dream of a life separate from his mother's that he would hide from her. Silently, through his seeming obedience and diligence, he began to work toward his escape.

Duncan's admission to Yale—on scholarship, after achieving the high marks that came easily to him, with nothing much else to do at home but study—meant he'd earned his way out of the Lowy house. He'd managed to achieve a place his mother believed would set him on the respected path she wished for him. For her, his acceptance implied security; for Duncan, it meant freedom. The future was wide open to him now.

Duncan had been thrilled to be at Yale from the day he'd stepped onto the campus. Every detail suggested an adventure: the wide, bright lawns and dim, echoing halls, the majestic Gothic buildings and the rougher streets of the city beyond. He wasn't the least bothered by the reports his mother delivered about New Haven's crime rate, nor by the roaches he discovered in his dorm room. He wasn't even bothered by his standoffish roommate, Blake Flournoy.

On first glance, Blake seemed like just the sort of spoiled prep school jerk that would end up playing pranks on Duncan, making him feel nervous and hopeless and destined to a despair as certain as the primrose path would be for blessed Blake, who'd arrived after him and still managed to claim the better top bunk.

"On your toes, buddy," Blake instructed, piling his clothes inside the larger bureau. "You're not living with your mommy anymore."

Blake was patronizing and aggressive and smug. Duncan saw this right away, but with time, he discovered other qualities in his roommate that eventually endeared Blake to him. Blake was loose with boundaries; he took, but gave generously too: he lent Duncan his clothes, and paid for his drinks when they went out, knowing that Duncan was in the work-study program. He also readily made up excuses to Duncan's mother, reducing her control over her son in ways Duncan was eager to discover.

Blake's glibness about the truth came as a relief to Duncan— there was great relief to be had in giving up on being good and pleasing people, and, for the first time, through Blake, Duncan was acquainted with some of the more selfish and darker sides he hadn't yet acknowledged in himself.

He had much to learn from Blake.

Alongside his roommate, Duncan discovered, finally, how to get what he wanted, especially from women. On the weekends, after they'd slept late and then Blake had beaten him at squash,

Blake would take Duncan out for dinner and drinks at Yorkside Pizza, or else at local dives that didn't card, and Blake would go up to any girl he wanted to and pull her from her chair to dance. On weekday evenings, with Blake as wingman, Duncan would have his chance at the girls, practicing on the piano in the college common rooms—for the express purpose of attracting female interest. His experience with Lillian had taught him that at least a certain kind of girl might be drawn in by his talent, and anyway, this was the only trick he had. So he and Blake would arrive around dinnertime, when dozens of coeds were coming and going from the dining hall, and Blake would call them over to notice the sweet-faced boy who played so nicely.

"The maestro here's named Duncan," Blake would say when a girl settled in to listen. "I have to make the introductions because he's a bit shy."

Duncan had been furious with Blake the first time he had said this, but after getting over his embarrassment and observing how the girl made an effort to draw him out, he soon saw the value in Blake's method. To his surprise, his being shy and sensitive counted in his favor with a fair number of girls—so many, in fact, that it soon became a problem. At first he was so flattered by the interest he was getting and so afraid of disappointing anyone that he went out with every girl who asked him. Some of these weren't too pleased to learn about the others—feelings were hurt, and, out of guilt, Duncan committed himself to a string of girls he didn't especially like. Finally, by the spring of his freshman year, he swore to himself he wouldn't get involved with anyone he wasn't head over heels for. He stopped playing piano in the common rooms and began to practice, privately, on a piano in one of the campus performance spaces. Then, one April evening, he heard music coming from a room down the hall. Inside, a girl was dancing on the stage.

She was facing the wall as she moved, her bronze curls swaying behind her. He watched her for a while before she turned and looked up, and he was suddenly aware that he hadn't spoken or moved away, but had just stood there, maybe twenty feet from her, watching. One stage light was on, but the rest of the room was dark—could she even see him?—and she looked so completely caught up in what she was doing, in a trance. As she began to dance again, she let out a small laugh—it might have been at him, or maybe at herself, at her own pleasure. But he found himself overcome with the desire to hear her laugh again.

He began rehearsing with practiced dedication, mostly out of the hope that he might cross paths with the girl again. When she didn't come, he'd stay and practice, secretly waiting, finding himself idly experimenting for hours. One evening, a melody took shape, and soon he'd come up with most of a sonata, a single-movement work rich with melancholy yearning, but punctuated with a lighter theme that he'd come to think of as the girl's laughter. He quickly jotted down the score, and waited a few days before he dared replay it.

When he did, his hope was confirmed: for the first time in his life, he'd written an original and rousing piece of music.

Summer break arrived soon after and, despite reminders from his mother that he was at school for a practical degree, he signed up for his first composition class upon returning in the fall. He spent time perfecting the sonata, and presented it as his midterm assignment, impressing his instructor so greatly that he suggested Duncan offer a recital. In November, Duncan performed his composition in Woolsey Hall, a space so grand he was lucky to see a third of it filled. Secretly he hoped the girl might be among the listeners, but he could hardly believe his luck when, after the show, as he was met by admiration and outstretched hands, the girl strolled past him with her bronze, wavy hair swept over her shoulder. Up close, she was shorter than he'd realized, more petite. She wore a white peasant dress, not the sort of clothing that most of the girls on campus wore. Her name, he'd learned from Blake, was Gina Reinhold.

She was a dance major, Blake told him with obvious contempt. Duncan could guess his thinking: what serious person would waste a Yale education performing pirouettes? Duncan didn't dare tell him, then, how his experience performing and hopes of meeting Gina were already tempting him to spend more time on his music. Soon he was spreading the word around that he'd be interested in composing for dancers. Not long after, he received a call from a student choreographer who was arranging a show; he immediately agreed to come to a rehearsal. Nervous, hopeful, Duncan arrived at the rehearsal space the next evening, and onstage among the many dancers, there she was, Gina Reinhold.

Gina was toward the front, possibly because she was smaller than the other dancers, but also, he was sure, because the choreographer had recognized she was the most commanding. The piece, the choreographer had told him, was meant to capture the struggle for human connection. At this point, the dancers were improvising, moving in and out of sync, engaged in cautious, stilted reaching, but Duncan kept his eyes on Gina, who was different, winding among the other bodies, sending one and then another dancer into a series of elated whirls across the stage.

Her energy riveted Duncan. He had the sensation, watching her, that everything he longed for in himself—conviction, liberation, transcendence—was here distilled within a five-foot-two-inch frame.

He wanted to amaze her, and so spent the next days trying to come up with a gorgeous and profound piece of music. But nothing he wrote seemed any good. He began to panic at the prospect of failing; he'd acted impulsively to get closer to this girl he admired, and had agreed to do something he couldn't. The next morning, he came by rehearsal early to meet with the choreographer and discuss his change of heart. When he arrived, though, the choreographer was running late, and the only person waiting was the person he most feared to see: Gina.

He must have looked ready to bolt, because right away she asked him what was wrong.

"I just came to say that I can't do this. Do this show. Can you relay that for me?"

"Well," she said, frankly, "first, I'd like to know why do you think you can't?"

He was surprised by her question, hadn't expected he'd need to confess his limits to her. "I . . . I can't force myself to do it. Melodies just come to me sometimes. It's not anything I can control."

He'd expected her to drop the matter, but Gina seemed to be as bold offstage as on.

"So when those melodies do come to you, how does it usually happen?"

He explained himself, his way of starting with another person's work, experimenting with deviations, building up from there. One exception sprang to mind, but he was too embarrassed to acknowledge that much to her then: the piece he'd written about her had been different. The idea had come to him all on its own.

"Have you ever worked with another person before? Another musician or a dancer?"

"No," he admitted, "never."

She went on to describe the way the pianist at her dance school in Santa Fe had worked. She would watch the dancers perform a sequence several times and then come up with music to accompany their movements. "Should we try that?"

He agreed to try, dubious as he was, because he couldn't imagine denying her. She bounded up to the stage and he sat down at the piano to watch her dance. Without the other dancers present he imagined she'd be hampered, but she launched in unreservedly, her form contracted into loneliness, then surging outward, searching. For his sake, she exaggerated the sentiment in every move, so that he could better grasp the tone, and he let his fingers run to keep up along the keys. A song began emerging.

After a moment, Gina stopped him. "That's pretty there, but maybe too pretty? I'm feeling the movement is more uncertain, even strained."

"Oh, okay. I see that. I'll try that then." He added more ambiguity in the form of suspended and diminished chords and quickly decided that yes, Gina was right. He continued until, a few moments later, Gina stopped him again.

"Here, though, the tone shifts. There's less ambivalence, more daring."

"Maybe this way." He tried a bolder, major-key passage.

"More tender, dreamier."

He slowed, taking in her words. Until now he'd been struck

by Gina from afar, by the intensity that she projected, but here, working with her, he began to get a feel for what sort of spirit animated her. Gina's instincts were so sharp, her confidence in them so total, that every phrase and motion to come from her seemed singularly persuasive. Her vitality hit him in a way that made him feel she was more real to him than he was to himself.

He proceeded to follow all her suggestions, and it startled him to find, in the end, when he played the piece over, incorporating her changes, that it was far better than he'd even imagined.

You're brilliant, he felt like telling her—the pressure of this private admission, this revelation, was so great his heart began to thump. He could feel himself blushing at this thought that gripped him: that Gina elevated him, brought him closer to the best that he might be. Something miraculous had taken place, and he didn't know how to convey it or what to do with all the energy stirred up in him, and so he played the piece for her again, this time with more fluency, and more quickly. Gina kept up, inventing new moves that matched still better with his notes. When they were finished, she was panting, and he was too, and both of them, not sure what else to do, began to laugh.

From that day on, he knew he had to find some way to get Gina in his life.

He had three weeks of daily rehearsals during which he might grow closer to her—though this setup didn't lend itself to privacy. He began to linger by the piano after rehearsals, while she changed into her regular clothes, and he'd pretend to take notes so that he could time his exit with hers. If she knew what he was doing, she spared him the embarrassment of letting on; either way, in his determination he found he didn't care. After a few nights of this charade, he saw her holding the door for him as they left, so they might walk onward together.

Gina was friendly to him, and, though he was shy around her, she easily filled the quiet as they walked down the campus streets.

"I've been wondering when you started playing. To be that good, I'm guessing young."

"Oh, five or six. I don't remember exactly. I always tinkered a little. There was a piano in the house—my mother played—and there wasn't a hell of a lot else to do at home." He was bungling things already, he thought, as if describing a childhood that was painfully dull could make him seem interesting. He quickly turned the focus onto her. "But I'm more interested in your story than my own."

As they strolled slowly across the Old Campus quad, she told him about herself, how she'd grown up in Santa Fe, the only child of two artists. "Not famous or anything, but my dad lives for it, paints every day."

"And your mom?"

"She had a stroke when I was nine."

He didn't know yet what this meant—had her mother lived or died?—and he was too afraid to ask. He was too afraid to ask her also how this event might be connected to her dancing, and to her intensity onstage—but he'd had an intuition, an image that came to him of a child Gina dancing while her mother sat stiff, as if that overabundance in her came from absorbing all the liveliness her mother couldn't express.

He'd felt such tenderness for her then. His whole body seemed to tingle in the cold.

"I'm very sorry. For your mother and for you."

Gina looked at him, taking this in. Her eyes were wide; probably she was surprised, herself, at letting a virtual stranger come so close, so fast, to what must have been such private pain.

"Thank you," she said, her voice ragged with emotion. "I'm sorry also, for my mother. But for me, I don't know, there was something that her accident taught me. It forced me to wake up and realize, there's no guarantee of a tomorrow, and no such thing as a safe choice." She slowed her pace as if contemplating the gravity of this thought. "You can lose it all in a minute. So why wait? Why compromise? If you want something, you grab it!"

"Right! Absolutely!" And yet those hands that wished so much to grab her remained buried in his pockets, pressed in so deeply he might tear the seams. She was right: if he wanted her, he ought to do something about it.

The more they talked, the more he realized just how well she knew herself and her future already. By her sophomore year in college, she'd figured out what sort of life she wished to lead. After graduation she meant to move to New York and join one of the experimental dance companies downtown. She planned to dance until the age of twenty-five, then have a child, take off a year, and resume dancing for as long as she was able. "Hopefully until I'm forty."

"And after that?" he asked her, teasing. "Don't you have the rest worked out yet?"

"Oh, I don't tend to think past forty. Who knows if I'll even make it beyond that?"

She said it lightly, without fear or self-pity, or even much awareness of how strange a sentiment this was. He began to think it over, to piece together the few details he'd collected so far of this lovely young woman. Her mother had suffered a stroke when

Gina was just nine. Maybe forty was the age she'd been, and maybe Gina envisioned her life unfolding the same way. Perhaps this explained the urgency he'd sensed in Gina; her determination to live presently, recklessly even, issued from her fear that her time here would be brief.

He looked at her again, vibrant and cheerful, any sadness in her kept far from the surface, where he had no right to touch it. Silently, he took hold of her hand.

Gina wrapped her fingers around his but said nothing. Brightly, lightening the tone, she filled the silence he'd let linger, lost in his thoughts.

"And what are *your* plans, then?"

"You mean for my life? I don't think I've got it worked out like you." He was too ashamed to tell her that his notions of life after college were quite practical and dull. He'd get a job in finance to pay off his loans. "I'm not sure yet what I'll do. But I'll have debts to pay off to begin with. And I know my parents are hoping Wall Street or law."

By now, Gina and Duncan were standing at the entrance to Pierson, her college, at the end of the path, beneath the redbrick tower. He wondered if she might say good night and go in, but Gina stood there instead, facing Duncan, her breath forming clouds in the air that seemed to linger magically.

"Don't they recognize your talent in music?"

"I mean, sure, somewhat, but music isn't a career to them. There's pleasure and there's work. They see those as two very different things."

"And do you?"

"I don't know, myself, but I can understand where they're

coming from. They've struggled financially and want more for me, that's all."

"But what sort of more?" she pressed, becoming agitated. "Don't you think what they want for you is to be happy?"

"Hell no. Happiness would just make a mess of things," he joked.

"You don't believe that!" She'd challenged him, and he'd grinned wider, because no, in Gina's presence, he didn't believe it. With her he felt that happiness was the only thing that mattered, and that it meant always having her near.

"Of course you won't actually give up your music in the end," she told him brashly.

"And why won't I?" he asked her.

"I won't let you."

He laughed, thrilled by her behaving as if his fate mattered to her.

"You remind me of my father," she went on to say, and Duncan, taken aback, couldn't decide if this was a good thing or the very worst.

"Until he met my mother," she went on, "he didn't imagine that he'd ever pursue art. He was meant to go into the family business. But my mother wouldn't let him. She told him that she had no interest in being with somebody who wasn't true to himself."

Talk of true selves, such intense romanticism—this would have struck Duncan as false or off-putting in anyone else. He'd been raised to be a skeptic—the worst could always happen, and most likely would—but Gina made him feel like this was precisely the reason to take risks.

"The only point in living is to follow your passion," she concluded.

He wanted to do just that, wanted to take the big risk, which was to tell her how he felt about her. He thought about it constantly in the next days: during breaks in rehearsal, or when he waited for her, as he soon did openly, outside the changing room. But every time he was about to get up the nerve, his heart would pound and he'd start sweating, until, at its worst, he'd need to take a jog around the theater so that she'd think this was the reason his face had turned red.

On the third-to-last night before the show opened, he made up his mind to admit his feelings once and for all. Each block they traversed on the way back, he'd order himself to make his move before the curb, but by the time they reached her dorm at Pierson he still hadn't done it. He must have looked so miserable standing there that she'd taken pity on him and suggested that she walk him to his dorm at Calhoun instead. They'd nearly made it there when he felt her hand on his shoulder, and then the other on his cheek. She turned his face to hers and he saw, in the second before his eyes closed, her lips rising to meet his.

They kissed so long his toes started to go numb, though he hadn't noticed this until she finally pulled away and said goodbye to him near the entrance to his dorm. He went bounding, giddy, up the dorm hall stairs. He couldn't feel his fingers, his feet were throbbing, and the blood was pulsing in his head so much he felt he might explode.

Gina Reinhold wanted him! It was the single most amazing fact of his young life. Every difficulty he'd ever faced, every lonely moment hadn't been suffered in vain any longer. All that emptiness he'd filled with music was preparation for the day when he'd meet Gina. All those disappointing events were put in place to lead to this point when he'd find Gina and fall in love and his real life would begin.

He and Gina were inseparable the next weeks. In the beginning, they took turns sleeping in one another's rooms, but soon they stopped going to his because Blake began complaining.

"You never made a fuss with other girls," Duncan pointed out, but Blake wasn't up for discussing the difference. Of course they both knew there was a difference between Duncan merely sleeping with a girl and getting carried away, the way he was with Gina.

"I've had crushes before, sure, but I've never had anyone get inside my head like this," Duncan made the mistake of confessing to Blake one afternoon. "It's like I wasn't fully awake before Gina. She's done something amazing to me."

"She's pussy-whipped you," Blake replied. "It's really not that complicated. Take a break, hook up with someone else. You'll be cured."

But Duncan had no interest in anyone else and no desire to be cured. Instead, he craved access to more of her, and became drawn to anything that interested her: an exhibit she wished to see at the art gallery, a lecture series that compelled her, a new novel she'd been reading. There was hardly a free moment when he wasn't engaged in exploring with her some new passion they could share.

"What's Gina got you up to now?" Blake would say when he and Duncan crossed paths, more and more briefly. Blake's hostility toward their relationship surprised him. Could Blake be jealous? Over time, Duncan began to have an inkling as to what his friend's envy might be about—Blake had lost his sidekick and had his place as Duncan's role model usurped. Before Gina, Blake had been the one to free Duncan from his inhibitions, the person to help him become braver and more alive.

Or perhaps there was more to it than that. As time went on, Blake's distrust of Gina deepened and he began making accusations against her, citing facts about Gina he'd uncovered from a girl he'd begun seeing too, a girl who, not coincidentally, thought Duncan, happened to come from Gina's hometown.

"In school, you know, she had a reputation as a liar," Blake announced to Duncan one afternoon. "It was so bad, the school shrink had to see her."

"For God's sake, her mother had a stroke. She went through hell. What would you expect?"

"You'll find any reason to excuse her."

"And you'll find any reason to condemn her," Duncan told him. "Whatever's behind this"—he didn't have the courage to speculate—"whatever's got you acting so crazy, I don't want you insulting my girlfriend."

"I think you do need it," Blake retorted. "You refuse to see what she's about—"

"Stop," Duncan had ordered firmly, and proceeded to set out the policy that would allow his friendship with Blake to survive. "You don't have to like Gina. You don't have to hang out with her. Think what you want about her, but if you want to spend time with me, if you want this friendship to continue, Blake, I don't want to hear it."

"Your choice," Blake agreed, "but I'm only trying to protect you."

Protect him from what? Despite himself, he began to wonder

if his love for Gina—and by now he was certain it was love—was in some way throwing him off course.

Even if she was innocent of blame, it remained true that since meeting Gina he'd been neglecting most everything but her. As winter turned to spring, he scarcely made it to any class outside of his musical studies. After a year-end meeting with his advisor, who warned him he was in danger of losing his scholarship, Duncan admitted his trouble to Gina.

"I don't know what's been happening with me. I can't get myself to give a damn about my classes, or about anything except being with you."

They were lying in her bed after sex in the later afternoon, Duncan still in the pleasure-fog he fell into with her. The sun was bright, the sheets damp with their sweat. Gina was flushed along her cheeks and chest, adorable that way. The pressure of desire turned into a different sort of love in such moments, one that didn't seek an easy resolution, and was more overwhelming for that fact. He didn't know how to have her more than he already had, and yet that wasn't enough.

"I'm sorry if I've let that happen," she began, but Duncan quickly assured her that none of this was her fault.

"I think it's just the fact that feeling strongly for you, it's made me see more sharply what I don't care about. So much of what I've been doing is stuff I don't really want to do."

"So what do you want to do?" she asked him, propping herself up sideways on her pillow. Her pleasure at what he was saying showed in her face, encouraging him to go yet further.

"I love music and I love you," he said, that phrase still new and wild on his lips. "The rest is nothing to me, really. That's the truth."

She began kissing him then, kissing him and kissing him until they both fell backward in the bed, until he had to pin her down just to contain the excitement in him.

For the first time in his life, Duncan resolved to live more according to his desires. Though he kept his economics major to appease his mother—and his scholarship funders—by senior year he was singularly enthralled by composition. In his spare time, he joined Gina in fifteen campus productions. Soon, the pair of them had become a phenomenon, a super-couple bound for stardom. It began to seem inevitable, simply assumed, that after graduation they would move to New York together, he pursuing music, she dancing. And yet his mother's practical voice lingered in his mind.

"At some point you'll need to make clear to your family what it is *you* want," Gina pressed him, unable to grasp how it was that Duncan could keep his parents so much in the dark about the parts of his life that mattered most—his art and her. By then, they still hadn't met Gina, nor did Duncan bring her up in conversation again after his mother—much like Blake—referred to her as a *distraction*. In some ways, he envied Gina's inability to grasp the rigidity of his own parents; of course he could hardly expect that she would understand, as a girl whose father approved of her every move and from whom she hid nothing. It had always disturbed him, and frankly made him envious, to come home and find Gina on the phone with her father, with disturbing regularity, recounting the day's events just like she would with him, or, worse, turning to her father with her frustrations over him. "If Duncan can't stand up for what he loves, how strong can that love be?" he'd overheard her say once.

He'd confronted her about it, finally. "If you complain to your dad about me, you'll only succeed in turning him against me. Is that what you want?"

"At least my father knows that you exist," she'd retorted, letting her hurt be known.

And so, two weeks later, on a rainy May Sunday, he and Gina made the trip by train to Toms River. He was giving Gina the family introduction that she wished for, though he wasn't at all sure that it was smart. He feared that being faced with his parents, with their modest achievements and immense anxieties, would only make Gina less admiring of him. The parts of him that were hesitant or pessimistic, the parts that were uneasy accepting pleasure, believing in his entitlement to happiness, all these would come out more strongly once she'd seen their source. His immediate concern, though, was that Gina would say something to outrage his mother or his mother would say something to outrage Gina. They both held such strong and opposing positions, he was afraid the tension between them that he'd so far carried inside him would become external, real, and disastrous.

They arrived at his modest, cheerless family home at noon, in time for lunch. His mother brought out plates of lettuce, bread, and tuna salad, and for a time, while they ate, they were all on their best behavior. Duncan's mother asked the mostly polite questions she might direct at any of her son's friends. Still, even during this exchange, his mother found three occasions to observe that Reinhold was a German name.

"I never thought of my father as German," Gina said the first time. The second time she explained: "He's American, a mix."

The third time, Duncan's mother made the remark to him instead. "It must be Rheingold, originally, like the opera, right, Duncan?"

"I don't know, Mom. I wouldn't know." Though of course it hadn't really been a question. Clearly his girlfriend shared the same name as the Wagner opera, Wagner being the one composer Duncan had always been forbidden from playing in the house. And now his mother meant to convey a similar message about Gina—*This girl does not belong here*—which Gina had naturally sensed.

How ashamed he felt of his mother's tribalism, how offended for Gina's sake. Yet Gina was unfazed. She'd kept her wits no matter how his mother tried to provoke her—asking after her political opinions: Had she followed the violence in Germany, the attacks on immigrants? Did she maintain the same stupid optimism about reunification as president Bush?

"I'm in favor of freedom, generally," Gina replied, "for those in East Germany, and those in New Jersey too."

She'd smiled at Duncan then, a gesture of complicity, and he understood that now was the time to do what he must do: here, with Gina in his corner, let his parents know that he would not be going on to law school or pursuing a career in finance either.

"Gina's a dancer," Duncan explained, coming around to his admission slowly. "She's a very talented one, enough to be professional. After graduation, she'll be moving to New York."

"That sounds exciting," said his mother, though she hardly said it with enthusiasm. "It's quite a struggle, though, isn't it? Life in the arts. Better if you have a partner engaged in something solid, I'd think."

"That hadn't occurred to me," said Gina calmly.

"Well, then I hope your family has money," his mother pressed, to Duncan's mortification.

"Esther," Duncan's father cautioned from where he sat, on

the other side of the room, reading the paper. Gina looked over at him, though Duncan's mother took no notice and simply went on.

"The phrase 'starving artist' exists for a reason."

"My family has some money, yes," Gina replied, simply, "and I don't deny that gives me a certain freedom. But that freedom can be Duncan's too. He's an extraordinary talent. I know that parents can't always see what others do, but others do see it, Mrs. Lowy. I certainly see it, and intend to do what I can to encourage him. I'd like to help him."

"Help him?" His mother's expression turned grave. "And why would you need this woman's help, Duncan?"

"I don't. I mean, we support each other, that's all. In the things we want to do." Here it was, he must say it, though it was bound to break his mother's heart. "I've been thinking, not that I'll necessarily rule out finance as a career forever, but I'd like to spend my first year out of school trying my hand at composing. See if I can make a career of that."

His mother's face was pale. He studied her: her hair, which she refused to dye, had turned prematurely white, her worry lines etched deeply between her brows. She was as marked by life and as hardened by it as Gina was unblemished and elastic.

He couldn't help but feel pity for his mother then, and some remorse for what he'd done. He understood how fearfully she clung to her idea of security, what a challenge, in her own life, feeling safe had proved to be. And here he was dismissing this, her hard-earned wisdom, and all the effort that she'd made to give him the peace of mind she'd never had.

"I know you're disappointed, Mom, but I felt you deserved to know how things stand. Gina and I will be moving to New

York after graduation and I'll be trying to establish myself as a composer."

"This is her idea, I take it?" His mother was demanding an answer, and he'd become instantly flustered.

"N-no, it's not her idea. It's what makes sense for me, what fits me. She's just come to help me see it. We've come to this together."

"No, no." His mother shook her head. "I don't believe this is what you want."

He could feel his anger rise, his frustration driving him to snap at her for one of the first times in his life: "What the hell would you know about what I ever wanted?"

After lashing out, he'd been frightened that his mother would crumble, but instead she'd surprised him that day. Without tears or theatrics, sitting calmly, she'd addressed him. "You're right, Duncan, you're right. It's my fault that you can't make choices for yourself and that you let this girl make them for you."

"I am choosing for myself!" He meant to be decisive, but his voice sounded childish, not at all the solid, manly tone he'd hoped to strike in front of Gina.

"If you want to rebel against me," his mother continued, "I can accept that. I'm old and fearful, I realize. But I will say this: I'm not a fool, and there are some things I do see." She turned her gaze almost imperceptibly to Gina, then back to her son. "She comes from privilege, and from people who've let her live inside a dream. If you give in to what she wants, you'll just end up in a dream with her, cut off from your true potential and what you might become. I can tell you right now what will happen. You'll go traipsing after her, and she'll lead you nowhere. One day you'll look up and realize you're lost."

He might have been shaken by this if he hadn't looked over at Gina and seen her then, so small and yet so huge, brimming with confidence, eyes flashing and cheeks ruddy, like something from a propaganda poster, an image of health and vitality and hope.

Seeing her then, he felt as if her daring had infused him, compelling him to throw himself into adulthood without any guarantee of safety. He would be reckless and single-minded; he would go after what he wanted, no matter if he or others suffered for it. All that mattered was to keep Gina proud and to keep her by his side. Whatever hardships they might face, he was ready to accept, because she was the one who'd saved him from a cautious and meager existence, who'd taught him, finally, at the brink of first adulthood, what it meant to be alive.

"So then I'll be lost," he said, looking his mother straight in the eyes. "And if I'm lost with Gina, I'll be lost happily."

Five

If Duncan's childhood was shaped by isolation and restriction, Gina's had been shaped by plenitude and loss. She'd grown up wealthy, in relaxed and sun-filled Santa Fe. Her fondest childhood memories were of dancing out on the back porch of her family home, where her parents would play records, and Gina would sway and twirl between the chairs and plants and flowers, under a vined trellis and a giant paper lantern, which she could jump up high and touch, her own graspable moon.

Music always seemed to play in that house, emanating from whichever room her mother was in, usually her sculpture studio, where Gina would come while her mother worked and dance beside her, watching herself in the gilt-framed mirror that stood on the floor, seeing herself growing until her head no longer fit under the frame.

She must have been around six when that happened, which was also the year that her mother began driving her to ballet classes five afternoons a week. Gina didn't recall ever deciding to be a dancer; in a household where both parents were artists, it was assumed everyone should have a creative passion. Only once she was older did she come to understand how unusual this was, how most other parents were occupied with jobs they held in order to survive.

Gina had grown up in a romantic universe, maintained by family money. Just before the Great Depression, her maternal grandfather had received the second state-issued oil and gas lease, allowing him to drill in southeastern Mexico in the Permian Basin. Within a generation, her mother's family had amassed a fortune. Her father's family was more modest, but they'd risen from laborers to business owners, running a small local shipping company that Gina's father was expected to inherit. His own artistic ambitions had been kept hidden from his family until Gina's mother had encouraged him to break away and become the painter she believed he was meant to be. Success had never seemed an issue—neither of Gina's parents, though talented, ever sold much work. They gave their art away, to the many friends who gathered in the years when Gina's mother was still fit to host them, when it seemed all the world's troubles were left at the threshold of their home.

That idyll had survived until Gina was nine.

She'd been in the fourth grade and attending a small private school where her mother worked as the art teacher. Every morning, they drove to school together, and though she'd made a fuss about not getting to ride with her friends on the school bus, the truth was Gina enjoyed the morning drives with her mother—sitting up in the front seat, with music playing on the stereo, Janis Joplin or Patti Smith, and her mother tapping the wheel, bracelets jangling. They didn't talk much—her mother had a mistrust of language, or a preference for quiet enjoyment. It was only later that Gina learned, from her father, that her mother was dyslexic and had been considered stupid by her family, in response to which she'd rebelled, running away from home five different times. She was the family hellion, apparently, though that side of her was hard to see in the mother Gina knew, who was devoted and warm, full of energy and appreciation for the beauty around her. When her mother wasn't working, she'd take Gina down to Abiquiu Lake or on long hikes; she was always the first one to dive into the water, always the first to crest a mountain peak. It was easy for Gina to admire her mother and long to be like her. She saw her mom as indomitable, until, suddenly, she wasn't.

One morning, Gina lay in bed listening to the sound of her mother in the shower. Every morning, after her alarm rang, she'd laze around in bed a while longer, knowing that she had until her mother shut off the water to get up, and then would have to rush to be on time. This morning, something was strange. Gina had woken, and then dozed, and then woken again to realize she was late. She'd called out to her mom and had gotten no answer. Finally, she crept toward the bathroom, where the water was still running.

The curtain rod was down. Blood was pooling in the shower. Her mother lay in the tub, unresponsive, with a gash along the left side of her head. Gina stood there shouting until her father came and called an ambulance. She'd been so terrified, so guilty—how long had her mom been lying there? At the hospital they learned that the fall had been preceded by a stroke, a severe one. There was nothing anyone could have done to prevent the damage, and nothing to be done to repair it either. What sort of damage? How would Mom be now? she'd asked her father. He hadn't had an answer for her. He'd only sat beside her crying, until she realized there would be no simple answers, or simple comforts, after this.

Following her mother's accident, the music stopped, the house grew silent. Words felt inconsequential—there wasn't anything to say or do to change the pain that weighed on her and her dad so heavily it blunted everything, made all else seem unreal.

Her mother continued to live at home, looked after by Gina and her father and by a nurse who came several times a week to check her vitals and perform tests of her progress—what little she ever made. Her mother's once-graceful movements were now stiff, her speech halting and basic. For the most part, she sat in her room, emerging only for the slow walks she took each day with Gina's father. Gina was uneasy around her, and found her mother's presence too painful a reminder of the woman who was gone. Now her mother never hugged Gina or kissed her, and it wasn't clear what emotion, if any, she could feel. Gina came to think it was a blessing if her mother didn't feel things; she'd have gladly chosen to feel less as well.

Eventually, Gina returned to classes, now dropped off by her father, who drove her to school seeking, in any way he could, to occupy her mother's place. And yet, as much as he was there, he couldn't possibly rescue her from the grayness she'd sunk into.

The only respite she could find was in the stories she told herself—of her mom's miraculous recovery, or of moving to some more exciting city, or of men appearing to whisk her off on some adventure. At points Gina's fantasies were so intense, it seemed she was confused between them and the life she was living. A neighbor's daughter, seventeen years old, had gotten pregnant, and soon ten-year-old Gina became concerned that she was pregnant too. When she mentioned this notion to her classmate, a teacher overheard and she was taken to speak with the school psychologist.

Her father came in for the meeting, which consisted of two parts. During the first, Gina sat alone with the psychologist, who had thick gray hair and a deeply dimpled smile. The woman asked her questions about the story that she'd told. Did she understand how a woman became pregnant? She had some idea: through being with a man. Had she been with a man herself? She hadn't, but she'd thought about it, she admitted, and wondered if in this case it was enough. And had she started ovulating? She had not. The woman assured Gina she was fine, had done nothing wrong, and then asked her to step into the hallway while Gina's father entered for a brief discussion, which Gina caught bits of through the thin door.

"She's always been dramatic," her father was saying, "but I'm worried she might be losing her grip on reality."

"My sense is that she doesn't really believe she's pregnant," said the woman, "but that this fantasy is playing a role for her, providing comfort. Maybe it's the idea of having a baby that would make the family a triangle again, and whole. Or maybe she wants to imagine she would mother this child to make up for the mothering she isn't getting."

After the meeting, Gina could feel her father's worry over her, and quickly decided to abandon the fantasy that had so gripped her. "Dad, I'm not crazy, okay? Sometimes pretending things makes me feel better."

"Of course you're not crazy. I know that. It's the loneliness, this awful loneliness without her." He reached out to take her hand and squeezed it, hard, in comfort and in need. "I feel it too."

Following their conversation, her father took an emergency

leave from his university position. Gina, he'd decided, required his exclusive attention.

"I think what we both need to get through this is one another. As long as we can trust in that, we'll be all right."

From that day on, her father had redoubled his involvement with her, to the point where others, she knew, might find their closeness strange. He'd seen to it that he was always home when she returned from school, always available for anything she needed—shopping trips and volunteering at the school, help with homework or conversations about puberty or boys. As she grew older, and her friends began dating, she failed to show interest in anyone. No one ever lived up to the figures in her imaginings, and finally she decided that her father was the only actual gallant man she knew. He'd adored his wife, had written her poems and painted her portrait over and over, with infinite care and fascination. When she grew debilitated, he maintained his devotion, looked after her and took her on those long walks each afternoon. Gina had asked him, through the years, why he didn't try to meet another woman, maybe marry again, and he would tell her that he'd had the two most extraordinary loves already in his life, with the family he had. Nothing else interested him.

Gina had given up her dancing for the past year, feeling guilty, perhaps, for exhibiting the vitality in her that her mother had lost—but now she came to feel this was precisely what she needed: an extraordinary love in her life. When she danced she had no thoughts, no memory, no wishes, no regrets. There was nothing to her but parts moving through space and the music that led her. She threw herself into dance like others might into religion. From ballet, she switched to modern, which was more improvisational, and better allowed her to become absorbed in what she was doing. Her dance school encouraged her to perform in small parts professionally, and by senior year she planned to attend art school and concentrate in dance. Instead, her college counselor persuaded her to apply to several liberal arts colleges as well. Her grades were good and there were several schools that had dance majors, including Yale. That spring, moved by her personal story and her success as a performer, the admissions committee offered her a place.

"New Haven is pretty far, though," her father pointed out, and there were other, closer schools. He stopped short of admitting how the distance would pain him, but she understood he found it hard to let her go. She felt awful about leaving—or, more precisely, guilty over the fact that she felt propelled to leave. All these years she'd never fully acknowledged her craving to be freed from her home and from the atmosphere of loss that hung in every room.

How exhilarating to arrive at Yale in the fall, where everything seemed grand and romantic in a way that spoke to the fantastical in her. She loved walking among the college courtyards, with their fragrant rosebushes and dreamy stone walkways hidden behind walls. She loved the dorm rooms with their dark wood and arched windows, the high-ceilinged dining halls with their raucous noise, and the sense she carried in them of having escaped Santa Fe and her small-minded peers to find herself among an exciting and worldly group of future friends. Within her freshman dorm lived a British aristocrat—an earl or duke of some sort—a daughter of an Indian diplomat, a son of a French politician, and a daughter of an Italian TV star. She befriended a few of them, but they proved less compelling than she'd hoped, and then she became involved with a young man, a guitar player, whose playing impressed her, until she realized nothing else about him did. She had to wait until sophomore year to meet the people who would really engage her, starting with a girl who was to become her best friend and set her on the path she'd follow years after their acquaintance: Violet Sharpe.

Violet was two years ahead of Gina in school, already a senior and the head of the college dramatic association. Everybody in the arts knew Violet: she was impossible to miss, a loping six-foot-tall Chinese girl with hair shaved on one side and the remainder dyed white-blond. Violet's face was also riveting, with thick, straight brows; full lips; and wide-set eyes with bold green streaks of shadow on the lids. Violet was the adopted daughter of two prominent figures in the world of New York theater; she'd therefore come onto campus with an automatic authority about the performance scene, and with the tacit promise of future connections—all of which caused those around her to seek her favor: the best actors turned down roles in other shows to work with her. The best crews attached themselves to her productions.

Gina knew of Violet, of course, even though their creative cliques only overlapped slightly—but sophomore year she'd noticed Violet coming to dance performances and showing up after rehearsals. The lure was a freckled brunette named Bette, whom Violet would continue to date on and off long after college. That October, Gina and Bette were in a show together, arranged by a student choreographer. The set designer had devised a system with screens lit from behind, which would make the dancers appear as silhouettes. The arrangement had worked during rehearsal, but during the second performance, one of the screens was kicked a little and brought too close to the hot lights.

The screens were apparently made of a very thin, dry paper and sprayed with flammable glue, so that in seconds the paper began to smoke and then curl into flames. The audience gasped and several of the dancers ran off. Gina had the presence of mind to return with the fire extinguisher—and then continued dancing. No intrusion from reality could sever her connection to her art. The audience sat bound by her singular force, lured back into the illusion, as one by one other dancers crept back in around her.

The next time Violet arrived at dance class to meet Bette, she drew Gina into their conversation.

"That was quite a performance last week," Violet remarked, tugging Gina's sleeve.

Gina shrugged, her smile knowing, even flirtatious. "What's a little fire to get in the way of a show?"

Violet was studying her, those green-painted eyes fixed. "I'd always thought you seemed a bit too normal, honestly, but I was wrong. I see it in you now. You've got some real crazy in you." Violet had grinned at her, revealing large teeth with a gap in the center, the sort of oddity her parents had known, in their circles, it would be best not to correct.

Gina supposed she might have been offended; there was a time when being called crazy would have frightened her, but now, with Violet, she felt relieved, accepted, seen. She'd known she contained the extremity that Violet named, but she'd never, until Violet put it that way, considered it any sort of gift.

"We're going to New York this weekend," Violet remarked with an air of casualness. "If you want to come."

"Love to," Gina told her, feeling the urge to leave behind the sheltered world of the campus and go exploring. "Though I don't have anywhere to stay."

Violet assured her that she had a place Gina would be free to use. "Anytime, really." The invitation carried the promise, already, of future adventures.

In the city, Violet took Gina to a dance performance downtown. The theater was at First Avenue and Ninth Street, a plain auditorium with columns obstructing the view. The outside was redbrick, institutional—it didn't look like a theater at all. In fact, she learned, the building was an abandoned public school.

The show she'd seen that night had confused and then astonished her. It seemed to break with every expectation she hadn't realized until then she'd been bound by. The dancers had looked so mismatched, tall and short, gangly and thick—each in distinct costumes that might have been their real clothes. At times they stopped dancing and sat and even talked to one another, or to the audience—dancers had voices!—and there were steps within the performance that might have been mistakes, and which Gina realized were intended to look that way, to break confidence in the dancers, to rouse in the audience a doubt, which would then be mocked by some act of virtuosity. The whole notion of a dancer, of what a dancer was, had been thrown up in the air that night, and Gina felt at once unsteadied and amazed.

"That was incredible," she'd effused to Violet after the show, though Violet was less impressed. It would take Gina longer to understand the history of such work, how much had been borrowed from other, greater figures in the dance world, but none of that altered the wonder she'd experienced that night when she was too young and unschooled to form a more measured reaction. Measured reactions could come later—wonder was what she needed then.

"It was incredible anyway," she insisted, persuading Violet

too in her enthusiasm, grabbing the girl's arm. "I want to dance that way someday."

"I'm sure you'll do whatever you want to," said Violet, impressed with Gina's determination, and infected by her reverie. "I can see you in a few years, gently bending the whole world to your wishes."

Gina laughed, both gleefully and guiltily, sensing Bette's discomfort with what was happening between them, Gina's effect on Violet. A change was taking place, a magnetic sort of friendship quickly binding these two young women together.

From the performance, Violet whisked Gina and Bette off to a party, somewhere west. A single small lamp underneath the drinks table served to light the whole space, so that at the edges of the room people disappeared into darkness. Every now and then Violet would come clutching Gina's arm to introduce her to a choreographer or to announce that Laurie Anderson had just been through. Is that Eric Bogosian? Oh my God, is that Grace Jones? In the dark it was nearly impossible to make out faces with any certainty, and everybody in the room had the look of someone famous, an aura of consequence about them. Even the people who were ugly were gorgeous.

If Violet's intent had been to hook Gina on the scene, she had succeeded. By the end of the night, Gina believed that there was simply nowhere else for a dancer like her to be than in New York, working wherever these people worked, living in a loft like the one Violet's fathers lived in, with exposed beams and brick and light streaming in through white curtains in the morning.

Gina had seen her future clearly, how the next decade should look. The only part she hadn't filled in yet was Duncan.

It was possibly sheer chance that, the week after she'd joined

Violet in New York, Gina was invited by a student choreographer to see a composition by a fellow sophomore. She'd found the music lovely, and was also taken with the boy onstage: shy, handsome, serious—someone whom she'd somehow never seen before. Though, hadn't she seen him? It had been briefly, the previous spring, in the rehearsal room where she'd stopped to try out an idea. As she'd danced, she'd caught him watching her, this stranger, and now here he was again, half a year later, no longer hidden in the dark, but in the spotlight, center stage.

She'd had an instinct about Duncan. She couldn't have said quite what it came down to, but some curiosity in her had been aroused—enough to persuade her choreographer friend to enlist Duncan to compose for a dance performance he was mounting. Duncan had agreed, but on the first day he was to join in the rehearsal, he lost his nerve and came in early to relay his apologies. Only Gina was around.

"I can't do this, I've never done anything like this," he'd admitted shyly.

Of course he could! She felt she knew this, that the young man she'd seen performing his extraordinary piece had far more talent in him than he acknowledged, or was even aware of in himself. In his sudden apprehension, she spotted something new in Duncan, a critical voice that interfered with his being the great musician she'd been so taken by before.

"There's no harm in trying at least, is there? I mean, maybe I can help."

She wasn't sure, once she'd said it, exactly how she might do that, but she sensed that what Duncan required was encouragement, and she felt, stirring in her, some desire to spur him on. And so she invented a story about a composer who wrote music while watching dancers dance—she hadn't really known one, but it seemed plausible enough.

She'd danced for him that morning, a solo performance with an air of dangerous intimacy. Maybe it was the strange nervousness arising in her—she liked this boy, wanted *him* to like *her*, and his opinion therefore mattered—or maybe it was the parallel fear she sensed in Duncan, the risk that he was taking in playing for her. As Duncan played, he seemed to grow more confident, and she became surprised by how the notes he chose fit to whatever she was doing. At first, it was imperfect—she found it necessary to adjust her movement, or suggest an adjustment to him, but soon it all seemed automatic and instinctual, the way his melody traced her movements, supported her and held her. She'd been startled by it, uncertain what it meant, this wordless resonance between them, but afterward, she couldn't get the experience out of her head. Dancing had been her escape, but a lonely one—before Duncan.

Most every night for the next weeks, Duncan would wait for her after rehearsals, pretending, at first, he was busy with his work, and then abandoning the pretense. He was nervous with her, his hands thrust inside his pockets as they walked, as if expressing the wish of his whole being to hide. But why? Could he be so blind to everything remarkable in him? He seemed not to realize that he was handsome, for instance, his dark hair pulled back from his thoughtful, lovely face, those red lips he'd sink his teeth into when he was thinking hard. Nor did he recognize his own talent, just how rare a gift he had, to be able to draw beauty out of thin air.

When he played music there was this boyish effortlessness about him, so different from the seriousness with which he spoke.

As they walked and talked, long pauses would open up while he considered his opinions and searched for what he meant to say, until, sometimes, she'd chirpily fill them. She was clearly more brash, but she could see that Duncan didn't mind this. In fact, it seemed to relieve him when she chimed in while he was laboring to answer some question, like what he meant to do with his life— a question she'd brought up without realizing it would send him into a tailspin. He considered all the factors—his parents' wishes, his sense of obligation, his notion of what was respectable—until she'd easily gushed her opinion: "The only point in living is to follow your passion."

"Tell me what you really think," he'd replied, laughing, and she could feel that he was grateful to her for speaking up for his desire, for briefly eclipsing the many stifling voices in his head.

If he felt lightened by her, perhaps he could have the same effect on her. She found herself relaxed with him from the start, and only more so as time went on. He was so enamored of her boldness, she felt bolder still. It became easy to tell him things she hadn't allowed herself to admit to anyone—not even Violet—like her urgent wish to have a child. Violet, who considered domesticity imprisonment, would have cringed to learn that Gina had been fantasizing about pregnancy since she was a girl. Catching sight of a mother and child together she'd feel an ache, or sometimes, just on her own and without cause, she'd envision scenes that she'd shared with her mother, but recast. She'd take her little girl swimming and let the small body cling to hers. She'd teach her how to swim and dance, and all those small, sweet childhood skills, how to tie her shoelaces, recite the alphabet, skip rope.

She hadn't let Duncan know what was behind her wish, had only mentioned motherhood, and her own mother, in passing, but it seemed to her that Duncan caught on to the sentiment behind it. After she'd told him, he'd grown thoughtful, and reached out to take her hand.

After that one touch, he hadn't dared touch her again, so it had been up to her to take hold of him one night outside his dorm, and stand on her toes to kiss him. It was the sort of kiss she'd hoped for, receptive, connected, like the way they were when she was dancing while he played. He held her tightly in the cold, the pair of them shivering after a time, from the cold and the import of what was happening.

Her daring seemed to kindle, slowly, the same within him. Sensible Duncan became more romantic, impulsive. He began showing up at her door with surprise invitations—to performances on campus and movies in town, anything she happened to mention she was curious about, his style of dating being much more quaint than that of other boys on campus, who simply showed up in girls' rooms for an evening of fun. He even made an effort to fit in with Gina's friends, though Violet made clear her suspicion of him from the start. An economics major, friends with a guy like Blake Flournoy, who represented every chauvinistic, conservative materialist Violet had set herself aggressively against—"How can you want a guy like that? He's not even an artist."

"He is," Gina insisted. "He's a brilliant one. He's just finding himself still. And he's changing."

Two weekends later, Duncan confirmed this hope in her when he arrived at her door with an invitation to a piano performance.

"The woman performing was my teacher when I was younger. Lillian. She was the first person to think I had talent, so my mother fired her, of course." He smiled at this, gloomily, then grew earnest again. "In a way she reminds me of you, or set me on a path to you, inspiring me."

"We'll go, of course," Gina told him, pleased by all the ways Duncan was embracing his musical self, loosening up his rigid devotion to his classwork, and by all the ways she was affecting him to do this. Now here was another woman who had encouraged him, long before her, and likely aroused his fantasies too. The small twinge of envy Gina felt was more than matched by her curiosity.

They took the train into Manhattan Saturday, and ended up in a small room at a library where the concert was being held. The teacher was older than she'd seemed from Duncan's descriptions, with streaks of gray in her hair and glasses that hid a pair of warm and pretty eyes. When they met after the show, Lillian hugged Duncan with such obvious affection that Gina might have been jealous, if she hadn't felt so sharply how Duncan cared for her, and how lucky this other woman thought her for that reason.

"He's an extraordinary person, this one," Lillian said, beaming, and Gina was sure that it was true, sure from how shyly grateful he seemed around them both, and for how sweetly he ended up playing, over coffees after, with Lillian's little daughter, a girl of five who hung over Duncan, enchanted.

That night, since it had gotten too late to take the train, Lillian invited Duncan and Gina to stay at her cramped Chinatown apartment. Lying curled up together on a futon, Duncan admitted something to Gina that he'd been embarrassed, before, to say. "That first piece I performed at Woolsey Hall, I wrote it for you."

Gina turned to look at him, incredulous. "But you didn't even know me yet."

"I'd seen you, though. And when I thought of you, that song

just came. I thought if I told you that, you might think I was crazy."

"You are crazy," she said, laughing, not letting on how much this thrilled her. How delighted she was to know that Duncan, with his reasoned and balanced arguments in each direction, his pragmatic future plans, Duncan, whom she feared might be a bit too sensible for her, had some madness in him too. Of course they each had to be a little crazy to fall so passionately for each other. Without passion, there could be no art and no love either, and they were going to build their lives on both. They were going to forge a love story that would be bigger and braver than either of them could ever dream up apart.

Six

Duncan // Vienna

June 1996

Duncan woke to knocking on the door. In his half sleep he called out, "Who is it? Who's there?"

"*Polizei,*" the voice replied.

He thought he must be dreaming, that this had to be a nightmare, a fabrication of his unconscious, images and ideas he'd somehow imbibed from his mother. Guilt and persecution, authorities with hard German accents shouting, and he in bed with lovely Gina, which was itself a sort of crime.

"Allo? Police!" the voice called from outside. "Please open the door!"

Duncan stood, shaking, seeking a way out. Their hotel room was on the top floor, and he wasn't about to go crawling through the windows anyway, with Gina standing near, looking at him worriedly, wondering what could be wrong—why the police would be knocking on their door and he would be standing with an expression of such guilt and fright.

He took the few steps to the door and paused, exhaling and

breathing in again, accepting his fate. Here it was, the moment that he'd imagined must come at some point, in some hotel or other. That he should meet such an end seemed a fitting punishment for having been greedy over his happiness. His conscience had such a hold on his perception then that it didn't occur to him to look for other explanations for what was happening, more plausible or more mundane, until he heard Gina's voice behind him. "The police. The hotel clerk must have called about the mugging."

He had to refocus his attention. The incident with the drunk from the train. Might that be all this was about?

He opened the room door and two officers strolled in, one a tall woman with a beaked nose, the other a bald man with a red moustache.

"Duncan Lowy, is it?"

"Yes, that's right." He was trying to stay calm, though it gave him a jolt to realize this officer knew who he was. The man looked at him, skeptically, it seemed. "We're sorry to be barging in on you. But we were told you were the victims of a crime last night."

"That's right," Gina replied, behind him. She'd risen to her feet, dressed in just a shirt.

The male officer averted his eyes. "We've come too early, I apologize, but we hoped to speak with you before you headed out. Maybe take a few minutes to dress, miss?"

A few minutes, Duncan thought, that might give him the time he needed to craft his responses in advance, to ready himself for whatever eventuality he might face next. The officer's English was remarkably good, as if the department had gone out of its way to send the officer most equipped to deal with Americans. And to send two officers all this way, and have them banging on a hotel door—it made no sense to go so far simply to apprehend an incompetent street thug.

The officer tapped on Duncan's shoulder and urged him to step out into the hall. Apparently he found Duncan's shirt and sweats a perfectly adequate outfit in which to continue with their interview.

"Again, apologies for catching you this way," the officer began, "but tourists like yourself, you come and go, which is why a criminal will choose to pick on you the way he has. We've had a number of such crimes reported in the area, and it's been awfully hard to get information before the victims have left. Of course, I understand it's the last thing you wish to be bothered with on your vacation."

"It's the right thing to do, though. I'm glad you've come." Duncan smiled, though inwardly he was positively furious with himself. If this really were the reason the officers had come, he'd been a fool to let it happen. He ought to have handled things better, to have made clear to Gina he didn't want the crime reported, and before that meddling clerk heard what had happened. "We should have called you ourselves, I know, but I admit that I was worked up last night."

"You're better now, then?" The man pulled a small notepad and pen from his back pocket. "Able to write up a statement?"

"Yes. I think so."

"Good. If you'd just give me your passport so I could copy down your information meanwhile."

"It's back in the room."

"I'll need you to get it, then, it's standard," the officer replied, which seemed plausible enough, and yet, as Duncan crossed back into the room to retrieve his passport, he found his thoughts drifting to more dangerous scenarios. The clerk had tipped off the police to his staying here, and they had discovered who he was and what he'd done.

Inside the room, he looked over at Gina, who was dressed now and speaking with the female officer. It seemed to him that Gina avoided meeting his gaze.

"Very good, sir," said the officer, once Duncan had returned with his passport and handed it over. The officer copied down the information and then offered Duncan the notepad. "Please write down anything you can recall of the event, every detail, especially of the assailant."

Duncan scribbled a few sentences, not wishing to be especially helpful. He had no desire to see these officers apprehend the man in question and drag this matter out. "I'm afraid I've forgotten so much. The shock of it all maybe. And to be honest, I'd had a few beers. And the beers here are twice the size they are back home."

"Do what you can," the officer replied curtly, and then went inside to confer with his partner. When the officer returned a moment later, he was examining their passports.

"I see the two of you came over to Europe separately? You and your wife?"

"Yes, um, yes." He hadn't thought the officer would take notice of that, though it wasn't too hard to account for, really. "I had to start our trip a little later." He lowered his voice, aware that Gina likely couldn't remember they'd come to Europe separately. "I had some work to finish up back home. Is that relevant in any way?"

"Only in case you are ever called in to testify. The Viennese authorities will need to be able to reach the both of you. So I did wonder if you'll be traveling together."

"As long as I don't piss my wife off, right?" He was trying to make light, though the prospect of Viennese officers keeping tabs on their movements alarmed him. He cleared his throat. "We'll be traveling together. Yes."

"Very good. And if the two of you could be in touch with our department when you settle in next, we'd like to have a record of where you are, so we can reach you if need be."

"Do you really want to be apprised of our every move?"

"Is that a problem?" The man's expression became stern. "I realize it's an inconvenience to you, but we do take criminal activity seriously, sir. That man attacked you. I can't imagine you'd want the same to happen to the next tourist who comes to town."

"No, no, of course not." It wasn't as if there was a way for this officer or anyone to enforce the requirement, or to know, if Duncan did offer the name of a certain hotel in a certain city, whether he was telling the truth or not. The smart approach would be to smile and agree to everything asked of him, then lie later on. "My wife and I like to be spontaneous, is all. But I don't see why that precludes my telling you where we do land."

He handed the officer the notebook with the statement he'd written up, feeling that, hoping that, their interview was over.

"Good, sir," said the man, and apologized again for bursting in upon them. "I hope it didn't give you any sort of scare."

"Well, it's a pretty effective wake-up call."

At last the officer smiled, and Duncan began to feel relieved. Cheerily, he stepped back into the hotel room, where Gina and the female officer had also evidently finished speaking. The woman tucked her notepad into her breast pocket and shook hands first with Gina, then with Duncan. The group moved over to the door, where the male officer withdrew a card and handed it to Duncan.

"When you do choose to make your next move, this is the number to call."

"Actually," Gina put in, "I think we'll leave Vienna today."

Leave today? They hadn't spoken of leaving; on the contrary, they'd discussed several destinations in Vienna they were intending to see. Suddenly, Duncan didn't know where Gina was coming from. They were moving out of sync. He turned uneasily to look at her, but she again avoided meeting his eyes. She continued to address the officers.

"We're off to Prague. I've a friend there we planned to visit."

"You have this friend's address?" the female officer inquired.

"We have a place she can be reached. Her name is Violet Sharpe, and she gets her mail through the National Marionette Theater, 1 Zatecka Street."

She knows the address, Duncan suddenly realized with dread. When and how had Gina come across it and decided on her plan?

At last the officers stepped out and Duncan closed the door behind them. He felt a nervous urge to laugh, to discharge the energy he'd been holding in, but Gina's face was grave.

"Something wrong?" he asked her, his thoughts returning to the tension of the night before. She'd had so many questions about Marina—had even managed to guess correctly that she was the person whom he'd phoned from the hotel by Lake Walen.

He stepped forward now, seeing Gina back away, and then the paranoid thought came that perhaps while he'd been led off into the hall, the other officer had been speaking to Gina about the real matter at hand. "Did that woman say something to upset you?"

"What could she have said?"

"I have no idea, I'm just asking. But suddenly you're insisting on going to Prague, announcing Violet's address. Which you couldn't even remember yesterday."

He was fishing, seeing if she might give herself away—had she been looking through his papers? Though he'd thought it wise to hang on to Violet's address, in case circumstance required that he reach her, he should have copied the information down, in hidden form, elsewhere. How careless he'd been to keep that postcard with their things.

"Memory's funny that way, isn't it?" She was staring off at the wall, still with that fixed and humorless expression.

"Gina, what's this about?" He was trying to contain the panic mounting in him. "You're acting strangely."

"*I* am?"

"Yes. And I wish you'd just open up to me. Tell me whatever's on your mind." She was still facing the wall when he came forward to touch her. As he did, she turned and looked directly up at him, so that, he later imagined, she could catch his spontaneous reaction to her question, one that shook him far more than the police had.

"Who the hell is Graham Bonafair?"

*   *   *

It was in early April, just a few months before he departed for Europe, that Duncan was home alone preparing dinner when he heard the front door buzzer. "Who is it?"

"Graham Bonafair," said the voice through the crackle.

"Do I know you?"

"Not directly," the stranger answered, "but we know someone in common. Gina Reinhold."

Duncan buzzed the man inside and stepped from the kitchen

to the door. He took a look around his living room, self-conscious suddenly, aware that he was being visited by a person—a *man*—who knew Gina, and who might report back to her what he'd observed. Since Gina had left, he'd done nothing to remove the evidence of her former presence. The postcards from their performances, the photographs of them together: these still hung on the walls. He felt a pang of shame and sadness too, thinking of the past seven months, how paralyzed he'd been. He'd written no new music, had abandoned his commission from Marina and sought no others. The house was filthy; he rarely cleaned. What did it matter? And then cleaning would involve putting away the things that Gina had left here, it would involve admitting that this was no longer her home, that she was gone. He wasn't ready to admit this, and he had a premonition that this visitor was here to press the point.

The front doorbell rang and Duncan answered, coming face-to-face with the young man out in his hall. Graham was tall and lean, his build similar to Duncan's own. He was good looking, if in a generic, bleached-out sort of way. His hair was longish, blond. He wore corduroy pants, torn at the knees but not cheap, and a linen shirt. Duncan noticed then the necklace Graham was wearing, braided leather with a turquoise stone. "Did you come up from Santa Fe?" Duncan ventured.

"That's right!" Graham offered a big, white-toothed grin. "How did you know?"

He had an open way about him, Duncan thought, the sort of openness that came from an untroubled life.

Duncan only smiled, and gestured toward the sofa for Graham to have a seat. "You and Gina, you're related? Or old family friends, is that it?"

"Sort of. My granddad was a big investor with her granddad.

But really my connection is through her dad," Graham explained. "I'm a painter. I studied with him for years. He's an amazing guy."

So Graham was Mr. Reinhold's pupil, properly admiring and obsequious. No wonder he and Gina's father got along. "And how long have you known Gina?"

"About six months. We met a few weeks after she left . . . um, New York." Graham looked away awkwardly and appeared to spot one of the photos of Duncan and Gina on the wall. He frowned before he caught himself, and Duncan sensed the reason. He could feel his mood rapidly souring, wasn't sure he wished to know anything more about this man's relationship with Gina.

"So what brings you, then?" he asked a little curtly.

"I know it's awkward, my coming by like this," Graham said, sitting forward in his seat. "Maybe I should have called instead, but I wanted this meeting to be in person."

"That's fine, you've found me."

"Okay, right. I'll get to it, in that case." Graham leaned over to pick up a bag he'd carried in with him. There were papers in it, printed, stapled. He handed them over to Duncan. "I met with a lawyer myself, to save you the hassle and the fees."

"These are divorce papers." The sight of the documents shocked him. They'd been married so briefly, he and Gina, it was a fact he'd only begun to accept when, suddenly, they were together no longer. And yet on paper, legally, he was bound to Gina still. He went searching through the pages for Gina's signature, the mark of her approval, but he found none. "Gina hasn't signed?"

"Well, I was waiting to ask her. I mean, I knew if I showed her the papers she'd wonder why I was doing this. I'd tip my hand. I'm hoping to propose, this June."

"After knowing her six months?" He was overstepping, sure, Duncan knew that, but here was this man he'd never met announcing his plan to marry Duncan's wife—it seemed to him he was entitled to be impolite.

"I realize we can't marry for a while. There's the matter of the divorce and all that. But I wanted Gina to be aware of my intentions and how serious I am."

Offering these statements to the man who'd occupied most of Gina's past—it would be cruel if it weren't a product of Graham's guilelessness. Gina couldn't possibly be satisfied by someone so naïve, Duncan thought, however well-meaning he might be.

"You're a direct sort of person, aren't you?" said Duncan.

"I guess I am." Graham appeared to rethink this. "You feel I've been too blunt with you."

"It's not an indictment. It's good to be up front."

"Well, you know. The truth was going to reach you anyway. And this seemed the more respectful thing to do, talking to you directly. I don't see why we can't be amicable. Gina never made out like you were a bad guy."

"Oh? What did she say about me, then?"

"Excuse me?"

He could see that he was making Graham uncomfortable, but to hell with it. Let him be uncomfortable. This was Duncan's chance to get some answers, after six months of uncertainty, six months during which Gina had refused to speak with him, or explain her behavior to him. She'd left him in such a state of bafflement, he couldn't bear it. Now, finally, he might understand Gina's decision to abandon him and their life together—for what? For this bland and callow stranger seated across from him now?

"I'm asking what she told you about me. About what happened. Why we split. She must have said something."

"She, um, she didn't get too detailed. There was another woman, I guess. A friend of hers."

"You mean Marina."

"She said something went on between the two of you."

"Nothing went on between us."

"Look, I, um. I'm only reporting what she told me."

"Right, sure you are." Duncan smiled to hide his irritation. He was feeling his old anger arising at the unfairness of it all, and at the uselessness of trying to convince this man of his innocence. It was a conversation he ought to have been allowed to have six months before instead, with Gina.

Looking uneasy, Graham started to fumble with his bag. "Anyhow, the papers. Why don't we get on to that, then, so I'll be out of your hair. Just a few spots for you to sign."

But Duncan wasn't letting the matter go that easily. "And what are her plans now, if I can ask? Now that she's with you?"

"Her plans?" Graham lowered the papers and exhaled. He didn't wish to answer, that was clear, but there was a favor that he wanted, and so he must have felt obliged to indulge Duncan's curiosity a while longer. "We were talking about her joining a dance studio in Albuquerque."

"Albuquerque. And you don't think that will feel like a step down, after New York?"

"Maybe that's not the worst thing. New York can wear a person out."

"Not a person like Gina. She loved this city."

"Maybe her feelings have changed."

"Maybe she wants to think they have."

"Well, you're not there with her to say one way or the other, are you?"

He could see Graham growing unnerved, offended by the implication that he knew Gina less well than Duncan. But so what if he was offended? It was the truth, wasn't it? Wouldn't Gina—his wild, marvelous Gina—be bored out of her mind living in New Mexico, with a man like this? Duncan sat there, facing his rival, determined to insist on the reality of the woman that he'd loved. "No, I'm not there with her now, but for the past six years, I have been. I think I know Gina a little."

Graham paused, as if perhaps realizing Duncan was correct, and then offered a simple "Anyway," with a sigh. "If you wouldn't mind signing the papers. That's what I came here for."

Graham handed the pages to him once again, and this time Duncan accepted them. "All right, then, I'll look these over and get back to you. How's that?"

Graham didn't appear pleased. "Don't you want to sign them now?"

"I don't sign anything without running it by my lawyer." He had no lawyer, but it had seemed the thing to say—that was what people did in such cases, consulted lawyers. The excuse would buy him time.

"I'm not sure why you'd need a lawyer, unless this is about money. Her father might be willing to arrange something for you. A little support to carry you over."

"I don't want money, for God's sake," he snapped at Graham, not meaning to, but this was really more than he could take. Had Mr. Reinhold made him out to be that desperate?

Graham hurried to apologize. "Right, I'm sure. It wasn't my intention to imply—"

"Not to worry." Duncan rose and put out his hand jovially, thinking it would be best to end the meeting now, while the mood was mostly cordial and he was coming out on top. He was feeling that he'd held his own, considering—not only because he hadn't done the thing Graham wanted, but because he felt he'd glimpsed the insecurity of the man's position with Gina. Graham had performed this errand on his own, which meant it wasn't necessarily something that Gina herself wanted—or at least it might not be.

Early the next week, Graham called to ask if Duncan had met with his lawyer yet. Duncan told him that he hadn't, and when Graham called again, he said the papers must have been misplaced. Graham offered to send another copy. For several more weeks Duncan evaded him, claiming he was still waiting on his lawyer, until Graham threatened to show up at his house again. He was leaving for Europe in two weeks with Gina, where he hoped to propose and have the paperwork finished beforehand.

"Where in Europe?" Duncan asked, explaining that he had a few meetings there himself. In fact, his good friend Blake had moved to London, he explained, and he'd be visiting Blake to interview for a job at his London ad firm. "For their music department, you know. My friend's been asking me to do it for some time."

"Too bad, we'll be in Germany," Graham replied.

"Ah, well, if my lawyer doesn't get to this before you leave, I'll come over to Germany and deliver the papers."

"Why would you do that?" Even Graham had begun to grow suspicious. "That's a lot of trouble."

"Well, I've caused you a lot of trouble, haven't I? It seems the least that I can do."

A week later, when Graham announced that he was leaving for Berlin, he'd given Duncan the name of his hotel: "Hotel de Rome. Near Potsdamer Platz."

Duncan, meanwhile, gave Graham the name of a hotel in London. In fact he had no intention of visiting London and no hotel reservation, but he assumed, and had been right to assume, that Graham wouldn't bother to check. It made him feel guilty to be lying in this way, but he told himself he wasn't duping Graham entirely, that he would give the man what he wanted and sign the papers, finally, if it turned out that this was what Gina wanted too.

But first he'd have to learn: *was* this what Gina wanted?

He devised a plan. To start, he'd told Graham that his path of travel would only take him through Frankfurt for a connecting flight, and not Berlin—could Graham meet him there instead? Graham consented, though his tone over the phone suggested an increasing amount of irritation over an otherwise simple transaction. Not that Graham's mood was Duncan's big concern when Duncan arrived in Berlin just as he calculated Graham must be leaving, and took a cab straight to the hotel. He was thinking only about Gina, worried she might have traveled with Graham and might now be in the wrong city; but Duncan relied on what he saw in Graham as a predisposition to be overly sentimental—he wouldn't ruin the surprise of the engagement by telling Gina that divorce papers were what awaited them in an excursion to Frankfurt. What excuse he gave to Gina for his quick solo jaunt hardly mattered to Duncan; all that mattered was that she trusted Graham enough to stay behind.

Arriving at the hotel in Berlin, Duncan asked after Graham at the front desk, just to make sure that the man had really gone.

"Mr. Bonafair set off this morning."

"Oh, that's a shame. A last-minute meeting, I guess. He said that he might have one."

"Are you a friend of his?"

"Of his and Gina Reinhold's. We went to college together. I assume that she left with him?"

"I don't know, sir. If you'd like to give a name, I'll call up to her room."

"Thank you, yes." He'd given the man a name, not his own—instead he'd mentioned the choreographer that had enlisted him to compose for his first show—the classmate who'd brought Gina and him together.

The desk clerk lowered the receiver. "Ms. Reinhold says she'll be right down."

He'd waited, pacing the lobby, and then forced himself to take a seat in a large leather chair, facing the elevator bay. At last an elevator opened and Gina stepped out, with an expectant look. She'd cut her hair shorter, and with the curls less weighed down, they were more girlish, her face more youthful, as if time had moved backward. She breezed through, glowing, awaiting a surprise, an old friend, ready to laugh and throw her arms around someone familiar in this very strange part of the world, having just been left alone in an unfamiliar city by her lover. And then she saw Duncan and stopped smiling. She stopped altogether, stopped right in her tracks and simply stared, her arms crossing slowly over her chest.

"What are you doing here?" she said as he approached.

"I'm sorry to catch you like this. I had to talk to you."

"*Catch me* like this? How did you find me? Who told you I was here?"

"Graham told me. He reached out to me a few weeks ago."

"Reached out to you why? Does he know you're here now?"

"No, no, that part he doesn't know. But like I said, Gina, I had to talk to you."

This discussion had all taken place in the romantic hotel lobby, between marble columns and velvet sofas, amid a cast of European characters that made it all feel that much more cinematic and unreal. He'd felt a bit ridiculous, making these grand statements, which didn't seem at all to suit him, but Gina they did suit. Another woman might have been embarrassed by the high drama, but he knew that, more than anything, Gina loved a bold gesture, and so he hoped that what he'd done might be judged favorably by her.

"Just hear me out," he told her. "Graham came to me, asking me to sign some divorce papers. He planned . . . Well, he wouldn't want me saying."

"I assume he wouldn't want you doing any of this."

Gina's sharpness threw him off. She seemed so angry that he'd come. Why should she hate to see him when seeing her aroused in him only longing and regret? "Look, I know it's selfish of me, but I had to tell you how I felt—how I *feel.*"

The meaning of all of this was dawning on Gina. "You sent him off on this Frankfurt trip."

"I had to, I—"

"For divorce papers. And why would he keep this a secret? Oh God, he's going to propose, isn't he?"

The way that she said this, not eagerly, but with a note of embarrassment even, gave Duncan the confidence to continue.

"Yes, he's going to propose. So he came to ask me to sign the papers and I didn't want to do it. I don't want to be divorced.

Maybe the marriage was a mistake in a certain sense—it was too soon, we were unsteady, and I think we both scared ourselves. But even if we were afraid of what it meant to be together, that doesn't mean we didn't want it. I know what I want. I still want you."

He awaited her reaction, tears, fists, something, but instead, Gina turned and walked away to reception, said something to the man behind the counter, and then stepped out through the revolving doors. Duncan was unsure what to do, whether to wait or run after her. In retrospect he should have run, but at the time he'd been confused and stunned still by their meeting. After a moment, he went up to the man at reception and asked what the young woman had told him.

"That she's gone out and you shouldn't bother waiting."

Still he waited. Useless as it might be, he was too miserable to do anything other than sit slumped in a chair and reflect on all the ways that he'd gone wrong. Hours went by—long enough that it occurred to him Graham could be on his way back from Frankfurt already, furious, even more furious to learn from Gina, who might call, that Duncan had accosted her. After another hour, he began to wonder whether Gina had assumed he'd go on waiting and never intended to return. Could she be so determined to avoid him that she would check in somewhere else, maybe have her luggage delivered after her? Twice he approached the staff behind the desk to ask if any messages had come from Gina Reinhold, but they assured him that none had.

After several hours spent pretending to read the paper or walking in circles outside, Duncan began to feel that he was crazy. He must be, to have come all this way to tell Gina something she didn't care to hear. She didn't wish to give him another chance.

She'd found a different man to love, and this man, unlike him, hadn't given her any cause to feel he would let her down.

Despairing, he stood, about to leave, when he saw one of the receptionists coming toward him.

"You're the one who's been waiting for Gina Reinhold, yes?"

"Yes, right. Did you hear from her?"

"Not from her. But from the hospital. Ms. Reinhold has had an accident."

He'd rushed to the hospital by taxi—it was a lucky thing, really, that he'd been notified at all. Gina had been carrying her hotel key, and whoever found her had phoned the hotel with the room number and told them to notify anybody staying with her. The receptionist had asked Duncan if he knew how Ms. Reinhold's partner might be reached.

"She told me he's out of the country. Until he's back, I can look after her."

At the hospital, a building on Luisenstrasse, the desk clerk informed Duncan that no one except family members could get information on Gina's condition or speak with her doctor. Duncan announced, truthfully, that he was Gina's husband. Shortly after, Gina's doctor stepped out to explain that she had fallen at a construction site on Potsdamer Platz and had suffered a concussion and intracranial swelling. She'd been unconscious for several hours and had woken about half an hour before, disoriented and unable to say where she was or how she'd come to be there.

"It's impossible at this stage to determine how temporary the damage to her mental functioning might be. I tell you this so that you won't be alarmed when you do see her. It's likely she won't even recognize you."

He felt as if the ground were dropping out beneath him—was

she gone, the Gina he'd known? Was he to blame? Possibly she wouldn't have taken that walk had he not appeared, or she wouldn't have been in such an agitated state after seeing him and she might not have lost her balance. In his selfish inability to let her go, he'd destroyed her, the most wonderful woman he'd ever known.

He entered the room, hardly able to bring himself to look at her, though when he did, he was relieved to find that she didn't even appear injured. There was a bandage around her head, but her face was unchanged, lovely still, and the expression she wore was remarkably focused, calm, and kind.

"You poor thing," she said to him, which had surprised him utterly, her sympathy for him, at such a moment.

He'd gasped a little, and felt a warm tear roll down his cheek.

"Oh, don't cry," she said, "I'm fine, baby, I'm fine."

He'd looked up at her, startled by the warmth in her face. He hadn't seen a look like that in so long, not since she'd left for Vienna the summer before, the summer that had ended them. Until he'd seen it, he hadn't felt so acutely how much he'd longed for exactly this.

"I'm just a bit confused," she told him. "They tell me I'm in Berlin."

"You are. We're in Berlin."

"Have we taken a trip? Our honeymoon?"

He stared at her, trying to make sense of what she was saying. Did she believe they'd come to this place together, that they were a couple still? Could she have forgotten the past year, his mistakes, all those stupid events that had come between them?

The sense of unsteadiness was overwhelming—she believed that they were starting their shared life. She had no notion that this possibility had been destroyed. He stepped forward and took a seat at the edge of her bed. He thought what he must tell her next to stop this—she was confused. She'd long ago stopped wanting to be with him.

But how could he tell her that when he could see now, in her eyes, how she did want him? Gina was brimming with emotion— the terror of her experience had woken her to what mattered, and pushed her to say things she wouldn't otherwise have dared.

"I want to start our life, to move forward, to have a child. Let's make a child on this trip, our child. Let's do that, please!"

He searched her face, that lovely mouth open a little, expectant, the half-closed eyes that begged him to join her in forgetting. He moved closer so that he could smell her sweet, familiar breath, and before he could form any words of objection, before he could collect himself enough to point out her misunderstanding, she leaned in toward him, reached for his face, and, like a figure from his dreams, drew him to her for a kiss.

He'd known he couldn't keep Gina in Berlin, and not, certainly, at a Berlin hospital. Graham wouldn't be gone long. By now he certainly would have realized he'd been stood up. Perhaps he'd guessed the reason, perhaps not, but regardless, he'd likely call the hotel to leave a message there for Gina, and also, very likely, when he did, he'd be informed of her injury and would catch the first flight back. It would all happen very quickly, and Gina's doctors were telling Duncan that they wished to keep her for more tests and observation. What might be done? He didn't know the workings of this country, had no connections here, hardly spoke the language. He'd realized that he needed help, and considered where to turn.

There was one nurse who'd distinguished herself in just those first hours. Her name was Greta and she was older, knowing, an East German. To ingratiate herself with him, a privileged American, she'd begun to offer favors: she might get Gina better bedding or an extra pillow, she might bring her some nicer food from a restaurant. Here was a woman, Duncan quickly sensed, who'd made her way through deprivation and had learned a thing or two about survival. He'd chosen to take a chance and told her—not the whole truth, he wouldn't dare do that—but as much as was needed to communicate his wishes. "I wondered if you could advise me what to do if I needed to get my wife quickly and quietly out of Berlin."

Knowing better than to ask questions, the nurse suggested he identify another clinic in another region and give a reason for her transfer. He might say Gina had a familiar doctor there, or friends or family in the area who wanted to be able to see her.

The next few hours were frantic. First, he'd enlisted Greta's help in finding a small clinic in Switzerland that seemed suitable. Then he went back to Gina's hotel and informed the receptionist that Gina would be needing her things at the hospital. The receptionist allowed him to go up to her room and pack, and Duncan had thrown everything inside the suitcase and hurried out. After, on the ride back to the hospital, he went through Gina's belongings and removed anything that might put an end to the illusion: a fresh postcard to Violet she hadn't yet sent; Gina's address book, which contained information for the new contacts she'd made in Santa Fe—colleagues at her dance studio, friends she'd made through and with Graham. He'd had to throw away her journal too, inside of which he'd found plenty of accounts of her new life. He'd felt guilty reading over her private entries, but he told himself that if he found something in her writing to persuade him what he was doing was clearly wrong, that she was happier with Graham than she'd been with him, then he would dispense with his deception.

Instead, he came upon a passage that gave him just the hope he needed to go on.

Each morning I wake up with him in Santa Fe it feels like I'm in the wrong place. It shouldn't be birds that I hear from my window, but the honking of Manhattan streets. It shouldn't be Graham reaching to stroke my hair, it should be Duncan kissing my sleeping mouth. When will it change? When will this life feel like my life?

After reading this, he knew he had to act. He must get Gina out of Berlin before Graham found her, but to do this required money. The clinics were expensive, travel was expensive, and he couldn't afford either. So he'd done the thing he'd never planned on doing. He called Marina Du Bellay.

"Duncan Lowy?" She'd been surprised to hear from him. They hadn't spoken in six months, not since he'd left the project she'd commissioned. That conversation had been brief: he'd let her know he couldn't see her or be involved with her in any way after what had happened, and yet she still insisted upon paying him at least a part of what she'd promised.

He'd refused her money, not wishing to exploit her guilt—and now here he was, forced to do precisely that.

"Hi, Marina, I'm, um, I'm sorry to call out of the blue."

"You okay? You sound agitated . . . is something wrong?"

He wasn't sure what to say; he didn't want Marina knowing

too much, just that he was in Berlin and in need of money he couldn't hide. "I'm in a bit of a jam, I guess. Otherwise I wouldn't trouble you." He had to pace the room, so tense was he that day, and overcome by the familiar and now painful cadence of Marina's voice.

"I'm glad you've called. I've felt so badly about you and Gina."

And here, he sensed, was the point to work from, the way to ask for the favor he needed.

"Actually, this is about us, Gina and I. She finally seems maybe ready to forgive me. I'd like to take her on a trip, a fresh start, that sort of thing. But trips cost money, and, well, I never did feel right accepting what you'd offered before. . . ."

"Ah, I see." Marina sighed. "I understand."

Duncan had sensed, perhaps, some small hurt he'd caused her, which aroused his regret. But he felt he had no choice, no other way of going forward. Marina promised she would wire thirty thousand dollars to a Zurich bank.

From the hospital, he and Gina took a taxi to Potsdamer Platz Bahnhof and boarded a train bound for Zurich. He'd been nervous all the way, envisioning police or checkpoint guards pulling him aside with questions, but in fact, no one approached them or even asked to see their passports. It had dawned on Duncan, as they made the passage, that for the first time in history, a visitor to Europe might move seamlessly from one nation to another, might slip unseen among twenty countries. The plot that was taking shape—to escape with Gina, crazy as it was—might also be possible.

In Zurich, Duncan breathed more easily. The culture of

anonymity that defined Swiss banks seemed to be shared by hospitals too. He'd let the head of the clinic know that privacy was a great matter to them, implying that Gina was someone of note back home. Thanks to Gina's status, as a budding starlet or heiress or whatever they imagined, she was a Swiss Jane Doe on the books. No one in Berlin knew where Gina was—he'd deliberately left the name of a different clinic with Gina's doctor there. Even if Graham were to call around to clinics in the surrounding countries, it was unlikely he'd find this rather obscure one, and once they'd left the clinic, he and Gina would be harder to find still. A detective might check the larger European hotels, but no one had the resources to keep up with the smaller guesthouses. It would be better to stick to quieter areas, regardless, for a time, in case Graham had brought his story to the press as well as to police.

In the next days, Duncan took care of smaller business. He located a jeweler and stopped in to buy two secondhand wedding bands. He'd held on to his own band, but hadn't thought to bring it with him, and he hadn't the first idea where Gina's might have been. At the store, he'd found two that looked much like the pair they'd picked together, but when he'd given hers to Gina that day, he'd been distressed to find it was too loose. After this, he arranged for an answering service to deliver his messages, in case Gina thought to check the machine they'd once shared. He was beginning to believe he had succeeded in his escape, especially since the papers he checked had nothing about Gina's disappearance. It seemed his malfeasance wasn't of interest to anyone. Only then, that night out dining in the Walensee, that pink-cheeked man at the corner table had recognized Gina.

"Sorry for staring," the man had said when Duncan went to

speak with him while Gina was in the bathroom, "but the lady you're with looks just like the girl from the Berlin papers." So her story—the accident, the disappearance, or both—hadn't gone unnoticed. In fact, it had gotten coverage significant enough to reach Switzerland. Still worse, her picture had been included with whatever was written.

He could imagine the sort of story it could be: Graham had offered up some vacation shot of her, lovely and smiling, and the tabloids had gone mad for it. *Romantic Holiday Hijacked!* the headline would read, and then below, they'd describe a young tourist who'd lost her memory and been abducted, unknowingly, by an obsessed estranged husband.

"What girl in the papers?" Duncan had asked the man, attempting innocence, heart pounding.

"There was a girl who had an accident and lost her memory. When her fiancé returned she'd been hurried off by another man."

"That's a lot of effort to make to avoid marriage," Duncan said good-heartedly, and to his great relief the man had laughed.

"You've got a point there," the man said.

"I hope my wife doesn't find marriage to me so awful."

"I'm sure not!" The stranger laughed again and apologized for staring earlier. "Obviously I mistook your wife. I'm sorry if I bothered her."

"No, no, not at all. I'll share the story with her, she'll find it funny."

Duncan shook hands with the stranger and then walked away to join Gina, all the while concealing his panic.

Gina's story was out. Anyone, any stranger at any other time, might recognize her. If he allowed himself to stop and think about the risks, really think, he'd not be able to continue. He had no long-term strategy, no inkling of how this deception could end happily for anyone, but for the time being he was focused on the here and now, on whatever machinations were required to keep from getting caught. His goal was just to make it last a little longer—the love Gina seemed to bear toward him, the bottomless devotion he felt then toward her.

To do this he'd have to manage Gina's correspondence. Her father, Violet, Graham . . . any contact with these people would easily cast suspicion on him, if not expose his ruse entirely. He'd luckily managed to convince Gina that calling home might upset her father, but he still must intervene with the letter she'd planned on sending. Instead of the actual letter, he'd given Ms. Arner an empty, misaddressed envelope, and he'd held on to the original in case he should need to write another one in Gina's hand, on her behalf.

Later, on his first night in Vienna, after hearing Mr. Reinhold's message, Duncan had decided it was time to write a letter to set him at ease. After he'd returned from his phone calls, he read Gina's letter over, gathering clues about the style she employed with her father:

Dear Dad,

I'm writing to you from the countryside not too far from Zurich where Duncan and I have been resting up after Berlin. Berlin was thrilling and exhausting. I'm sure you'd be inspired by it. Everywhere the past is being smashed and rebuilt. Imagine a whole city intent on erasing history. . . .

Duncan had to smile, reading this—Gina, who had no memory of Berlin, was lying too! True, she was doing it for the best of reasons, to spare her father worry over her injuries, but she wasn't just adjusting the truth a bit, she was *embracing* the lie. So much of her letter was false that he was able to keep most of it, excluding just the references to his being with her. From this beginning, which he wrote out again, he added two more paragraphs in her excited, rounded script.

I've been wracking my brain over how much of this to tell you,
since we're apart and you might worry. Though I promise you,
you have no reason to. I'm fine, really better than fine. I think
you probably need to hear that from me, especially since Graham
might come to you—might have come to you already—and give
you a different impression. I can imagine what sort of speculation
Graham might have engaged in, and probably triggered in you
too. So I want you to hear the story from me.

After this, Duncan had described more or less accurately what had happened in Berlin, that Graham had gone off for a meeting, that she'd taken a walk and been injured:

I'm sure it must be very scary to hear that—and Graham might
have suggested that I've only left him because I'm not myself. But
I am myself, Dad, I really am. That accident gave me a shock.
I woke up, like a stranger to my life, and suddenly it seemed so
clear—I've been living in a way that doesn't fit me. One thing
that I felt, with some sadness, but also relief, because I'd caught
myself in time: I don't want to be married to Graham Bonafair.

He's a good person, I know that, and he loves me, and maybe I even love him a little. But not enough. Not the way I want to love the person that I marry. As for Duncan . . .

He left off there, thinking over what precisely would be the thing to say about himself. He might, for instance, choose to tell Gina's father that the two of them were reunited and traveling together, but he worried that to do it now might add to Graham's alarm. "You see," Graham would say, "she's clearly not in her right mind if she ran back to Duncan so quickly." Whereas if Gina were to travel on her own for a few weeks, and then decide to give Duncan another shot, well, who could find fault with her, really, for that?

I'm well aware that Duncan's hurt me in the past. But this accident has made me feel that I need to give myself some time to sort through my emotions. I've decided to travel for a while on my own now. I might go to Rome or Paris or Budapest—I'll write to you again or call once I'm more settled, but, for now, I want you to know that things are good with me and you don't need to be concerned.

Meanwhile, I hope you're staying cool in the Santa Fe summer. Wear a hat—maybe I'll pick one up for you, something stylish from Paris or Rome. Miss you, Daddy, and love you.

Your girl,
Gina

When he was through, and having thought it over at some length, the letter seemed to him the right one to send. Certainly it offered a more plausible explanation for those events Graham might have outlined to Gina's father already. Was there really any question which account was the more likely? That Gina had chosen to go off to contemplate her future, taking time to consider Graham's proposal, or that she'd been kidnapped by Duncan, kept in a state of permanent illusion? This story sounded so outrageous that, if he hadn't been living that wild reality daily, he wouldn't have believed it himself.

The letter had come out so well—even the penmanship matched Gina's—that Duncan imagined he would be writing again. For this reason, he'd held on to Violet's postcard, too, in case he should see a motive to write to Violet as he had Gina's father. It hadn't occurred to him what a great risk he was taking by keeping these items with him, how one day Gina might stumble across them and he'd face a moment like he was facing now.

*   *   *

Standing before him, in their Vienna hotel room, unsettled yet determined, Gina was describing the events of the last night that had led her to ask after Graham Bonafair.

"I couldn't sleep and I'd thought I'd write a letter, so I'd gone to look for paper. I couldn't find the stationery, but I know you keep some in your folder, so I thought I'd take a sheet. I'd only picked it up when a postcard fell out, with Violet's address and a return address from the Hotel de Rome. You hadn't mentioned that we'd stayed there, so I called them, out of curiosity, and they told me I had a message waiting. From someone named Graham Bonafair."

He stood there, hearing all this, sweat broken out over his lip. He was an instant from confessing the truth, which he was sure she must have discovered already. If she'd gotten this far, then nothing would keep her from speaking with Graham, who would tell her the whole story. And even if they hadn't spoken, Gina must have deduced the truth on her own. He took a breath and studied her more closely, her brow knit and eyes wide. There was confusion in her face, fear and hope, and, he sensed, some tenderness.

She doesn't know, he thought. He might survive this still.

"Graham's a friend of your father's. A former student. A painter from Santa Fe." He was impressed by how matter-of-factly he offered up this information.

Gina too seemed somewhat disarmed by his neat explanation. "And why is a friend of my father's calling me?"

"Gina," he said gently, gaining time, "I can see whatever you're thinking right now isn't good. I guess you're wondering if I hid that postcard on purpose. And you must be thinking that if I did, that means I'm hiding other things from you."

"You never sent my father's letter," she fired at him. "I found that in the folder too."

"All right, yes. I can explain all of that. I intended to—I wasn't planning to keep you in the dark forever, but you'd suffered a trauma, and I didn't want to overwhelm you right away." He took a step from her, arms crossed, contemplating. He must think quickly. "So, to start with Violet. You're right I kept her address from you for a time—though I only held on to it because I knew we'd make the visit at some point, when you were ready. But Violet's a loose cannon, and if we were to visit her, I couldn't know what she might say."

"Say about what?"

He took her hand, leading her over to the bed—giving the

impression he meant to proceed with care, though really he required the extra seconds to formulate his answer. "It hasn't been an easy year for you, and after your accident, more disorientation wasn't what you needed."

"Well, I can handle it now," she insisted, though worried wrinkles appeared across her forehead. "Whatever happened, I want you to tell me."

He sighed. "There was an argument."

"The one with Violet?"

"No, I just said that to protect you. The rift was with your father."

"My father?"

"You weren't speaking, which was why I couldn't have you calling him or sending him letters. Or seeing Violet either, for that matter, since she's not one to keep her mouth shut."

Gina was peering at him sideways, incredulous. "But what could my father have done that was so terrible?"

"I didn't say it was terrible. He's human, he's got his own selfishness too." What had begun as a lie told out of expedience was becoming, Duncan realized, a small act of revenge. There was a time he'd begged Gina's father to help soften Gina's anger against him, to move her to forgive his failings, but the man had only turned him away.

"Tell me what happened, Duncan," she asked, growing impatient.

"I really hate making you relive this, but all right. You'd gone down to Santa Fe to visit him and he was trying to persuade you to stay. To get out of New York for a while. You know how he's always pushing for more time with you, and he was eager to have you to himself, away from me."

"So there was an issue with *you*, then?" The suspicious look was back again.

"No, no. I mean, he's not my greatest fan, you know this, but your fight had nothing to do with me." Gina seemed so ready to blame him. He must not give her any grounds to do so. "While you were staying there I had a call from the artistic director at PS 122. He wanted you to produce a piece for their spring festival and I tried to get the message to you, but your father chose not to relay it. You'd have had to come back to New York, and he didn't want you leaving."

He watched her take this in, knowing how meaningful that invitation would be, and knowing how much conviction the story possessed because it was mostly true. PS 122 was the venue she'd first visited with Violet back in school; the performance she'd seen there had inspired her fantasy of moving to New York. To stage her own work there would be to fulfill one of her dreams.

"So what happened?" Her voice was tentative now, smaller, childlike.

"What happened was the spot was given to someone else." He nodded and exhaled, as if he were finally letting go of all his secrets. "You were so hurt and angry after. There was a fight about it, with your dad. You didn't tell me details, just that you'd realized he was interfering in your life in ways that were not healthy and that you needed to get distance from him. That was part of the motive behind this trip, to get away. We both knew the situation would be less painful if you were distracted, and your dad wouldn't be able to get ahold of you. Though naturally he would try. I can only assume that's why this Graham Bonafair person was calling. To persuade you to get back in touch with your father."

"This is crazy. Some stranger phoning because my father won't."

"That's how bad it got between you."

Gina spun about the room, moving restlessly, as she always did when something upended her understanding.

"You can call the theater to confirm this if you need to. The artistic director will remember."

Gina heard this and slowed down. It must have occurred to her that he wouldn't lie about a detail that could be so easily checked. Moreover, even if Gina hadn't objected to her father's efforts to control her, she'd begun to recognize them, over time.

"No," said Gina, speaking more calmly. "I believe you."

"Gina, I'm sorry." He *was* feeling sorry then, for so many things. "I'm sorry I didn't tell you sooner. I hated to lie, but with all you were facing, to make you doubt your connection to your father seemed too cruel." He meant this, he really did, and so the words came across with conviction—which was really the most awful part about it all. It *was* cruel to make Gina doubt her father in the midst of all the uncertainty she faced, and yet this was precisely what he was doing now.

For several minutes after hearing what he'd told her, Gina sat quietly at the edge of the bed, and he assumed her thoughts and mood had finally settled. But then, rather suddenly, she moved to the hotel dresser and began tossing their clothes into the suitcase.

"You're packing?" He tried not to sound nervous, though this action could mean different things: that she meant to leave Vienna or Europe altogether—or that she meant to leave *him*. Had she not believed him?

"Like I told the officers," she replied simply, "I'd like to get moving today."

"To Prague, then?"

"Unless you have some objection. Now that I do know the truth," she went on, "there's nothing to fear from my meeting Violet, is there?"

She turned then, with a strange smile on her lips, and in that instant he knew that his success in convincing her—if in fact he had convinced her—would be short-lived. Prague would be the end for him. If Gina managed to find Violet, their meeting would allow her to test every lie he'd told her until now. And Violet, who'd never liked him, would be only too happy to reveal his hoax. He'd barely survived Vienna—Astrid Du Bellay, the mugger, the police—still the police might come back for him, and yet he'd have preferred staying where they were to traveling to Prague. As it was, he was only trading in one set of dangers for another that was worse.

Seven

Gina // Prague

June 1996

They left for Prague from the Westbahnhof station. Tired from her sleepless night, Gina curled up in her seat and managed to doze for nearly all of the four-hour ride. Her exhaustion was so deep she wondered if more might be behind it—the shocks of the past day, Duncan's lies and the explanation that he'd given, her estrangement from her father. She would call her father, she'd decided, the first moment she found herself alone—so as not to clue Duncan in on her doubts about his story.

Now and again, while she dozed, when the tracks would squeak or someone would walk past her and stir her from her sleep, she would open her eyes and observe Duncan, staring out the window in the seat across from hers, handsome, caring Duncan, whom she'd loved and trusted more than anyone for years, and whom, it panicked her to think, she wasn't sure she should trust still.

They arrived at Hlavni Nadrazi station around one, and Gina suggested they head straight to the National Marionette

Theater, to see if anybody there could provide them with Violet's address.

"Before we go searching the city, we should at least drop off our bags."

Duncan's point was sensible enough, though this meant they'd need to locate a hotel and book a room. He took an especially long time calling around from the station before Gina finally insisted on a spot—a small guesthouse on Kaprova Street, just south of the Old Town and walking distance from the Marionette Theater.

They took a taxi the short drive from the train station, through charming streets that were more crooked and individual than Vienna's, the buildings smaller, uneven, brightly painted in different pastel shades. After they dropped their things, Duncan proposed a short detour to the river on the way to the theater, and since this would only delay them slightly, Gina agreed. They proceeded north, to the pathway on the right bank of the Vltava River. The walkway was planted with trees and there were benches where one could sit and look out over the iron fence to the left bank of the city, at the neat white buildings with orange roofs, green trees spread throughout.

After walking for some time, Duncan proposed they sit and enjoy the view. They were near the Charles Bridge, and in view of Prague Castle, which was situated across the river, on a hill. Duncan read aloud from the guidebook about the castle, but Gina wasn't listening. The briny smell of the river was making her feel ill and she was eager to get on to Violet's. She stood, impatient, and pressed Duncan to go on.

The National Marionette Theater was only a short distance, in the Old Town of Prague, just below the Jewish Quarter. The theater itself was housed in a rather modern building on Zatecka

Street—the only hint this was a theater was the large puppet perched above the wooden entrance. Inside, a cluster of young people were chatting and smoking in the corner, and an old man with a beard was seated at a desk, behind stacks of books. All around him puppets hung slack at the ends of their strings, staring at whatever visitor should step up to the desk. Gina asked the man if he might know how to find Violet Sharpe.

"Violetta, the American, you mean?"

The man called out to the group of young people in the corner, and one of them, a man in a black turtleneck, gestured for Gina and Duncan to follow. They stepped out onto the street and went around the corner to a café, a simple space crowded with tables and ugly vinyl booths. The air was choked with cigarette smoke and a smell of grease so strong Gina feared she might throw up. She was in a hurry to get out, but the young man proceeded slowly, stopping to chat with his many acquaintances. The patrons were mostly in their twenties, a mix of nationalities, but seemingly at the same stage in life—between being students and adults, caught in limbo, she imagined, in a city that was caught in limbo too, stuck in a reckless moment between the solid past and the soon-to-be-defined future.

The young man stopped in front of a table at the back of the café and spoke in Czech to the five people seated there. One of them, a young woman, stood and introduced herself as Buella.

She was very tall, with freckled, pale skin and eyes an almost burning yellow brown—stunning, in that lizard-like way of certain Eastern European beauties, a model of impenetrable perfection. Unthinkingly, Gina glanced at Duncan, who quickly looked away from the stranger. She'd never felt awkward in Duncan's presence with pretty women in the past, but the events of the last day had upset her faith. As she more clearly began to realize, she still had misgivings about Duncan and Marina Du Bellay. Violet, hopefully, could tell her what had transpired.

"We're here to visit Violet Sharpe," Gina informed the pretty stranger.

The girl nodded and paused to light a cigarette. "The car is outside. I can take you."

They drove together in the very old, small car while the girl smoked in the front with the window down, the wind blowing the smoke back in Duncan and Gina's faces. They were driving to the Zizkov district, Buella explained, as they entered an area populated with cheaper, simpler buildings covered in graffiti. Between some of the buildings were open lots where homeless people had put up shanties. In the distance stood a very tall and narrow tower, white with a red-and-white-striped tip. It looked so much like a spaceship that Gina asked Buella to tell her what it was.

"The TV tower," Buella answered. "Under communism, people called it the ugliest building in Prague. But now it's different. Now the city is made beautiful for tourists and we begin to love the ugly parts."

Naturally Violet, Gina thought, would be drawn to the ugly parts of Prague, where the disgruntled and dispossessed were bound to be, those who didn't simply embrace the West and its smug improvements. In the ugly parts, where there would be unrest, there would also be the impulse to make art. It was a brave thing her friend had done, she felt, leaving the comforts of New York, where Violet had always been accepted, to seek her own place in the unsettled and unknown. She found it beautiful and also vertiginous, and marveled to think that Violet had made this move, leaving behind a place where she'd belonged much more than Gina could imagine ever belonging anywhere. In that instant, Gina experienced a slight tremor herself—a sense of her own disorientation, her distance from her home, geographical and emotional—caused by her doubts about her father, and about Duncan too.

The car turned onto a block of six-story buildings in light greens, pinks, and yellows. Violet's was a fading shade of peach. Buella rang the buzzer, and after a long pause, the door opened. A girl answered and at first Gina took her for a stranger, but then the woman spoke to her familiarly in perfect English.

"Gina! I had no idea you were coming today!"

The voice she knew—rasping, high. "Bette, my God!" She hugged her old classmate, surprised that Bette was still with Violet and embarrassed that she hadn't recognized her. Bette's curly hair was shorter, a thick, dark mane around her face, and she was plumper than she'd been before.

"Duncan." Bette looked him over, clearly taken aback. "A lot of surprises today."

Duncan stood, rocking on his heels, hands in his pockets, smile tense. "Sorry to drop in suddenly midday. I'm assuming Violet must be out?"

"She's at our performance space, a few blocks south. But she usually comes back home for lunch around two or three, so your timing's perfect. I was just finishing cooking."

Buella returned to the car and the others proceeded up two flights of stairs and into the apartment, furnished with cheap, old-fashioned items: a worn sofa, a threadbare rug, pillows piled on the ground. Gina was sure that if she were to sink into one, it would release a plume of dust. She headed for a sliding door across the room, which opened up onto a balcony. She needed some fresh air.

"You can wait outside if you like." Bette pulled the door open wide and gestured to the four chairs gathered around a rain-wrecked table.

The balcony floor was made of tiles, many of which were chipped or loose. The guardrail was missing for about five feet at the end of the balcony closest to the street—though Gina assumed that even where the rail stood, it offered at best an illusion of security. Below the balcony was a patch of ground overrun with weeds, and a pile of rotten boards that must once have formed a walkway or a fence. When Gina turned to peer over the edge, she felt her heart beat faster.

"It's not much now," Bette said, gesturing to the open lot below. "But Violet has plans to make the whole building a residence for artists."

"She owns the entire building?" Gina asked, impressed.

"This and the theater space, yeah. Where Violet is now."

"Maybe we should call her and let her know we're here," Gina proposed.

Bette smiled wistfully. "Oh, now you're reminding me of home. We don't much do phone calls in Prague. I mean, hardly anyone that we know has a working line. It takes six months to get a phone installed, and that's assuming you're lucky. Nothing to do but wait, I'm afraid. But if you're hungry, we can at least start eating. I'm sure with some bread and rice we can stretch things out to four."

In fact Gina was ravenous, hungry in a gnawing way that seemed strange to her—as if she'd just run miles.

Bette entered the kitchen and returned again after a few

minutes carrying two platters of food, one piled with dumplings, the other with potato pancakes.

They'd only begun setting out the dishes when there was a noise in the next room and Violet came strolling in. Her hair was different—cut jaggedly and then dyed orange—but otherwise she was eternally the same: tall, bold-faced, and smiling. At the sight of Gina she tipped her head back and grinned, revealing her large, gapped teeth. She crossed the room in two grand strides and pulled Gina in for a powerful hug. "I don't believe it. No way. Gina Reinhold. The one and only."

When Violet finally released her, Gina saw her look over at Duncan—once and then again, clearly startled and far from pleased to see him there.

"I realize we came unexpectedly," he offered. "I hope we aren't putting you out."

"A visit from Gina could never put me out." Again Violet cast an assessing glance in Duncan's direction, while Gina sat, perplexed. Then, after an awkward pause, she pulled up a chair alongside Gina, and suggested to Bette that she bring out some cold drinks. "There's beer in the fridge," she said, and, turning to Gina, added: "People don't know that some of the world's best beers are from here."

When the drinks were brought and poured, Violet offered a toast. "To old friends and fresh horizons."

Bottles clinked around the table, and Violet's words seemed to echo in Gina's head. It was uncanny, really, meeting familiar people in an unfamiliar place. She'd been feeling so unsteadied by her accident, by the past that she had lost, that everyone and everything seemed to be floating, unmoored, like objects in a dreamscape.

Violet was watching her; she seemed to be guessing at her thoughts. "It's a strange meeting, isn't it, all of us here? I can't seem to make sense of it myself."

"Well, I think it's remarkable, really, what you've done. Starting from scratch somewhere with no connections. It takes enormous courage."

Violet closed her eyes, a gesture between modesty and the savoring of a prize morsel. "Either courage or just stupidity."

Across the table, Duncan gave a nod.

Violet noticed this and turned to look at him, eyes narrowed. "And what brings you here, Duncan? I can't say I expected our meeting again."

There was a beat, a tense silence, before Duncan replied. "A lot has happened since you and Gina were last in touch, I think. And, well, I should tell you. She had an accident not long ago. She's still recovering, so we're trying to take it easy."

"What sort of accident?" Violet turned to Gina now, abruptly.

"I had a bad fall in Berlin. There was some swelling in my brain."

"Oh no," exclaimed Bette. "Are you okay?"

"Fine. Some memory issues still, but fine." She didn't mention the dizziness she was feeling then. She'd had only a few sips of beer, but drinking in the heat of the afternoon and on an empty stomach had not been a good idea.

"She's doing well," Duncan confirmed. "We're just easing back into things, you know. It seemed like a good idea for her to be surrounded by old friends."

"Just how much have you forgotten?" Violet asked Gina, ignoring Duncan and leaning in, thick brows furrowed.

"Hard to say. It's getting better, though."

"Thankfully," Duncan added. "But I'm sure Gina doesn't want to just talk about her injury. Bette says you're opening a theater."

"Well, yes." Violet couldn't help but show excitement at the chance to talk about her project. "It wasn't something I'd planned to do, but the arts here are in jeopardy. The cost of property is skyrocketing, foreign investment is flooding in, so other forces need to assert themselves also. The city is so charming, people will to try to claim it, and you want it to be the people who genuinely get it and not, you know, *the guys who just want to take advantage.*"

There was a tone of challenge in Violet's statement, Gina observed, though she couldn't say quite what it was about, whether what was at play between Duncan and her friend was any more than the old antipathy.

Violet had been at odds with Duncan from the very beginning. Gina supposed that they were very different people, really. Violet had grown up with parents in the arts and had always operated as an insider and connector of people. Duncan, meanwhile, was by nature an outsider. That hadn't mattered much in college, but in New York people relied on contacts from music schools, which Duncan didn't have, nor was he capable of cozying up to those who could help him—like Violet, or even, though he'd finally, shamefully accepted her commission, Marina Du Bellay. There was just some stubborn part of him that refused to compromise or ingratiate himself, which Violet took as arrogance. More than once she'd let Gina know her view: that Duncan was rigid, dour, and selfish, and sure to hold her back.

In any case, if Duncan picked up on Violet's hostility today, he didn't let it show. Smiling, he congratulated her on her projects.

"It all sounds very impressive, what you're doing here. I'd love to see the theater."

"Yes," Gina chimed in, "I'd love to see it too."

"Actually, you can see the building from here." Excited by their interest, despite whatever other reservations she had, Violet rose from her chair and went to stand at the balcony's edge, a hand perched on the precarious rail. "It's in the direction of the TV tower, there on the right. With the yellow roof."

Gina came to join her, peering out over the city at the bright rooftops and spires, and the odd futuristic tower they'd seen as they drove in. A tile wobbled underfoot, and she made the mistake of looking down over the railing at the ground below. Suddenly her vision swirled and was flooded with light, and she had the sense that she might faint. She stepped back quickly and grabbed onto a chair for support.

"Are you all right?" Duncan asked her, on his feet now, holding her arm.

"Tired, I guess. Maybe the beer."

"Did you drink the water here?" Bette put in. "I was sick as a dog my first week."

"You look pale," Violet observed, coming closer to her. She took hold of Gina's hand. "Come inside for a minute. I've got a thermometer somewhere." Duncan began to follow, but Violet told him to stay put. "You all finish eating. I've got her."

"I'll be fine," Gina said, though she had a momentary fear that she might not be fine, that these symptoms might be connected to the light-headedness and nausea she'd felt after the accident. She hadn't had such symptoms in almost two weeks, and her memories were beginning to feel less foggy, but still the fear gripped her. The issue could be neurological; this was a residue of childhood, her dread, back to a time when every headache and dizzy spell made her jump to the word *stroke*.

Violet entered the bathroom first, where she rummaged through an old cabinet with a cracked mirror. After a minute, Violet was cursing. "I swear we had one."

"Never mind. I don't think I have a fever."

"Something's wrong with you," said Violet, "I can see it."

Yes, Gina knew this to be true, even if she couldn't say what it was. The sensations were familiar, eerily so.

"I think I should just lie down for a few minutes," she told Violet, who led her into her bedroom, which was stuffy like the rest of the apartment, with musty, heavy furniture, lace curtains, a floral rug. Candles stood on the bedside table, alongside an odd little sculpture of an enormous woman, which Gina stared at while she breathed in deeply. She was trying to focus on the room, on where she was, but images began crowding her thoughts: She was in a room that seemed to spin around her. There were mirrors on the velvet walls, and hanging lamps. People were laughing, hardly noticing when she stood from the table and walked out. One man followed her, the Frenchman she'd met in Vienna. He'd asked if she was feeling well: *You look like you might faint.*

She felt the same way now, thoughts coming to her as in a fever. She jerked upright at the impression that the sheets around her must be bloody. She searched the floral pattern, but there was, of course, no blood.

"What's going on?" Violet was sitting on the bed beside her, watching her, concerned.

"I . . . I don't know. Probably it's the water, like Bette said."

"It's not just that," Violet said, lowering her voice. "I mean all of it, your showing up like this, with *Duncan*. Is it the accident? Just how much have you forgotten?"

"I don't know."

"Our talks last fall? The time you called me crying?"

"About my father?"

"No, not your father. You really don't remember?"

"How's my girl doing?" Duncan's voice startled her. Gina hadn't seen him enter the room.

Violet turned to face him, impatient, even hostile. "We're managing fine, thanks."

Duncan ignored this and came to sit ahead of Violet on the bed. He put his hand to Gina's forehead. "Maybe I should get you back to the hotel."

"We're not done talking," said Violet.

"That can wait, can't it? Probably it should wait, if Gina's not well." Duncan peered down at her, studying her as she studied him too, the thinly veiled anxiety behind his show of care. "I think maybe she needs a doctor," Duncan concluded.

"If she needs a doctor, I'll call a doctor," Violet countered.

"I think I'll be all right," Gina spoke at last, addressing Duncan now. "I'm fine, just need to rest a bit. I'll join you out there soon."

Violet heaved a sigh as Duncan stepped out of the room without shutting the door behind him. He walked away, and through the opening Gina could see him moving hesitantly toward the balcony.

"You said I'd called you crying," she resumed in a whisper, trying again to concentrate on Violet. Violet began to answer, but Gina hardly heard her, for in that instant, a very strange thing occurred. At first, she imagined it was another illusion, a product of her illness. Duncan was there, across the room, on the balcony, and then he wasn't.

She'd never been so frightened in all her life. The only event she could compare it to was that awful day, when she was nine, when she'd found her mother fallen in the shower. A terrifying moment, but then she'd only heard the crash and come in after, whereas this time she'd turned to look at Duncan and caught sight of him at the precise instant he'd leaned back on that perilous balcony in a spot where there was no guardrail to hold him.

She'd seen his body tip backward into the air, and, disbelieving, she'd seen it sink out of her sight, soundlessly, arms out as if wishing to be caught in a saving embrace.

Eight

Duncan // Prague

June 1996

His body hit the ground with such a powerful jolt it felt like the breath was sucked out of his lungs. He felt nothing but a buzzing numbness; he heard nothing but ringing in his ears. When he slowly opened his eyes he saw blue sky above, and then Gina's panicked face above his own. She was speaking to him, asking him if he was okay. Her voice came out muffled. His was a gasp.

"Gina."

"You can see me? Hear me?"

"Yes."

Her hand was trembling as she reached for his. "Are you in pain?"

"I don't know. What happened?"

"Ask him if he can move," said Violet, standing out of view, some feet away.

"No, don't!" Gina ordered him, pinning down his arms. More calmly, she explained: "I think the rule is to lie still until the paramedics come."

"Is that right?" Bette's voice now, Duncan realized, coming from somewhere near. He was afraid to turn his neck to see.

"Somebody needs to call an ambulance!" Gina shouted, looking up to where the other girls must be standing. "Please call whatever 911 is here, tell them what's happened!"

Duncan was dimly aware then of a discussion taking place around him. The ringing in his ears was growing dimmer, and he could make out phrases, even those spoken in a hushed voice, at some distance. "The hospitals in this city . . . who can say when or even if . . . but we know someone . . . a real doctor, absolutely. . . ."

"All right, then, get him," said Gina, and came again to crouch by Duncan and take his hand in hers. He was squeezing her palm, holding on for dear life. He felt her grip against his, squeezing back. *He had her.* And so, he told himself, even if bones were broken, even if the damage was worse, what he'd done was worth it.

"Duncan, eh?" A stranger was kneeling above him now, with his thinning black hair pulled into a ponytail.

"Duncan, yeah," he croaked.

"My name's Terry," said the man, in a thick Australian accent. "I'm the next-door neighbor but I'm also a doctor, right? And I'm gonna give you a little look-see, eh?"

The man leaned down next to him and peered into his eyes. He then wagged his fingers back and forth in front of Duncan's face, and asked permission to check under his shirt. "This hurt you, mate? When I press here?"

Duncan writhed away. The pain was searing.

Terry slapped his knees and stood, addressing Gina. "Your friend's bloody lucky he landed somewhere soft." Turning back to Duncan, he explained. "You've got some bad bruising in one spot on the side there. Possibly a fractured rib, but there's really not much to do about that except stop falling off of buildings."

"Thanks," said Duncan weakly.

"Pick up a thermometer," the man resumed, facing Gina, "and if his temp goes above thirty-nine, or if you notice some red or yellow in his eyes, you get him to a hospital. Other than that, get your hands on some good painkillers and he should be all right. So, anyone got a ciggy?"

The Australian went to get a smoke from Bette, and Gina came to tell Duncan that Buella would pick them up by car. When Buella arrived, Duncan tried sitting up. A shooting pain in his chest made him cringe, but other than that, he seemed to be all right. He rubbed the back of his head to be sure there was no blood.

Soon Gina and the Australian were helping Duncan into the back seat. Gina sat beside him, telling Buella to take them to a hospital.

"No hospital," Duncan insisted. If he were admitted, he'd be stuck there, a sitting duck, while Violet would be free to tell Gina everything, to uncover his ruse and call Graham or Gina's father, or else notify the police to come pick him up. "You heard Violet's opinion of the local hospitals. And that doctor says I should be fine."

Gina eyed him, concerned. "You could have a concussion, internal injuries."

"If anything goes wrong, we'll go then." He didn't wait for Gina to agree, but sat achingly forward to give Buella the address of their hotel.

As Buella started the engine, Violet and Bette stood looking on, Violet frowning, obviously frustrated by all that she still wished to say. Meanwhile, the Australian doctor leaned down to Duncan's open window to offer some final advice.

"Don't forget to stop at the pharmacy first, pick up the strongest painkillers they have." He reached in to clap Duncan on the shoulder. "And don't be stinting, mate, because that's gonna bloody hurt heaps later on, eh?"

When Duncan awoke his mouth was dry, the sheets were wet, and his entire body ached so much he was terrified to move. He'd fallen asleep before nightfall, as soon as he and Gina got back from the pharmacy to their room, when the pills he'd taken had kicked in. He'd taken three times the recommended dose, and that was of the strongest formula he could buy without prescription. Still, by now the medicine must have worn off. Gasping as he did, he turned in bed to see Gina beside him, sleeping. The pills, he recalled, were in the bathroom. Digging his teeth into his bottom lip, he swung his legs down to the floor and sat up in bed. After catching his breath, he readied himself for the next jolt of pain, got to his feet, and tottered to the bathroom to collapse against the sink.

He studied himself in the bathroom mirror. There was a bruise along his left side, turned a deep purple. He was grimacing and he imagined that his jaw might be locking. Could it be tetanus? Had he ever had a tetanus shot? What if there had been rusted nails among the dirt and rubble where he'd fallen? Was tetanus fatal? Was he putting his life at risk by failing to care for himself properly? He swallowed two more pills with bottled water and stripped off his sweaty clothes—stiffly, painfully—dropping them on the floor. He felt like an old rusted nail himself. Wrapped in a towel, he sat down on the toilet seat to wait for the pills to take effect.

His thoughts were racing, circling over the madness of the last days, the sheer insanity of this thing that he'd done—throwing himself off of a building. It *was* an act of insanity, and yet he'd been so rational in his thinking just before. He'd seen no other way to stop Violet in that moment, other than throwing Violet herself over the balcony. She was going to tell Gina everything and his blissful time with her would be over. What, then, was there to hold onto, what more really was there to lose? He'd looked down at the ground below, the weeds and threadbare shrubs. Then he'd come to stand in the place without any railing, closed his eyes, and leaned back, as if to brace himself against the rail he knew would not be there. He'd felt his body pitch backward, a sickening thrust in his stomach as he fell, his foot scraping the balcony's edge. Falling, he'd told himself not to be stiff, to let gravity deposit him however it might—if he were lucky, at the feet of the woman whose love he would risk his life to keep.

The pain had subsided a little but he couldn't stop shaking; his mouth was so parched he felt like he'd swallowed sand. He ought to get himself some water—he'd gone through the only bottle he and Gina had picked up, so he'd check the lobby. He slipped out of the hotel room, dressed in a robe, unable to stop shivering as he staggered to the stairwell, taking a full ten minutes to make it down three flights of stairs.

As he neared the lobby landing at the bottom of the steps, he heard a voice, a young man's voice, distressed, speaking English.

"Let me call up, please."

"I'm sorry, sir," said another voice, softer, official. "The phones don't work in all the rooms. And anyway, we can't allow our guests to be disturbed in the night. Not unless it's an emergency."

"It *is* an emergency. You're harboring a criminal, you understand? If I have to I'll come back with someone from the embassy."

He knew this voice. He'd imagined words like these, a scene like this—so much so that he had to wonder if it might be a feverish hallucination. He had to have a look, as risky as it was to step into view where he might also be seen. He tiptoed silently and peered around a pillar and into the main lobby. There the man was, looking much the same as he had when Duncan had met him: linen shirt, shaggy blond hair, but with a newly strained and weary expression on his handsome face. Graham Bonafair had found them.

Duncan returned to his room in a panic—how stupid he'd been to give Buella the address of their hotel! He ought to have considered the danger, the likelihood that Graham had reached out to Violet, or that she, grown suspicious, would reach out herself. He'd led Graham right to their door. Now he must think of a way out. Perhaps he ought to wake Gina, make an issue of his injuries and insist on going to a hospital. Though the risk was that Graham would intercept them, and even if not, he'd probably come looking for them at hospitals next. There had to be a solution, but Duncan couldn't come up with one. As he took a seat on the bed, his mind felt thick from medication and from sheer exhaustion. His body seemed weighted, sucked against the mattress. At some point he gave in and lay down, intending to rest only briefly, clear his head—instead, he fell into a sleep deep.

He awoke to morning light; the sun was coming in hotly around the shades. The sheets around him were dry; his fever must have passed. He stretched and felt some aches, and sharper pains in his chest. When he turned over, slowly, he realized that

Gina wasn't in her place in bed beside him. He stood up with a throbbing jolt. What if, in the few hours when he'd foolishly allowed himself to sleep, Graham had found his way to Gina?

"Gina!" he called to her, and then, when there was no answer, he hobbled to the bathroom: she wasn't inside. When he returned to the bed, he saw, on his bedside table, a small note written on hotel stationery.

Didn't want to wake you so I've gone out walking. Back soon.
You rest.

He took a deep breath. Maybe she'd simply gone out for a stroll. Still, it seemed odd, her leaving him alone in his condition, and dangerous besides, her out and about when Graham was looking for her. What if he'd waited for her in the lobby all evening? In his agitation, Duncan crumpled up the note, and some of the ink came off on his hand. The ink was wet, which meant Gina had just left. He might still catch her. Grabbing the room key and pushing his feet into his shoes, he hurried, wincing, to the lobby. There was an unfamiliar woman at the front desk. Duncan asked her whether she'd seen his wife, a young auburn-haired woman, leave that morning.

"My shift only just started. But I think there was a woman leaving as I came."

"And was she with a man, by chance? About my age? Tall, light-haired?"

"I don't believe so," said the woman, to Duncan's great relief. "Were you expecting a visitor?"

"Yes, I think he may have come by, possibly he left a message. Room nineteen."

"There is something, yes." The woman produced an envelope from the row of cubbyholes behind the desk. The envelope was unsealed: Duncan pulled the paper from it, expecting to see Graham's name at the bottom. But the signature was Violet's.

Dear Gina,

I need to speak with you in private, as soon as possible. I wish I'd been able to say more when I saw you, but I've only realized what's happened since I've spoken to your father. He explained everything to me, and I need to explain it to you too.

If you can get away alone and meet me at one by the hotel entrance, I'll be waiting. You'll need to find a way to meet me without Duncan around. You'll understand why when I see you.

Violet

The situation was even worse than he'd thought. Now Graham and Violet, and possibly the police as well, were trying to reach Gina. He must get to Gina first, must use what he knew of her to anticipate her movements. She might have returned to the banks of the Vltava River, maybe even continued over the Charles Bridge, but she'd been that way already, and what she hadn't seen was the Old Town, Staré Mesto, which was just five minutes north of their hotel. He returned to the room to load up on painkillers before setting off again, along Zatecka Street. Each step pained him, but he hurried as much as he was able, soon stumbling into what had to be the Jewish Quarter, since he counted five synagogues on his walk through the cramped streets. The most prominent building among these was the Old

New Synagogue: an awkward construction with yellowed plaster walls and an oddly proportioned triangular brick roof, the whole effect like a child's imitation of an elegant church.

The strange building attracted him, and he stepped in, briefly diverted. There were several older people at the front of the chapel, heads bent, under shawls, praying. In all his life he'd never prayed, not even in those moments of silence in the temple as a child, not even on the holiest of days, Yom Kippur, when he joined the congregation in the ritual of beating their breasts as he counted off the many sins that he, at the tender age of eight or ten, should admit to committing. As a boy, it had troubled him that he couldn't summon any of the emotions he knew to be proper, not contrition, not humility, not faith in a greater being in whom his action would inspire pity. He'd come to feel wretched for his failure to feel guilty, as a result of which his mother took him to be guilty in the right ways and would comfort him and hug him. He'd accepted her embraces, so in a sense he'd lied even in this moment of confession, and had been convinced by this of his depravity.

Something must be wrong with him, he'd thought, and now had the thought that he'd been right. This thing he'd done to Gina, this way that he'd misled her and terrified the people who cared for her—it was more than a crime. It was a sin. He wished to feel remorse, to feel that if Gina were discovered by Graham or Violet ahead of him, so be it. Why else was he drawn to this temple, if not so that he might confront his error and accept the punishment of losing Gina forever? He ought to feel this and to pray for forgiveness, but if he were to pray, he knew, he would only ask that she be brought back to him.

Without quite believing he was doing such a thing, he brought his hands together and lowered his head to the fingertips. It felt good to him to have his head bowed, to accept his weakness in the face of what forces were upon him, to admit that he loved Gina, would always love Gina, and would endure whatever mad adventure and whatever loss or pain loving her might bring upon him. His love was stronger than his will—he couldn't, no matter how he might wish to, stop adoring Gina for her courage and her beauty and her vivid pure desires. He couldn't find a way to think of life without her as any sort of life at all. He might seem to have Gina as his victim, held by the illusion he'd created, but he knew that, finally, she was the one who had and always would have control over him. He yielded to her power, to becoming a subject of her love. This was his form of devotion.

He offered these thoughts up to whatever forces might be listening, and then he opened his eyes again and turned to pass among the worshippers and back outside, into the light.

The time was approaching half past noon when Duncan found his way from the Old Town and began his slow and dreadful walk back toward the hotel. His back was so stiff it was like glue had seeped in under his skin, and shooting pains assaulted him at every step.

He reached the entrance to the hotel at ten to one, ten minutes before Violet had vowed to meet Gina, though, assuming Gina hadn't read the letter, she had no notion of this, and might be wandering still, or might already have returned to the room. He went into the lobby to check with the woman behind the desk, but she insisted his wife hadn't returned. Through the window, as he stood there, he noticed Violet waiting across the street— a foot taller than most, her hair as orange as a traffic cone, she was thankfully easy to spot. As he looked on, she checked her watch and started off toward the hotel. His heart thudded. If he stayed in the lobby, Violet would see him. If he stepped out, Violet would see him. If he went up to his room, Violet might come up after him.

He hesitated, then turned to the clerk: "If a young woman comes asking for Gina, please send her upstairs to our room."

Taking the room key, he headed for the stairwell. At the second floor he exited and waited the amount of time it would take, in his imagination, for Violet to ask for assistance, then climb the three flights to their floor. He waited until he believed she'd reached the top, then reentered the stairwell and started down. A minute off and he'd have met her on the stairs, but he had not. He hurried out onto the street and, almost exactly as he did, he noticed Gina walking toward their hotel. So she had read Violet's letter, Duncan assumed, until, to his surprise, he saw her stop several doors over from the hotel and enter a storefront. He hurried after her. The business she'd wandered into was a travel agency.

"Duncan!" She spotted him across the room and came over, concerned. "I thought you'd be resting. Are you strong enough to be out like this?"

"I'm better, much better." He stepped up to her and kissed her and she kissed him back, as if all were well, though on closer inspection, he wasn't sure. Her cheeks were blotchy and her eyes were red and overbright.

"Have you been crying?"

She turned away and shook her head, making him wonder if the worst had happened—she'd read Violet's letter or come across her and discovered the truth. But then she drew up against him, pulling his arm around her.

"I'm sorry I went off like that. I didn't want you to see me so upset but I had to let it out, all the emotion from yesterday. It was terrifying. I thought you were dead."

She buried her face into his neck and he held her, until he became aware of people watching, the employees of the agency. Three of them sat around waiting, decked out in yellow uniforms.

"Can I help you with something, then?" asked one employee.

"Yes, thank you." Gina seemed to recall herself and let go of Duncan, heading over to the desk. Duncan followed behind her, uncertain what had brought her to this place.

"I was just walking by and saw the advertisement for the Palio up in the window. Do you by chance sell tickets?"

"The Palio?" Duncan turned to Gina as the woman behind the desk searched her computer.

"It's a medieval horse race in Siena," Gina explained. "I overheard a couple talking about it this morning and it's one of those things people come from all over the world to see. The race is tomorrow and I thought if we left Prague today, we might make it. Assuming, obviously, the idea appeals to you and you feel well enough to do it."

He studied her, searching her eager face. Yes, of course it appealed to him. There was nothing he wanted more than to get the hell out of Prague, and as fast as possible. The plan was perfect. So perfect, he couldn't quite believe it.

"But I assumed you'd want more time in Prague?"

"Maybe afterward we can return, visit Violet again. But yesterday was too much. I feel I need to get out of here, find some distraction."

"Absolutely. Yes." He felt so immensely grateful he could hardly contain his glee. Thanks to Gina's whims, he wouldn't need to come up with some new story to justify a sudden move.

Until this moment, when escaping together was actually beginning to seem possible, he hadn't let himself admit how dire things had become. With Graham and Violet looking for them, there was really nowhere in this small city where he could plausibly keep himself and Gina hidden.

The woman behind the desk returned, having spoken with the tourist bureau in Siena. "I can book you passage, but the tickets for the race are only sold inside the city. Hotels too are all booked—officially. Though I'm told unofficially is something different."

"Very good," said Duncan. A city in chaos where all the arrangements were done on the sly—this seemed precisely the sort of place where he and Gina might escape discovery. "And if we were to head to Siena now, what would be the fastest way?"

The woman consulted her computer and announced there was a train to Vienna, then Rome through Chiusi to Siena, leaving in a little more than an hour.

"We haven't packed." Duncan turned to Gina. "We'd need to rush."

Gina appeared undaunted. "I'll order a car while you throw our things into the suitcases and bring them down."

"Yes, good!" How he adored her then, for her adventurous spirit and determination, for all those qualities in her that led to her unwitting cooperation. He kissed her hard on the mouth before heading out the door, where he spotted Violet at the café across the street, smoking a cigarette. He ducked back inside, considering how he might arrange the next few moves. His great fear was that Gina would come outside to the car and be spotted by Violet.

Heading back to the desk, he suggested Gina call a cab from

there, since probably the agent could arrange a better price than they'd get on their own. Then, while she was distracted with the call, he asked another agent for a piece of paper and a pen. He scribbled a note, then headed back outside in search of a messenger. He spotted an older man with a dog, holding up a sign offering tours of the old city.

"Do you speak English?" Duncan asked him.

"Few words."

"You see the girl over there, with the orange hair?"

"Yes, I see her."

"Could you give her this?"

He handed the note and some bills to the man, who showed more interest in the money than the message. Even if he were to read the note, Duncan didn't think he'd detect anything wrong: *Don't want to run into Duncan. Can you meet me three blocks north of the hotel? On the northeast corner. I'll be there. Gina.*

The next ten minutes proceeded like clockwork. From a distance, Duncan watched Violet turn and walk in the direction his note instructed her to go; then he got the key from the hotel front desk, bounded up to his room, and tossed his and Gina's things into a suitcase. All the while, below, the desk clerk prepared their bill. Duncan paid quickly, and by the time he emerged onto the street again, really too weak and stiff to carry a single bag, let alone two, he was so high on adrenaline that he felt briefly invincible. The car was waiting, an unobtrusive tan sedan. Gina saw him and got in as the bags were shoved into the trunk. He climbed in beside her, onto the cool leather seat. The car was new, with a smell that made him think happily of motion.

"To the Palio!" Gina exclaimed. "The race begins. And they're off!"

As the car pulled out, Duncan turned to gaze at her, her pretty face giddy and grinning, recalling earlier days, when they were first launching their young lives. So much had since gone wrong, so much to dim that wild, eager smile, yet here it was before him, fresh, as if no time had passed.

Nine

Gina // New York

1993–94

These were the unforgettable days. Gina felt that way even eighteen months after graduation, waking up each morning in the bed she shared with Duncan five feet in the air. Their studio walk-up contained a bunk bed, to provide some living space below, and she supposed a part of her attraction to the place was the reminder it offered of the dorm rooms of their first years together. Duncan might have preferred a more mature arrangement, but she enjoyed the playfulness of their studio, as if she and Duncan were children engaged in a game of house, acting the part of adults, finding amusement where true adults encountered obligation and routine.

Sitting up in bed, with only a foot between her and the ceiling, she could see Duncan in the kitchenette, drinking coffee while packing songbooks and composition paper into his bag.

"You're leaving already?" The clock on the wall beside her read only half past seven.

"Did I wake you? You sleep more." Duncan came over to kiss

her. When he stood at his full height, his head rose just above the barriers at the mattress edge.

She ran her fingers through the hair at the nape of his neck. "Or you could come back to bed."

"Don't tempt me," he said, smiling around their kiss. "I really should go. I think I might have an idea for something."

"Do you?" She hoped she hadn't sounded too surprised, but it had been a while since Duncan had spoken of any new musical ideas. These days, he was too tired for inspiration—or that was the excuse he offered—and given that he was working multiple jobs, she could hardly blame him.

"Go, then. Go. That's great."

He grinned at her, clearly roused by her encouragement. He grabbed his bag and paused again, to kiss her a last time on his way out. "See you in a bit."

She watched him leave, the door shutting as the neighbor's dog, on cue, began barking behind him. When they'd signed the lease on their apartment, which they'd thought an improvement on their rat-infested first one, they hadn't known about the dog. The neighbor must have been out with him—possibly the landlord had seen to it she was—so it was only after they'd moved in that they'd realized there would be constant barking through the day.

"You can't work like this," Gina had announced early on, though Duncan wouldn't admit this right away.

"Maybe I'll go deaf like Beethoven."

"Let's see if we can find a happier solution."

The solution they'd finally arrived at, after earplugs and a noise machine, was that Duncan would work at Blake's apartment over in NoHo, which was free during the day while Blake worked up on Madison Avenue. She supposed it disappointed her a little that Duncan wasn't inspired to creativity by the home they shared; she knew he'd agreed to the apartment because she loved it, and she was grateful to him for wanting to give her the sort of life she'd wished to have. And giving her the life she'd wished for, he insisted, brought him joy.

Hers was precisely the sort of New York neighborhood she'd imagined living in for years—downstairs from her apartment was a Laundromat that always smelled of marijuana and had posters in the windows for guitar lessons and missing cats. Next to that, on the corner, stood a diner that exuded the scent of bacon all day long. Across the way, an older couple sat up on their balcony, a small, bearded Jewish man and a Jamaican woman with a miraculous Afro, the pair peeking down and catching Gina's eye as she went by on her way to work, past the tattoo parlors, secondhand clothing stores, and book and record shops. The first internet cafés were springing up, with used furniture spilling out onto the street, occupied by young patrons and older bohemians too. Everyone looked like some sort of artist, and everywhere Gina went there were postcards advertising some new gallery or cabaret.

So much was happening around her. Experimental theaters were multiplying and there were several dance companies doing just the sort of work Gina wished to do. She'd been exceptionally lucky to have been granted introductions, through Violet, to artistic directors and choreographers at Danspace and Dance Theater Workshop and Trisha Brown. In her first round of auditions, she'd landed small parts in two companies, and by the end of her first year, she'd become a regular in a dance company that worked out of a progressive church on East Tenth Street.

She'd been thrilled with her place there: the church felt like a refuge from the bustle of the city, a quiet corner surrounded by trees and filled with young artists, some involved in dance, some with the poetry project or experimental theater troupe that also were hosted by the church. She'd performed inside the chapel, in a grand white space with high arched ceilings and balconies and stained-glass windows.

What better place was there to dance than inside a house of worship? Dance was her religion, after all. She aspired to live all her life as a dance, gracefully, in the moment, without fear of the future or ghosts of memory.

Daily rehearsals were held at a separate location, an old factory floor a few blocks east of the church. Gina arrived at nine, changed inside the dressing rooms, and then joined the other dancers to warm up. There were twelve others in her troupe, most around her age, though they seemed to her younger than she was, overwhelmed by the big city, happily and sometimes unhappily adrift, whereas she had Duncan to provide her a sense of stability.

The four-hour rehearsal went by quickly as they always did, though for the last hour she began to watch the clock. At one, when their class broke for lunch, she'd be able to see Duncan, who worked most afternoons in a studio upstairs. He'd been hired about a month before, through her, to play piano for one of the choreographers who preferred rehearsing with live music. The pay was less than he'd gotten at the temping jobs he'd had before, but the job gave him time to practice on the piano—and then the chance for them to see each other in the middle of the day.

As soon as the dancers were dismissed for lunch, Gina darted upstairs and spotted Duncan, his back to her, already at the piano. She crept up behind him to kiss his neck.

"Ladies, please, I'm taken."

"Hilarious."

"Oh shit, Gina, it's you."

Turning around, he laughed and reached to pull her onto the bench beside him. She'd have liked to kiss him again, but the dancers were entering and the instructor too, and they weren't college kids anymore. She supposed one of the pleasures in Duncan's working with her was the chance to feel again like students, meeting for a moment between classes. She liked being reminded of those simpler days—before they had rent to pay, or thousands of the country's most creative youngsters to compete with, when they were still a charmed couple bound to do great things.

Standing to go, she caught sight of Duncan's lunch up on the piano—a cheese sandwich and a banana. He didn't even have the money for the deli salad bar she was on her way to next.

"You want me to pick up something for you from the store?"

"No, I'm fine. You should probably have dinner without me too. I've got five lessons after this. Doubt I'll be home before nine."

She felt a wave of sadness on leaving, thinking of Duncan setting off from here and crossing the city back and forth, giving private lessons house to house. Sometimes when he got home he'd be so tired he could barely hold a conversation. But this, she told herself, was the reality of living in New York and working in the arts, an experience they were both glad to be sharing—though sometimes she wondered just how glad Duncan really was.

She'd have liked to make his life a little easier, to further his success, and it was partly for this reason that she planned to visit Violet that night.

From rehearsal, which ended at five, Gina took the train to

Tribeca and walked to West Street, where Violet lived in a giant open loft with six roommates, all of them male—a set designer, a DJ, a cinematographer, a painter, and two sculptors.

Outside the building, a metal ramp led to the entrance, and a freight elevator took Gina up to the tenth floor, where she stepped into the front area, reserved for the original tenant, Hector. Hector stood six foot five with a curly black beard that peeked out beneath the face shield he wore to work. When Gina entered, he was shooting flames at a hunk of metal—that was how she often found him. Violet was in her room, walled off by a Japanese screen, sitting cross-legged on the floor, chatting away over the noise with another roommate, Donovan, the cinematographer, a slender boy with a snub nose and full lips.

"The snake was harmless, I'm completely sure," Violet was telling Donovan. "At least my fathers' lawyer says that I'm completely sure. . . ." Violet left off as she spotted Gina at the entrance. "There she is, my favorite diva."

"I thought *I* was," Donovan teased, and stood from Violet's mattress. Gina gestured for him to stay, but Donovan brushed past her. "Oh, enough babbling. I've my opus waiting for me."

Donovan passed behind the screen, and Gina could hear him a ways off, getting caught up in banter with someone else. "What is that hideous smell?"

"Your opus?"

"No, seriously."

"Lucas is making vegan chili."

It was always like this at Violet's place—endless chatter, music playing, hammers pounding in the background. For the life of her, Gina couldn't fathom how Violet managed to get anything done in such conditions, how she could work or think or sleep, but she found it an admirable feature of Violet's, her enjoyment of creative bustle, the way she was enlivened by her friends.

Violet grinned to see her. "I'll get us drinks. You want some chili?"

"Thanks, I ate before."

Violet left to get the drinks and Gina pulled up the step stool that was the only thing to sit on in Violet's room besides the mattress.

"So what's the latest with the snake fiasco?" she asked Violet, who returned with the drinks, taking her seat again on the floor. Gina preferred not to launch straightaway into the subject that had led her here so for a while she was brought up to speed on the incident that had closed Violet's last show, a modern retelling of Adam and Eve, during which the live snake she'd employed had escaped into an upstairs apartment. The woman in the apartment had suffered a panic attack—or so she claimed—and afterward, the family lawyer had encouraged Violet to lie low for a bit, so she'd taken advantage of an invitation to participate in a theater conference in Prague. While there, Violet had met a group of young Serbs and Croats fleeing the Bosnian War. When she returned to New York, she carried audiotapes of their testimonies, which she meant to have played alongside a dance piece. She wanted Gina to choreograph and to perform.

"Good news on the Bosnian refugees," Violet launched in, changing the subject. "I submitted the proposal, and, get this, the Kitchen wants it as part of their Fall Festival program."

"That's fantastic!" Gina slapped the floor, joining in with Violet's excitement, hoping that this good feeling would incline her friend to generosity. "I've been thinking about the show too, working up ideas, but I have to say I'm at my best when Duncan and I collaborate together."

For a moment, the whole space grew implausibly quiet. Gina was relieved when the hammering resumed and Violet spoke up again.

"Trouble is," Violet replied at last, "I already talked with another composer."

"Whoever it is, I can promise you they won't do a better job than Duncan."

She didn't know how to ask any more directly, and yet, as helpful as Violet was to her, on this point, Gina wasn't sure her friend would yield. Violet wouldn't be eager to work with Duncan, whom she took to be inflexible. Even Gina had to admit that collaboration sometimes proved difficult for him, though he was perfectly capable of it with her. If only he had the chance to work with her again, that might give him the boost he needed.

"Look, all I'm asking is that you let him try. If you don't like what he comes up with, you go with your other person. And I'll defer happily to you."

Violet looked at her and cocked her head. "It's funny, really. Of all the people I know, crazy, loud, pushy people, I don't think any of them is harder to say no to than you."

"Thank you!" Gina almost shouted, and before Violet could possibly insist that she hadn't yet said yes, Gina rose from the step stool and tackled her friend into a hug.

Later that night, at home, Gina presented the opportunity to Duncan. They were on the battered sofa they kept under their bed, and Duncan, drained from the day, was idly flipping through TV stations.

"I don't know if you'd be interested," she began, "but Violet has this new idea for a performance piece. There's already been interest in it from the artistic director at the Kitchen. She's got the concept, but she needs choreography and music. That's where I said we could help."

"*We* could help?" Duncan lowered the volume and turned to look at her. "By us, you mean you, but you twisted her arm to include me."

"Does it matter? Won't it be fun to come up with something great together?"

He was silent, the TV lights playing on his troubled face. She sensed his pride might get the better of him, his reluctance to accept Violet's help and even hers. She climbed onto his lap, blocking the screen. "Wouldn't it make you happy, for us to have that chance again to show what we can do? I know it would make me happy."

He nodded and she kissed him excitedly, taking this for his agreement. He went along and then they had sex like that, her astride him, their eyes locked. It seemed to her a while had passed since they'd looked at one another that way, that mostly sex took place in the dark or with Duncan behind her or over her so that she couldn't see his face. That he could look at her now made her feel certain she'd done the right thing, that she'd correctly guessed he needed help from her, though he'd never have dared to ask.

The next week, following rehearsals, she and Duncan began staying behind after the others left, to take advantage of the few hours when the studio was free. In the course of several attempts, Duncan began to form a melody to match the tone of Gina's dancing—she'd come upon the idea first, to have a figure surrounded by violence, but dancing through it, half-aware. The piece Duncan composed was full of menace and chaos but then, when transposed to a new key, slowed and sweetened, became intensely romantic. A love song with the threat nestled inside.

"I think it's the best he's done," Gina boasted to Violet, when the time came to present the work to her. Despite herself, Violet was impressed, and, after she cast other dancers and brought in additional musicians, the show was as powerful as Gina had envisioned. On the first night they performed, at the start of June, the audience rose to its feet.

The following week, Violet called Gina and told her, in a voice choked with excitement, to go pick up a copy of the *New York Times*. Gina ducked down to the corner bodega and brought the paper back to the dining table, where the phone lay waiting, Violet still on the line.

"Do you see it?"

The festival had received a page in the Arts section and their show had been the main subject of the roundup: *"Gina Reinhold dances through the violence as though entranced, seemingly oblivious, yet moved by every shock. The mystery surrounding what she sees creates the tension and holds the viewer rapt."*

"You're famous now," Violet concluded, while Gina stood with the paper trembling in her hands. It was overwhelming to be recognized this way, but her own giddy pleasure was marred by her worry over Duncan: where was the mention of the music, of *his* brilliance?

"Doesn't she comment on the score?"

"Nope, I checked. And for that matter, not too much about the concept or direction. Just the choreography and dancing. You're the one they noticed." Violet went on, explaining the impact the coverage would have. "You'll get cast in better shows, invited to do all sorts of festivals."

Gina got off the phone with Violet then, unable to share in her friend's exhilaration, too preoccupied by how to handle Duncan.

This news would crush him, she felt, after all the struggles he'd been having. Though in other ways she could be brave, she lacked the capacity to say anything that would make a person whom she cared for sad. She was unable to do it with her father, whom she felt had suffered pain enough, and she was now unable to do it with Duncan, whose disappointment she only wished to quell.

She tossed the paper into the trash outside, thinking the best thing might be to allow Duncan to make the discovery himself. Once she'd decided on this approach, though, she was stuck with it, and had to endure an awkward Sunday during which Duncan moved silently around the house and she found herself unable to sit still. She was sure he'd heard the news somehow, but was pretending, as she was pretending, feeling too ashamed to admit his disappointment in himself. The next day, feeling trapped in the charade and unbearably antsy, she came back from rehearsal claiming someone mentioned that their show was lauded in the *Times*.

"*You* were lauded," Duncan corrected. He went then to get the article, which he had stashed in his bag, and she'd made out as if she were reading it for the first time. She'd read slowly, afraid to look up from the page and find Duncan grimacing, hurt. And then she felt his arms around her.

"I'm thrilled for you," he told her. "You deserved that."

"You deserved it too," she said, trying to hold him to her, but Duncan pulled away.

"Oh, well, you know, it's how it is. Can't expect to be loved by everyone."

"*I* love you," she said.

He'd looked at her then, and a quiver passed over him. "I hope so."

"Of course I do." Why on earth would he doubt that? Could he believe this event would in any way alter the bond between them?

"It's not that I'm jealous," he let her know. "Honestly, it makes me so glad to see you succeed. Even happier than if it had been me. I just worry sometimes. I'm not sure if I'm equally cut out for this, and if I'm not—"

"Of course you are! Just because a single critic doesn't see it means nothing. The audience saw it. I see it."

"And I appreciate that, I really do. But I'm just mentioning it because I know you have a certain vision of me, of us. I mean, if things didn't end up going that way—"

"They will," she said, feeling a sudden urge to shut the discussion down. "Right now you're just feeling disappointed."

"I can handle my disappointment," Duncan replied with a small sigh. "It's yours that worries me."

He didn't need to worry, she tried to reassure him, though she could feel that she'd misspoken. She ought to have told him his success didn't matter to her, that she wanted it only for the sake of his happiness, but she wasn't sure how to say this so it wouldn't convey loss of hope in him.

When, three weeks later, she was invited to Vienna to participate in the largest dance festival in Europe, she had a moment of similar dread. It seemed that her comparative success might, in fact, be driving a wedge between them. It took her several days to tell Duncan about the invitation, and when she did, she presented the trip as one that they should make together. Vienna was a center for classical music and there would be people from all over the world converging for this festival and for the Salzburg Festival that followed: composers, conductors, patrons. Going there might serve his needs too.

"What I really need now is to catch up on rent," he told her. "But you go, you should. It's a great opportunity for you."

In the weeks that preceded her departure for Vienna, though Duncan pretended they were fine, Gina could feel something had changed between them. Whereas before she'd wake to find Duncan on his way to Blake's apartment, pausing first to kiss her goodbye, now, most mornings when she awoke, Duncan was already gone. Was he actually writing music or simply choosing to avoid her? She was so distracted for most of the month, with performances at the church three nights a week, on top of daily rehearsals for the Vienna festival, that she could hardly bring it up. It seemed an act of mercy when, in the week preceding her departure, the chapel suffered an electrical problem just an hour before curtain, and the performance had to be canceled. Gina was given the night off, and she hurried home to enjoy her surprise freedom with Duncan.

When she reached her apartment, though, Duncan wasn't there. Instead, she discovered Blake, stretched out in her bed reading *GQ*.

"Gina." Blake glanced up lazily, peeking out over the rails. "You're not supposed to be here."

"I'd think that's more true of you."

Blake smirked and kicked his feet over the ladder. He'd worn his loafers in their bed. Seeing him up there in that top bunk, she was reminded of the cool treatment she'd gotten from Blake back in college, whenever she and Duncan had to stop off in his room. She'd never had any illusions that Blake liked her. Before she came along, Blake had been happily trying to remake Duncan in his image: lending him his expensive, preppy clothes; taking him on drinking binges; trying to get him to become some sort of slick womanizer.

Duncan had moved beyond all that once he'd met her, but Blake was still the same, going to clubs four nights a week in the meatpacking district, picking up bridge-and-tunnel girls who had nowhere to stay the night and were too drunk to drive back home. She supposed Blake missed Duncan—the only person Blake didn't treat as disposable. Such devotion to Duncan, from a man who seemed otherwise aloof, had made her wonder, at times, if Blake's feelings for Duncan were more than simply friendly. But whatever the motive for Blake's interest in Duncan and his choices, it was clear that Blake couldn't stand that Duncan was settled, with her no less, and had no interest in the sort of life that Blake was leading, working in advertising, schmoozing with execs, and bossing around creatives, people like her and her friends who never thought much of him, and whom he therefore treated with contempt.

"Duncan's using my place, so he said I could use his."

She didn't know Duncan to go to Blake's at this hour. "Is he writing now?"

Blake shook his head and crossed his arms over his chest. "I don't think he'd want me saying."

Of course Blake meant to arouse her worst suspicions, she knew that, and she hated to succumb to them. "Well, I can call him at your place and ask him what he's up to."

"No, no. Don't do that, you'll mess things up."

"Mess what up?"

"Look, if I tell you, can we agree this stays between us?"

She hesitated before agreeing, not sure she wanted to have to hold on to such a secret. But nor did she wish to interrupt Duncan and force the truth from him. "All right, it's between us."

"He's having dinner with his parents," Blake finally admitted.

It took her a moment to absorb the meaning in this statement, and to place it in context. Ever since they'd moved to New York, Duncan's parents hadn't been to visit once, despite being just an easy drive away. She'd raised the issue several times, wondering if Duncan meant to hide their circumstances, if he was ashamed of the life he had with her.

"It's not worth it to have my mother here," Duncan had replied. "Believe me, she'll only notice every little thing that's wrong and we'll both be irritated after. It's better not to have her, to send a message. As long as you intend to judge and reject, you don't get to be included in my life."

She'd been so proud of him for saying that, but how it stung her now to learn that he'd been lying, that in fact he *was* including his mother—but excluding her.

She looked over at Blake, who was smiling coyly, brushing a lock of smooth blond hair behind his ear. The only reason he'd admitted the truth at all was because he knew it would hurt her.

"You're pissed at him," Blake concluded. "And he obviously knew you would be. That's why he didn't want to tell you."

"If he'd *told* me, I wouldn't be pissed." She felt the urge to clarify herself, though it was Duncan, not Blake, whose understanding mattered. "I'm upset because he thinks he needs to lie."

"Oh, you can't be all that surprised," said Blake. She knew he was baiting her, but then, she was nonetheless eager for any insight into what Duncan's behavior could mean. From his closest ally, apparently, no less.

Blake stared back at her, his smugly handsome face with boyishly red cheeks, typically so unexpressive, now enlivened by emotion, by his loyalty to Duncan and his antipathy to her. "He's so desperate for your approval he can't possibly be honest." They stared at one another. "You know the guy, you know his history," Blake finally went on, after making her wait in that maddening way he had. "He's just doing what he's always done, being held captive to someone else's idea of him. How are you any different from the mother he's lying to right now?"

Of course she was different! In a thousand ways different. And yet, *was* Duncan entrapping himself in a life with her, the way he'd been entrapped by his mother at home? Was he simply reliving the old pattern, limiting his freedom so as to keep her happy, doing what she wanted of him, without considering, without beginning to know, really, what it was *he* wanted?

She'd never minded the compromises they'd been forced to make in the way that Duncan had. Yapping dogs and rats were things they'd laugh about one day when they were older and more comfortably settled. A fair amount of discomfort seemed part of the thrill of being young and bohemian in a big city, and she hoped that Duncan felt the same. Though she had to admit she wasn't sure when she'd catch a private, sullen look cross over his face now and then; was he worried that this was to be his lot forever? His parents had given him every advantage and here he was frittering away his chance at a comfortable life. Was that how Duncan felt about it? Was he simply pretending he was contented for her sake?

These questions seemed too much to ask him now. In three days she was leaving for Vienna, and she didn't want to fly off angry. It was an excuse to avoid the matter, of course she realized that, but she made use of it and chose to spend the next several days busy with packing, and, true to her promise to Blake, didn't mention that she'd ever run into him or heard from him what Duncan had been doing.

At the airport, she and Duncan exchanged awkward goodbyes. "I wish you were coming," she told him.

"Oh, I'll go when I have a reason to."

"I'm sure you will. Soon. Next time, probably."

"Right."

As the plane took off, later, she'd felt a jolt of panic. It felt dangerous to be apart from Duncan when she was already feeling distant from him. She'd have been worried over this throughout the trip, she was sure, if she hadn't been so distracted: sponsors of the festival, various interested parties with money and connections, took her and her fellow dancers out to expensive restaurants or on private tours. She'd enjoyed her time alone and hadn't missed Duncan in the ways she'd thought she would. This fact, and the guilt it inspired, made her dread calling him and feel like a liar when she offered assurances—"It really would be so much better if you were here with me." She was afraid to admit all that she was enjoying without him, concerned she'd arouse his envy or make him suspect she was as joyfully busy as she was. With so little to talk about, their conversations were flat, brief, and shadowed by the unsaid. Had this trip only brought into relief how they'd been drifting? Was the end for them nearing?

Naturally, here, circumstances intervened, as they tend to do whenever we imagine the course of things has been set. Just before the conclusion of the festival, Gina had a call from her father. Her mother had suffered a third stroke. This one, her last, was fatal.

Gina flew to Santa Fe. She could not cry, not until she was off the plane, when simply the smell of the summer air, the particular dryness of it that recalled home, loosened tears within her. Duncan had been the only one able to staunch them. He'd arrived before her and met her at the airport, while her father was forced to remain at the house with his guests.

"Gina," he said, palming her head, stroking her hair. Simply hearing her name pronounced in his voice while he held her erased the gulf she'd invented in her mind. This man knew her more deeply than anyone, knew what the loss of her mother must mean, and made her grief less lonely and immense just by his presence. She held him and cried, for her mother's vanishing from her, and from the near loss of him, which he must have feared too, and so held her more tightly still.

Those days, which never quite came into focus, seemed to consist of endless plates carried in and out, the heavy smell of flowers amassing in vases, bright sun and extraordinary heat, and a feeling of weightless emptiness, as if a hole she'd carried in her since girlhood had at last been uncovered.

That late August in Santa Fe, the pain of the present and the past converged: she became the nine-year-old she'd been, finally saying goodbye to a mother she'd mourned years before but hadn't been able to admit the loss of fully until now. No one would ever be the world for her as her mother once was—and it dawned on her, in those days, for the first time really, that the person closest to meaning this much to her was Duncan.

She'd felt her need for him more acutely than she ever had before. Her mother's death had occurred, it seemed, just to make clear at a moment when the doubts had gathered that she would never, in fact, be able to leave Duncan, that for all their struggles and for whatever their future might contain, she would remain with him, marry him, have his children, do all those things that felt imminent to her now.

From Santa Fe she and Duncan returned to New York with a sense of starting over. She never told Duncan of her discussion with Blake and set aside the doubts that had been raised. With the clout she still held following her rave review in the *Times*, she persuaded the head of Dance Theater Workshop to let her stage a piece, with Duncan as her composer. She and Duncan began work on an entirely new show, and Duncan began to write, almost immediately, with such fluency, often waking up in the morning with a musical line in his head.

A month or so after, she proposed to him—not with a ring or on one knee, but with a simple announcement, as they lay in bed before sleep, of her wish.

"I want to marry you," she said, hoping it would banish these feelings of loneliness and blackness engulfing her still.

Duncan turned on his side, tense. She placed her hand on his chest, felt his pulse.

"What do you mean? Eventually? Now?"

"Now. I want to be with you always and to make that clear right now."

"Really? Married?" He held the word, and she let him, let him get used to it and make it his. "Yes, I want to marry you," he said at last. "I want that too."

She reached for him, entangling as much of them as she could, connecting every possible inch of skin, and lay like that, feeling his body in the dark. Her grief surrounded her, but seemed held off by the happiness between them, as, unseen, the tears rolled down her cheeks.

The next morning, they'd discussed the realities that accompanied their promise. Gina didn't wish to wait, or make a fuss over the service. Her father had just emerged from planning her mother's funeral, and she didn't want to burden him with the responsibility of arranging yet another ceremony. Anyway the notion of a formal gathering felt morbid to her. "Can't we keep it simple, just between us?"

"And why not a real ceremony? I mean, this is the only time . . ."

Duncan was less certain, but she'd managed to persuade him.

"Think about it. Your mother, my father. They'll cast a pall. The day should feel like it's ours. Unspoiled."

Yes, the blunt truth was that neither of their parents would be thrilled by the fact of their union. Duncan's mother would sulk, and Gina's father was in mourning, and, though Gina often denied the fact to Duncan, each of them knew her father didn't care for him and would suffer their marriage as another loss. In his mind, Gina's ambitions aside, Duncan was the sole factor keeping Gina thousands of miles away.

So they agreed—they'd keep the wedding small, and private. They bought modest rings, applied for a license, and picked a day to visit city hall. For the celebration, they invited only twenty friends: Blake and Violet; a few of Violet's roommates, including Donovan and Hector; Gina's fellow dancers; the choreographer that Duncan worked for; even, out of a spirit of goodwill, the neighbor with the yapping dog. It had been precisely the sort of easy, raucous atmosphere that Gina needed: friends toasting them and laughing and dancing until Duncan forced them out so he could carry his new bride off to bed.

They'd slept together so many times in the last years that sex between them could hardly be expected to feel new. And yet that night it *had* felt new to Gina, like their whole lives and all their hopes were in their bed with them, creating a denser presence, more profound. In the next weeks, a sense of promise and fertility seemed to attend her and Duncan's every move.

As her mother's estate was settled, Gina learned that she'd come into a sizable inheritance, so that her and Duncan's financial struggles would soon be behind them. Shortly thereafter, the piece for Dance Theater Workshop was performed, and, as if in honor of the love they'd revived between them, Duncan's work was given favorable reviews by two critics, and artistic directors of several theaters began calling to enlist him in their shows. Suddenly the shift had happened, commissions came his way, and she and Duncan were both working consistently. Over the next months, they decorated the walls of their apartment with postcards of the many shows they'd done, some apart and some together—and she'd imagined that alongside the postcards would come pictures of the life they'd make, of them on honeymoon, of her pregnant, each of their hands cupping her belly, awed by the fullness of their future.

Ten

Duncan // New York

1995

It was the night of Violet's farewell party, and Duncan had promised to join Gina there after he'd finished his evening piano lessons. Violet's departure had come as a surprise: only two weeks earlier, she'd announced her plan to move to Prague—this just following Blake's announcement that he was taking a position at Ogilvy and Mather's office in London. Their friends' departures marked the end of an era, Duncan sensed, but though he would miss having Blake around, and was sure Gina would miss Violet still more, he had to admit he was also eager to make a break with recent history. The past year had been a tough one, with their estrangement and Gina losing her mother, but since their marriage especially, he and Gina had recovered their equilibrium and were delighting in each other again.

He arrived at Violet's in Tribeca around nine. What the building—industrial, neglected—lacked on the outside was made up for by the immense floor space within. The elevator opened onto a vast room, and, at the entrance, a giant metal sculpture shaped like a woman lay spread-eagled. Someone had placed a cup of wine on each of the breasts.

Duncan moved through the thick crowd, seeking out Gina. He spotted Violet instead. She was standing off to the side, by an exposed toilet. He wondered at Violet's exhibitionism: did she piss and crap in the open with her six roommates too? It was certainly a quirk of Violet, who had family money, to choose to live in such rough conditions, but he had to admit that boded well for her launching her new life in a country where Western comforts, including private plumbing, might not be taken for granted. Moving to Prague was brave of her, he thought, braver than he'd been willing to acknowledge Violet was before. Over the years, he'd been of the opinion that Violet, with her rich fathers and connections, made a show of being unconventional while operating free of risk. He'd resented the contempt he felt she bore him for his practical concerns, but tonight, possibly because his career was going well, finally, and perhaps because this was goodbye for now, he was feeling in the mood to put their differences aside.

He stepped up to plant a kiss on her wide and salty cheek.

"And one day," he said to Violet, "I'll tell the historians who ask me that the Prague theater renaissance actually started in West Tribeca."

"And you expect historians will often come to interview you in the future?"

"Why not? I'll be the husband of the great Gina Reinhold."

Violet smiled at this. Whatever competitive instincts he aroused in her, Gina did not. "Your better half is over there," Violet remarked, and pointed to where Gina was absorbed in conversation with a young woman whose name Duncan had forgotten. He'd seen her before, a dancer from college, a round-faced brunette with eyebrows plucked into crescent moons. Gina, thankfully, guessed at his difficulty and reintroduced the girl as Bette, Violet's ex-girlfriend.

"Actually," Bette corrected her, "we're sort of on again, Violet and me."

"Are you?" Gina covered her mouth, embarrassed. "I didn't realize, I'm sorry."

"No, don't be," Bette reassured her. "On this week, off next, that's what seems to fit with us. What I can't get is how you two are married. Permanence, that shit's insane!"

"I guess that's what we are," said Gina, and Duncan wrapped his arms around her waist, hoisting her off of the floor.

He was feeling so glad to see her in that moment, so glad to be her husband and even, just then, to be himself—young and strong and healthy, full of desire and hope. He loved this girl with her small body and huge spirit, her eager, laughing eyes. He loved her and was grateful to her, for holding fast to him when he was shaken by doubt, by that confusion and ambivalence she was so blissfully without. He was grateful to her for being steadfast when he couldn't be, for seeing to it that he stuck to composing, which he never could have done—never would have started with—if not for her. Gina was not just his better half, he thought; she'd made him ten times better alongside her.

"Actually, I think Gina and I haven't even cracked the surface of insane. I'm feeling like it's time for our next move, something crazier than marriage."

"What do you mean?" Gina asked, searching his face.

He wasn't entirely sure what he meant, but he imagined he was inspired by Blake's and Violet's setting off, that this had put him in mind of travel and adventure. They might move somewhere new, or maybe embark on some grander project. Possibly he could turn the piece he was developing into part of something larger, a full, modern ballet.

Once Bette had left, Gina told him, "What you said before, I've had a feeling like that too." She was looking up at him, her eyes glassy, and he had a frightening sense that whatever she was going to say next was something big. "The feeling has come over me lately, like this happiness should lead to something."

"To something?"

"To someone, actually. I . . . Well, you know it's something that I've always wanted, to start a family young, to have a child."

He'd tried with all his might not to reveal the tumult in him brought on by her words. A child. He'd known, in some abstract way, that this was something Gina wanted, something she'd mentioned to him now and again, but never in a way that made him feel that it was a pressing wish. It was a fantasy—and hers alone—he thought, a longing from her past that surely didn't fit in any way with the present life that they were leading.

Nor did it have anything to do with him. He hadn't given the slightest thought to parenthood and couldn't imagine himself up to the role. So much effort was going into hiding the dread that clutched him at the prospect, he wasn't able to focus at all on what to say, and stood there mute for a long moment, until Gina began to frown.

"You're not glad I brought it up."

"I'm surprised, is all . . . ," he stammered. She looked so hurt, so disappointed. He had to find some way to cheer her. "I'm not saying I don't want that. You've just caught me off guard."

"Well, right, sure." She brightened, the life returned to her face, her stiff body relaxed again. "I've been wanting to say something for a while. So maybe this was a bit shocking, but I'm glad I have. Now it's out there and we can deal with it."

"Right, that's true. Now we can."

Except that he didn't have the remotest notion how to deal with this. He'd only just begun to get his footing professionally, in the life he'd been fumbling along at until just months before. And that life, how was it suitable for a child? Both he and Gina were working day and night, trying to establish themselves. They barely had time to manage their own business, to do laundry or fix meals. They didn't even have the confidence to own a house-plant and now Gina was speaking of caring for a human being? Because of what? Because she was turning twenty-four and some childhood version of herself had formed a notion she'd be a mom by twenty-five? Could Gina be such a slave to her own girlhood fable?

Before he or Gina could say more, Violet came to join them, hugging Gina and causing Duncan to recall that this was an emotional night. He resolved to wait and see whether Gina raised the subject again. He didn't need to wait long. The very next morning, when he'd woken, Gina was up already, watching him.

"About last night, we were carried away a bit, so I just wanted to mention again what was said."

For an instant, he felt hope: Gina was going to tell him that, in the sober light of day, she knew a child was a mistake.

"I wanted to make clear this is something I've been thinking about for a long time now. Something you've always known I wanted."

"Gina, I realize it's an idea you've had, but ideas come and go."

"Not this one," she said sharply, looking stung. "If you know me at all, you have to know that this isn't some whim. I never got to have the time I was meant to with my mother. And I'm not about to let something like that happen again."

"Hold, on, hold on," he said, reaching for her, taking her into his arms. He could feel the heat of her tears against his neck as he held her like this, realizing how deeply and painfully this wish was rooted in her.

"What happened to your mom won't happen to you. You're going to live a long and great life. No pressure. No rush."

"It's not a rush." She looked up, her tone defensive. "It's just something that I really want. Why put off the things in life you know you want?"

Her lips were trembling as she spoke. She didn't just want a child, he realized now—she wanted one desperately.

"I love you more than anything, Gina, you know that," he began cautiously. "Which means that I want more than anything for you to be happy. I swear I do, but I need to be sure it's the right thing for you—and for *us*. This year has already been a whirlwind; so much has been stirred up in you. It seems to me we ought to wait, see if your feelings change."

"They won't change," she said, sullen. "You're only hoping that they will."

"Gina, please, let's at least try to understand better what's behind this."

"There's nothing to understand. It's the most natural wish in the world to want a child. If you don't want one, why don't you try to understand the fear that's behind *that*?"

Her voice was hard, her face flushed. She was angry with him, a rarity. Whatever disappointments he might have caused her in the past, she'd never blamed him for them—but this, this was different.

Gina wanted something from him and he wasn't agreeing to give it to her. After all she'd done for him, he was choosing to hold out, and though he firmly believed he should hold out, that bringing a creature into the world was not something to be done lightly, still the simple fact of Gina's displeasure, and the knowledge that in some way he'd caused it, was really more than he could bear.

He hoped, at least, he wouldn't need to bear it for too long, that Gina would calm down and that the things he'd said might slowly penetrate her thinking. The next day, though, Gina remained remote. She didn't kiss him back when he kissed her; her tone with him was clipped and she scarcely caught his eye. At last, he tried to engage her to speak with him about it.

"Can we acknowledge what's going on here?"

"Sure, it's acknowledged. I'm upset and you know perfectly well why. What do you want me to say?"

He wanted her to say that this would pass, that she would come to see things his way and no longer resent him. Of course it was his problem, he told himself, that he was unable to stand disappointing a woman whom he loved. But even if he knew this about himself, he seemed powerless to change it.

After another day spent in the gloom of Gina's displeasure, he began grasping at anything he could offer that might soften her against him.

"I think you're right to feel my fear plays a role here. Maybe it's the fear that I can't live up to the idea of what a father ought to be."

She looked up at him, encouraged. "Well, let's talk about that, then."

"I feel, to be a father, I'd need to be more stable. Responsible.

Personally and financially too. Maybe it's old-fashioned, but I'm not comfortable just relying on your family money."

"I see." Gina looked off, considering. "But if you were working on projects that were better paid, if that could start to happen for you, that might help."

"Yes, sure. That might help a lot."

This concession, he realized only in hindsight, was the beginning of the end.

He'd said it because he'd have said anything, at that moment, to keep Gina speaking to him in the gentle way she was. Still, he didn't feel like he'd been lying. By the time his career had reached a stage where he could support a family, he might really feel emboldened to do what Gina wanted. It hadn't occurred to him that any such shift could happen quickly, or that Gina, who'd always encouraged him to ignore financial considerations, would switch her position easily.

A few days later, Gina announced they'd been invited to a party that coming Friday, where she could introduce Duncan to a young woman she wanted him to meet.

"Marina Du Bellay. We spent time together in Vienna. Her mother is a French aristocrat who sits on the festival board. Marina's in New York now, making her first film. A few months back I put her in touch with Violet's roommate Donovan, the cinematographer."

"And why do you want us to meet?"

"Well, you want to take on more lucrative projects. Seems to me that a film score would be a good place to start."

"You realize most independent film pays next to nothing."

"Marina's loaded," Gina said bluntly, uncharacteristically so.

The party was held at a town house on the Upper East Side,

hosted by the producer of a documentary Donovan had been working on all winter. The house was expensively furnished, and many of the guests were older, friends of the producer and her husband. None of the people looked familiar to Duncan, but, after stopping at the bar for drinks, Gina led him over to the one guest he did know, Donovan, who stood talking to a tall, striking woman with straight blond hair tied up in a knot.

"Marina," Gina said, as the woman turned and saw her, clapping her hand to her heart as if overwhelmed by the surprise.

"Gina!"

Marina was a few years older than Gina, long and angular, shoulders a little hunched. She had a high forehead and wide-set, blurry blue eyes. Duncan wouldn't have called her pretty, not like Gina, but there was no doubt she was arresting.

"This is Duncan, my husband," Gina let her know.

"Husband, my God. Benoit will be destroyed."

Benoit. Duncan had never heard the name before, and couldn't help but wonder who he was. That whole Vienna trip remained mysterious to him—so much of it never discussed in the wake of Gina's mother's death. This name made him anxious, but he tried to put his thoughts aside.

"Will you be going back this summer?" Marina was asking Gina.

"If they invite me, I guess I might."

"Oh, they'll invite you. You were the best dancer there."

"I was not, not by any stretch."

"You were! You were amazing!" Marina was effusive, even manic. She grabbed hold of both of Gina's hands. "I want to dance with you, amazing dancer. Let's go dance."

"But no one's dancing. . . ," Gina trailed off as Marina pulled her to a small, uncrowded patch between the sofas.

Duncan and Donovan stood watching the women as first Marina and then Gina began dancing to the music playing in the background, while the stiffer guests looked on. Donovan was smoking a joint, which he soon handed over to Duncan. Duncan inhaled gratefully, becoming aware of how much he required relaxation. Minutes later, as Duncan finished off his drink and eased into his high, he felt calm enough to confess to Donovan the reason he was there.

"Gina's got it in her head that Marina might hire me. For her movie. To do the score."

"Marina might, you know. She hired me almost on the spot. Goes on instinct, she says."

"And how's that working out for her?"

"Filming hasn't started yet, so hard to say." Donovan paused for a drag. "But hey, however it goes, the lady pays."

Duncan looked over at Gina and Marina, joined now in their dancing by a towering, bearded man and a woman in overalls who backed into a vase that was propped atop a shelf. At the noise of the crash, Marina grabbed Gina's arm and pulled her away, back to Donovan and Duncan.

Marina was laughing, but Gina was upset.

"I hope it wasn't worth a fortune," Gina said.

"They can afford it," Marina assured her. "Plus, the host's a bastard anyway. I know the couple. My mother had me meet them when I moved here because the wife makes films. Or pays others to make them. And her husband supports her hobby just so she won't leave him. He fucks everything, by the way."

"How do you know?" Donovan asked her.

"How do you think?" said Marina, grinning. "He fucked me."

As she broke into laughter, she fixed her eyes on Duncan. He laughed along, lightly, which seemed the safest thing to do.

Marina watched him, smiling. "You're not sure if I did it or not, are you?"

"I mean, I've just met you. Too soon to form any opinion."

Her smile widened. She was enjoying this, his nervousness, the chance to sound out his first feelings for her. She had to be aware of her effect on men. The height, the yellow hair, the wildness in her eyes, all these would garner her immediate attention. "I must have created some impression, though?"

"Well, Gina tells me you're a lovely person."

"Of course." She rolled her eyes at his careful reply, then took hold, again, of Gina's arm. "She's the lovely one, clearly."

"Both of you," said Duncan.

A brief silence fell over the group, which Duncan broke with an announcement that he needed the bathroom. The way Marina looked at him, the fact that he noticed and was pleased, set him on edge.

"Donovan, there's someone here you have to meet. Your future husband." With that, Marina pulled Donovan away, and Duncan and Gina were left standing together.

"Marina's high as hell," he observed to Gina. "I'm not sure I see any value in trying to talk to her tonight."

"Oh, she's always like this. She's chatting with you, it's going well."

Duncan shrugged and glanced over at Marina, catching her looking back at him. He headed off to the bathroom and took his place in the long line outside the door. After a moment, he noticed

Marina stepping away from Donovan and the other man, coming to join the line behind him.

"Oh, for fuck's sake, can't they open up another?" she griped, bouncing a little to suggest her need to go.

Duncan offered to let her skip ahead of him. Instead, when the room freed up and Marina darted in, she pulled Duncan along with her.

"I can wait," he stammered, but Marina had already locked the door behind them.

"I don't need the toilet anyway," she told him, and the next thing he knew, she was standing in the tub, hiking up her skirt.

"Jesus, what are you doing?"

"I told you the host's a bastard." Reaching for one of the silver soap dispensers on the sink, she unscrewed the top and began urinating into it.

"Marina, stop. Other people might use that. Not just the host, the party guests."

"Sssshh. You're making me mess up. Goddammit, you should do it. Women are useless pissers."

"I'm not going to do it."

A knock came on the door. "One at a time! What's going on in there?"

"Just a moment," Duncan called back. He wanted to get out of there, to unlock the door, but Marina wasn't done yet and the pressure in his bladder was intense. He unzipped his fly, relieved himself, and was almost finished when the door opened behind him. Apparently, Marina hadn't locked it properly and, to his horror, when Duncan turned, he caught sight of Gina standing just a few feet away.

She looked at him, confused and then distressed, and walked away. He caught up to her and drew her into a corner, out of Marina's sight line. "She just yanked me in after her. I didn't know what to do—that woman's crazy. You didn't tell me she was crazy."

"You might have kicked her out. Walked out yourself."

"I'm sorry. I didn't want to offend her. I guess I wasn't certain what to do, what you'd want me to do."

"What *I'd* want you to do? Were you really thinking about that?"

He nodded and her expression grew pained. In an instant she was crying. He was startled by her tears, wasn't sure what they might mean. He feared she might be terrifically upset with him, but then she took his face into her hands. "I'm the one who should be sorry. I've been twisting you in knots, haven't I? Thinking about what I want, making it all about what I want."

"I'll admit," he conceded, "this past week hasn't been easy."

"I know it hasn't. I got carried away, and I'm sorry. I promise that I'll stop now."

She had stopped too—quite suddenly, from then on, Gina stopped treating him like he'd hurt her, stopped talking of a child or of altering, in any way, his professional path. Over the next weeks and months, he continued playing piano at the studio, and giving lessons, and working on the same performance projects. The threat had passed, it seemed. He and Gina were at peace again and had returned to the pleasant pattern of their lives before.

In August, as Marina predicted, Gina was indeed invited to perform again in Vienna. Duncan had managed to escape another conversation about their future child before she'd left. At first he'd been grateful, but in the ensuing days of her absence—with phone calls even fewer and farther between than her last time in Vienna—he couldn't help but feel that he'd been too quick to assume their problems were resolved. Perhaps something larger had shifted in Gina, and between them. Perhaps this silence was her way of beginning to, gradually, let go—not of her dreams of motherhood, but of Duncan, of their shared future.

A week after Gina had left, Marina called, out of the blue, to ask him if he was still interested in composing for her film.

"Gina had told me you might be. And we're now in postproduction, so this would be the time to meet if you're still interested."

"To be honest, I'm not sure. I've committed to some other projects."

"I see. Well, up to you, then, but if you have some recordings, you might as well send them along to me and then, if I like them, we can discuss what I'm looking for and offering. I don't see the harm in that, do you?"

A voice in him warned that yes, there might be harm in that. After all, it was already suspicious that Marina was reaching out now, just after Gina's departure. Still, he'd never been much good at saying no, and all Marina wanted was a sample of his work. He sent this off and two days later Marina called again to invite him to talk. This time he conceded, meeting her at a garden restaurant near her home in Gramercy.

"I listened to what you sent me," Marina told him, after they'd exchanged quick kisses on both cheeks. "Obviously we wouldn't be here if I didn't think you have marvelous talent."

"Thank you. That's kind of you to say." He was being polite and careful, mindful, as Marina spoke, of the way she sat down in her chair so that her slender legs were stretched out to almost touch his, while the rest of her leaned back, appraising.

"Those were pieces for dance, am I right? And now you're looking to expand into film, is that true?"

"Thinking about it, yeah."

"I can't blame you. I'd imagine that in dance there's so little to be gained, so little money and recognition." She sipped her water. "It's hard to see why you'd even want to, except for Gina's sake."

"Actually, it's Gina who encouraged me to explore new possibilities."

"And do you always require her approval to explore new possibilities?"

"No, of course not."

Marina smiled, acknowledging her teasing, then grew serious again. "Though I would like to know that this is something *you* want."

"Right now I want some wine and a waiter to take our order."

They ordered, and while they waited for the food to arrive, Marina admitted that she'd done some investigating about Duncan, and had learned from her acquaintances that he was considered, at least by some, to be the best-kept secret among young classical composers. "You haven't done much and most people don't know of you, but the few that do admire you."

"That's nice to hear," he said, flushing a little. Marina might be exaggerating, but it was a rare pleasure for him, being offered praise. And now Marina was prepared to offer him money as well.

"Given the quality of your work, I'm willing to raise my music budget. How does sixty thousand sound to you?"

"Seems reasonable," he said, trying not to fall out of his chair. Sixty thousand was twice what he'd earned throughout the entire year.

"Good, good. So then we can start getting to the fun part.

There are a few musicians I'd like you to hear, artists who capture very well the tone I want for my film."

Over the next two weeks, while Gina was away, keeping busy, Duncan was kept busy by Marina. As he began composing, working every free moment he had, she invited him to several shows a week, some small bands at local venues, and some large orchestra performances. After one show at Lincoln Center, which she insisted was her treat, she introduced him to an elegant European couple.

"Duncan, I'd like you to meet Astrid and Riccardo. My mother and her fiancé."

He'd been caught off guard by this meeting with Marina's mother, and especially by the sly way her mother smiled at him. Still, he told himself that he was doing nothing wrong, that this was a business relationship—Marina was now his client, and paying him an awful lot, and so spending time with her this way was a perfectly fine thing to do.

He clung to this idea, even when she arrived at his door, two nights later, holding a bottle of wine and dressed in a blouse open far enough that he could see she wore nothing underneath it. He clung to this idea even when she put on music and flung herself across his sofa. Even when she was tipsy and again using this as an excuse for saying things she shouldn't.

"It's probably not my place to comment, but it honestly surprises me that you didn't accompany Gina to Vienna this time—I mean after the last trip."

"I've got projects I'm finishing, and this one . . ." He left it at that, not indulging Marina by asking her what she was alluding to about Gina's last visit. He recalled the name she'd mentioned before, Benoit—the man who would be crushed to hear Gina was married. "Anyway, I think it's a good thing for a couple to spend a little time apart. Miss one another."

"Not all men are so trusting."

"Gina's never given me a reason not to trust her."

"Oh, Duncan, you're too sweet. You really are. Gina is so lucky. Most men with your talent are egomaniacs, but you're as innocent as you are gifted. It's a good thing you've seen as little as you have. I mean a scene like Vienna, the conniving and exploiting. Gina can handle herself, of course, but that kind of thing would crush that pure spirit right out of you." Marina laughed and he tried to smile, though in truth he was shaken, reminded of the insecurity he'd suffered that past summer and which was now, in Gina's absence, stirred up in him again.

Duncan peered down at Marina, who was lying back on his sofa, now with her eyes closed. She was alluring, he couldn't deny it, stylish and worldly, and he supposed it flattered him that such a woman would see so much possibility in him. As much as Gina had encouraged him before, she'd also borne witness to too many of his failures to idealize him any longer. Lost in his thoughts, he continued watching Marina lying there until he wasn't even sure she hadn't drifted off to sleep. When the song ended, though, she sat up again and opened her eyes, looking at him boldly.

"It's an interesting piece . . ." He began to comment on the music, what little he'd had the presence to observe, while Marina stared up at him. An amused smile formed on her lips. Then she kissed him.

He didn't pull away—not at first. Sure, he'd been briefly stunned, if not surprised—but also he found himself excited, susceptible at that moment to interest from an attractive woman who wasn't his wife. Another alluring figure to mold and shape him.

He allowed her to open her blouse further, exposing herself, before he stood and backed away.

Just after he withdrew, Marina stood too and brushed past him, blouse still open, walking off to refill her wineglass in the kitchenette. "I shouldn't have done that. Gina's my friend. You're married. You must think badly of me."

"I don't. I—"

"It's just so obvious that you two don't fit together anymore. She's moved on to other things, and you really should too. But if you don't see that, it's not my place to insist."

Marina finally glanced up at him, but something else caught her attention. She looked over at the door.

The music continued to play, which must have accounted for the fact that he hadn't heard the sound of a key turning in the lock. He'd been too distracted too by Marina to notice the front door standing open. No one was at the doorway now, but Gina's luggage remained where, a moment before, Gina must have been.

He'd darted out to the hallway and peered over the banister just in time to see Gina two flights down, fleeing through the building entrance. What could she have seen or heard? He bounded down the steps, but by the time he burst onto the street, Gina was nowhere in sight. She must have slipped into a taxi and away. Later, after Marina had left with a flutter of apologies, he called up anyone he could think of in search of Gina, but she wasn't staying with her friends and no one knew where she was. He hadn't any idea how to reach her until a week had passed, when one of her fellow dancers let him know that Gina had flown home to Santa Fe.

All right, all he had to do was get Gina on the phone and explain himself—he hadn't slept with Marina, hadn't wished to sleep with Marina. He'd been indulgent with her, too indulgent, yes, but in the hopes of gaining a commission that would let Gina and him move forward in their lives together, do what they wanted. He'd come around to what she wanted. A child. He could be ready. No, he *was* ready!

Once she'd heard this, once she saw how sickened he was to think he'd hurt her, well, Gina would forgive him. Nothing unforgivable had happened.

"I just need five minutes on the phone with her," he told her father when he called their house in Santa Fe.

"I'm sorry, but she won't speak with you, Duncan. She's made it very clear that she wants to move on now."

"Look, Mr. Reinhold, I don't know what she might have told you, but it's all a big misunderstanding. If you'll let me explain, she'll see she's overreacting."

"It might seem like she's overreacting to you, but that's how Gina is. Other people, what they feel as a ripple, she feels as a tidal wave."

"But it's barely a ripple. It's a mistake."

"I'm sorry, son," said Mr. Reinhold, in a tone that might have suggested sympathy but was, Duncan was sure, bereft of any. "It's awful to lose someone you love," he said contemplatively, Duncan now growing angry that Mr. Reinhold would turn his grief as a weapon against him, "but I'm afraid that's what's happened."

Duncan hung up from the call in a state of baffled despair. None of this made sense. There must be some part of the story he wasn't getting, but he had no means of learning what. He turned to Gina's friends for understanding—perhaps her fellow dancers would have an explanation, but they were equally perplexed and frustrated by her disappearance. She wasn't speaking with them either.

It struck him then that she wasn't abandoning him only; she

was giving up on everything: her career, their apartment, her life in New York, that life she'd envisioned for them when she was just nineteen. She'd seen it all so vividly she'd made him fall in love with that life too, and now she'd just run off to Santa Fe, mysteriously, to let their life together die.

It all seemed so utterly unlike her, this behavior, as if she'd collapsed into some former, weaker, childhood self, dependent on her father, fearful and withdrawn.

A week later, Duncan received a call from the artistic director at PS 122. The man was calling to invite Gina to choreograph a piece for their festival that winter.

"Gina's paying a visit back home," Duncan told him, "but I'll be sure to relay the offer." He phoned Gina's house several times that day, but no one picked up his calls. Finally, he left a message on the house answering machine.

Two days later, having gotten no response, he phoned the artistic director to ask whether Gina had been in touch with him directly. After learning that she hadn't been, Duncan canceled his lessons for the next days and flew out to Santa Fe.

He arrived at the Reinhold house, unannounced, at 10 a.m. Mr. Reinhold came to the door and refused to let him in.

"I have something I need to say to Gina," Duncan let him know. "It's not only about me. A professional matter too."

The man stood and looked at him, breathing deeply, his broad chest expanding. He was larger than Duncan, powerful still. His red beard covered half his face, but Duncan could see his jaw was set. "I can't let you in, I'm sorry."

"Mr. Reinhold, she's had an offer from a theater that means a lot to her. It's the dance company that made her want to come to New York in the first place."

"Gina needs a break from New York for now."

"You mean she needs a break from me."

Mr. Reinhold made no reply, only stepped out onto the lawn and beckoned Duncan to follow.

"Listen," Duncan continued, walking beside him, "I didn't do what Gina thinks. I'd never betray her or disappoint her that way. That's the last thing I'd ever do."

Mr. Reinhold sighed, speaking slowly. "Duncan, a guy like you, you can't help but disappoint her. You're all promise and no follow-through; you'll say anything to please her, and even think you mean it, but you don't know what the hell you mean, 'cause you have no idea who you are or what you're about."

Duncan had always had a nagging sense that Gina's father didn't like him, but the man had never admitted it, or given any indication of the reason why. He'd had no proof that this was how Mr. Reinhold saw him, until now; he would need to work hard to keep his hurt from getting in his way.

"I'm about loving your daughter. That's what I'm about."

Mr. Reinhold's arms were crossed, his lips pursed, unyielding. But Duncan wouldn't back down either.

"With all due respect," Duncan went on, gathering his courage, "you don't get to tell me who I am or what I'm about, and you don't get to do that for Gina either. She's a grown woman. She should come out here and face me and tell me in her own words what she wants."

"I'm sorry you've come down here for nothing." Without another word, Gina's father turned inside, shutting the door behind him.

He should have pounded on that door, Duncan thought later. He should have camped out on that lawn until Gina came to see him, instead of walking away. Whatever was happening inside that house was wrong, he knew it was, that somehow Gina had lost her footing and her father had seized upon the moment to get her back—his daughter, who had always been his compensation for having lost his wife and whom he'd never wanted to let go. Thinking of Gina being kept here, he saw her for the first time as frightened, almost like the anxious, guilty boy Gina had spent the past five years saving him from being. It was his great mistake to leave her there, and for the next months, alone in their apartment, he was haunted by his failure.

Why had he yielded to Frank Reinhold? What sort of creature was he to be led around always by others? For most of his life, his mother had made decisions for him and told him who to be. Then he'd let Gina reshape him to fit as well as he was able into her vision for him, and when that went awry, and he failed to match her fantasy, he'd been intoxicated by the allure of something— someone—new, Marina, and his impulses upended the life he'd built and the only relationship that mattered.

Then—months later, that spring—chance had given him the opportunity to correct for all of this, when a stranger named Graham Bonafair had shown up at his door to remind him again of who he was and what that meant.

He loved Gina and understood that she was lost to herself, the way he once had been. Did he not owe it to her—and to them— to take control of his destiny and do whatever he must to bring her back to herself, to him, and her true home?

Eleven

Gina // Siena

July 1996

After a frantic drive to Hlavni Nadrazi station, Gina squeezing Duncan's hand at every painful pothole, they arrived with just minutes before the train to Vienna. Thankfully, there was no line at the ticket window, and, with a strained sprint down the platform, she and Duncan collapsed into their seats just as the train was pulling out. For some time after, Gina's heart kept pounding until at last she settled down and turned to watch the lovely, wistful city, even stranger to her now, rolling past her window and into memory.

Not since Berlin had she had such a feeling: that she was leaving a place a different person than when she'd come. The fog was clearing, replaced by a sharp sense of purpose. She wasn't yet ready to tell Duncan the cause, but she wondered if he felt a change in her. At times that morning he'd seemed to watch her with a puzzled look, and she supposed that it was odd, her insisting on this sudden trip, and that Duncan must be wondering about her motives. She imagined each of them at this instant, seated across from one another, silently guessing at the other's thoughts. Perhaps Duncan had formed certain ideas, but this, she told herself, shouldn't trouble her too much.

How wrong we always are, after all, when we believe we know the minds of those we love.

"I hope Violet won't be upset we left so quickly," she announced, breaking the silence, and her own reverie. She must keep on top of the situation—Violet would have her own theories on Gina's sudden disappearance, and it would be prudent to provide her friend with some answers.

Duncan hardly seemed to hear her: pale and worn out from his injuries, he was having trouble keeping his eyes open. Soon he was dozing, and Gina, meanwhile, fished her writing pad out of the suitcase and sat down again to write a letter to her friend.

Dear Violet,

I owe you an apology for leaving Prague the way I did, without explanation. It must be confusing for you—my showing up out of the blue, and then vanishing as fast, without reassuring you that Duncan is all right (he is) or stopping in to say goodbye.

There are things I could tell you about the past weeks— things I'd planned to tell you when I came to Prague. But then this morning changed all that. Changed my plans, changed everything. I should have suspected what was happening from my sickness yesterday, but I didn't know myself until I awoke today, tender in places that left no room for doubt. . . .

She left off there, distractedly, thoughts circling back to hours ago, when she'd left Duncan in bed and set off, in a tumult of feeling, to wander the Prague streets. Images had flooded her memory as she ambled about, losing track of where she was going, until, as if in a dream, she'd come upon this cottage-like building and had seen Duncan walking through the entrance. She'd been startled to find him—she'd left him asleep not long before—and had followed him into what she then recognized must be a temple. From the back of the room she stood and watched him, his head bowed and body rocking.

He was praying. Duncan, who did not believe in prayer. Duncan, rational Duncan, who'd so often put his pragmatism ahead of faith in what he loved—here he was, with such a penitent way about him that tears came to her eyes. She couldn't know what words he might be casting up to God, but she believed that they must have to do with them, that he must be seeking some means to keep them whole, to repair the harm they'd done each other. She'd left the temple knowing that what had happened between them was a blessing, her discovery that morning a gift of grace.

Now Duncan sat across from her, deeply asleep and oblivious to the fact that his prayer had been answered. He slept on like that, while she finished her letter to Violet and penned another, much the same, to her father.

In Vienna, they switched to the train for Rome, where they took a sleeping car for the overnight ride. It took Gina some time to shake off her thoughts and settle down to sleep, but she had slept, because soon it was morning, and Duncan was waking her to let her know they were approaching Roma Termini. As soon as the train halted, there was a great rush all around to catch the Siena train. A crowd had formed already on the platform, thick and loud and buoyant: young men and women flirted, rival fans taunted one another. Many passengers had brought along their lunch and sat down on the platform to eat; others poured glasses of wine. While Duncan waited among them, Gina went off to change money and buy the tickets and some food.

Rested and feeling better, Duncan devoured the sandwiches she'd bought, though all Gina could bring herself to eat was a slice of plain, dry bread. In Chiusi, they were required to change trains again, and for the last leg of the trip, the raucous passengers began to sing. The singing cheered Gina, reminded her that Prague was now behind her, and that what lay ahead was turbulent and unknown and, quite possibly, fantastic.

At Stazione di Siena, chaos was already erupting, people spilling through the front doors into the street in search of taxis. Without porters in sight, she and Duncan had to struggle with their luggage, and by the time they were outside, the line at the taxi stand was so immense, they despaired of ever getting into town. As they stood debating what to do, a young man in a cap approached them, asking in English if they wanted transit to the city center.

"*Sì, sì.*" Duncan nodded, and the young man took their bags and led them to a minivan filled with tourists.

The ride was hot and bumpy, but thankfully short, and soon the van pulled up along a brick wall with signs leading to parking lots and to the Piazza del Campo. From here on, the way was closed to vehicles, all but the few police cars that crawled among the throngs of pedestrians through the narrow, slanted streets. Vendors stood along the gutters selling mementos of the race and other items that might appeal to tourists—binoculars and hats, maps, bottles of water. An enterprising young man spotted

Duncan and Gina dragging their suitcases and offered his assistance.

"I can be guide and carry for you. Only ten thousand lire."

Gina insisted that they do it—Duncan was still in no shape for lugging bags—and the young man proved to be useful in other ways as well, full of information and advice. They would need to hurry to reach the *campo* by four, he let them know, because after that, only the entrance at Via Giovanni Dupré would be open. If they didn't already have tickets to the race, he would help them to locate the local men, *palcaioli*, who managed the wooden seats around the square.

The young man led them down one of the streets that radiated from the city center and soon they reached the square, paved in red brick and fronted by a circle of red medieval buildings and a palace with a tower casting its long shadow. At the center of the square, a great mass of people stood together, hemmed in by barricades. The narrow band of exposed ground between the crowd and surrounding buildings formed the track where the racehorses would run, and around the outside of the ring stood wooden bleachers, already packed.

After a long search, Gina spotted two free seats and their guide negotiated over tickets with the older man who manned the bleachers. For a hefty price, the man gave them tickets, but insisted the suitcases took up too much room and would need to be removed. Their guide suggested they try the Hotel Duomo, which might keep their bags for a fee, and he and Duncan started off then, leaving Gina on her own to hold the seats.

The time was half past three, the heat of the day was intense, and the red brick of the square blazed under the summer sun. As Gina stood amid the noisy, jostling crowd, breathing in the smell of sweat and dirt, she began to feel her eyes ache and her dizziness return. The scene around her seemed overbright: the fans dressed in the sharp colors of each district, blue and red and green. It was all so theatrical—the waving flags and pageantry, the picture-perfect ancient square—and for a moment, she couldn't quite believe that this was real, that this could truly be her life now, this mad adventure she and Duncan had begun.

All that day she had been running, speeding toward this race that would mark only the start of one much longer and leading who knew where. None of it felt possible, nor would it, she realized then, until she'd shared the news with Duncan. She felt seized by a desire to tell him what she'd been too overwhelmed and nervous to admit to him before, this secret she'd been holding, which she now felt the urge to name.

It was their future she was carrying, their future child.

Twelve

Duncan // Siena

July 1996

It took some time before Duncan and the young guide reached their destination: an elegant three-story building painted a mint green, the Hotel Duomo. Inside, the lobby was teeming with people, some on chairs and others standing, all gathered around a television that had been set up to broadcast the race for those who lacked the inclination to get a seat on the square. The group chattered in Italian—locals, from the look of them, mostly older people who had likely seen the race dozens of times and didn't find it worth the risk of heatstroke to witness it live again.

Duncan walked past them and up to the man behind reception. He introduced himself, asked the man if he spoke English, and then inquired whether, for a price, he might leave his luggage in the hotel during the race.

"I'm afraid we only hold luggage for our guests, signore."

"Well, as it happens, my wife and I are also looking for a room."

The clerk sighed heavily. "And I'm also afraid rooms this week are booked ahead for months, signore."

"I see."

"Then, of course," the clerk continued, "private citizens do rent out rooms for a price to help tourists. I do know someone with a room, a neighbor, or I might, but sadly the police are against this practice. Understand I risk a fine, giving you this information."

"And how much would this fine be?" Duncan reached for his wallet, selecting a twenty-thousand-lira note before the man could summon a larger number.

The man accepted the bill and reached for his desk phone. "I'll call my neighbor now."

Duncan waited while the clerk negotiated with his neighbor in Italian and then announced that the cost of the room would be two hundred thousand lire—high, but not outrageous, and certainly worth it in these circumstances.

"And the room includes a meal, signore. You'll have trouble getting food any other way. The restaurants are booked like the hotels." The clerk paused to let Duncan take this in, and then handed him a slip of paper. "If I might just get your names then, signore. Yours and your wife's. I will copy from the passports, is fine."

Duncan handed over the passports, and after studying them the clerk looked up, surprised. "Gina Reinhold is your wife?"

The question caught him off guard. How could this man have heard of Gina? So much time had passed since Berlin, and he and Gina had come so far, that Duncan had felt safe enough to stop consulting the papers. If a story had run about them, if the search had widened, he might have missed it. "That name's familiar to you?"

"A man came in an hour before, asking after her. He said to call him if I see her."

"A man? What sort of man?"

"Maybe fifty years, with red hair, tall, American like you. He said his name was Reinhold too."

Duncan was trying to stay calm; this might be a mistake, another Reinhold or Reinhart or Reynolds. "Did he have a beard, by chance?"

"He did, signore, a short beard."

Duncan felt his face grow hot.

But could it really be? He tried to sort it out, how Mr. Reinhold could have discovered where they were and gotten here so quickly. Was it possible that Violet or Graham had discovered the travel agency by the hotel, then, after learning he and Gina were headed to Siena, that one of them had alerted Mr. Reinhold? Gina's impulsiveness he'd always attributed to her mother, but perhaps Mr. Reinhold had a streak in him too—would he not learn this news and immediately book a flight from Santa Fe that morning, cutting them off? It was also possible that Gina's father was already in Europe, on the hunt, and had flown here from Berlin or Zurich or wherever he'd picked up their trail. A feat like this would require immense coordination, which meant that if what he envisioned was in fact true, Gina's father was sparing no effort or expense to bring his daughter home.

"I should be getting back to my wife," said Duncan, thinking of Gina then, sitting in plain sight out on the campo. He was furious at himself for his complacency, for speaking of his plans so openly in front of the travel agent back in Prague and now for leaving Gina unattended. Thanking the clerk, he turned toward the door.

"Wait, signore? Don't you require the address where you'll be staying?"

"Yes, right, of course." He hurried back to take the slip of paper with the address.

"And what shall I tell this man if he comes back asking after Ms. Reinhold?"

Duncan paused at the desk, long enough to withdraw another twenty-thousand-lira note. "You might suggest he try some of the other hotels."

"Yes, very good, signore."

The clerk took the money, and Duncan removed another bill to offer the young guide, before parting ways with him and rushing off in the direction of the campo.

The beat of drums sounded in the distance. The parade must be underway. Duncan headed toward the noise, walking as quickly as he was able with the pain shooting through his ribs. On his way he passed a group of laughing men and women, smelling of alcohol and dressed in costume—one man had his face hidden behind a carnival mask. Soon after this, Duncan ducked inside a shop selling local paraphernalia and selected the mask closest to the one the other man had worn—Venetian style, with white and red and gold—then doubled back and picked another mask for Gina. Moving under cover from there on, he felt safer, but not safe. Police were everywhere, gathered to manage the crowds, and perhaps the authorities had been notified that Gina's kidnapper was here. For all he knew, his picture and Gina's had been circulated among the dozens of officers he passed.

At last Duncan came to one of the openings onto the square, but an officer stood barring the way.

Paranoid, even if masked, Duncan felt he had no choice but to find an unguarded entrance, so he stumbled along in pain and the heat, trying his luck at the various streets that radiated from the campo. Two officers blocked the next entrance, but at the third, whoever was on duty must have stepped away, and Duncan simply squeezed past the barricade and inside the square. It seemed no one had noticed him, but if police or anyone had seen him and yelled for him to stop, Duncan wouldn't have been able to hear them anyway above the drums and trumpets and the chanting crowd. The parade performers were ahead of him, men in blue and white medieval costume, followed by a cart driven by oxen. Duncan slipped in among them, emboldened by the mask, searching the bleachers for Gina.

Having come from a different entrance, he wasn't sure which way to go. Each side of the square looked the same and it took him some time, as he scurried along the edge of bleachers, lost in the din of the crowd, to position himself with regard to the clock tower and identify the right direction. The bleachers were packed and most of the people were standing, no doubt obscuring someone as small as Gina. As he proceeded, searching, the call of a trumpet stopped him. Seconds later, a charge of men on horseback thundered past, wielding swords. Duncan hugged the bleacher wall, the ground trembling underfoot. After the horses passed, a brief calm descended, and then came an explosion so thunderous and ground-shaking that it took Duncan a moment to still his nerves and realize from the atmosphere of hushed anticipation that the race was about to begin.

"Duncan!" He heard his name being called—not by Gina, as he'd hoped, but by a man. He turned to look in the direction of the shout, peering out at the crowd at the center of the square. A man stood writhing at the edge, pushing against the barricades, tall, red-haired, and bearded, looking so determined that Duncan was gripped by panic. Mr. Reinhold had seen him.

Was it possible? Duncan still wore his mask, but when he looked down at his shirt, he realized he'd worn one of the few he'd brought with him, a blue and green madras that Gina had bought him, and that Mr. Reinhold had once envied aloud.

Another explosion marked the start of the race, and ten horses went careening around the square, with brightly dressed jockeys clinging to their bridles. Duncan quickly jumped over the short wall that fronted the bleachers. His body radiated pain and he had to stop and catch his breath as people nearby grumbled at him. He turned back to watch the race just in time to see the first jockey fall, and men in white shirts and orange pants run to scoop him from the path of the other horses. Beyond, Duncan could make out Gina's father, watching him, bristling behind the barricade, waiting for the race to be over so he might leap across.

The race was only ninety seconds long; Duncan had no time to waste. He had to move, but couldn't think how it would be possible in the stubborn crowd. He began climbing, thinking that perhaps he might slip back behind the bleachers and find his way to Gina by walking underneath the seats. Moving upward, cursed and shoved by those he passed, he heard mounting cheers, and then a whinnying shriek followed by a collective gasp. When Duncan looked back at the track, he saw another jockey fallen from his horse, but this time a horse was down as well, and a second man lay on his stomach a few feet away.

The medics were already on the track attending to the injured as, on the far end of the campo, the winner was met by hoots and cheers. Holding his breath, Duncan watched two of the medics come to the man prone in the dirt and help him slowly to his feet. Duncan supposed he'd already guessed who the injured man must be, even before the figure was mostly upright, a head taller than the two medics who held him, his arms around their shoulders, his head bobbing.

Had Gina seen this? Her father trampled before her? The crowd had grown so rowdy now that Duncan had no hope of finding Gina until the square had cleared a little. He waited for people to begin descending from the bleachers, and finally, when the seats were half-emptied, he spotted Gina, standing still at the center of so much movement, remaining as he'd asked her to remain, in the precise spot where he'd left her.

He called her name and waved. As he approached her, she looked at him blankly, until he realized that he was still wearing his mask. He took it off and held it in his shaking hands.

"Are you all right?" he asked her, trying to glean from her expression what she might have seen. She seemed far too calm to have noticed her father, let alone that he'd been hurt. Looking back the way he'd come, Duncan could see the horse down on its side. From here, Gina would have been able to observe the fall, but not the details, not, he hoped, the faces of anyone involved.

"That was horrible," she said, clearly shaken, though the abstract way in which she said this confirmed for Duncan that she had not seen clearly who the wounded man happened to be.

He pulled her to him and held her, hoping she couldn't feel him trembling or sense his terror—Gina's father was here, and he was wounded, maybe grievously, because of him. It was too awful to keep from her, though if he told her, he knew this would be the end. All his hopes were collapsing. If he'd ever entertained the fantasy that one day Gina might finally forgive him for his lies, he knew that she would not forgive him what had happened on this day. So unsteadied was he by this realization that he was afraid he would trip as they climbed, side by side, across the bleachers. He recalled his injuries of the last day, his fever and his aches, and felt as if this new shock had made him ill again. When they reached the ground, he was sure it must be shaking still with the rush of hooves.

From the campo he stumbled on, borne along by the steady current of people that fed into the surrounding streets. He didn't bother giving Gina her mask, since the mood between them was too somber and he doubted anyone could spot them in the throng. For a time he simply followed the crowd without thinking, until Gina asked after the address of their lodgings, and Duncan withdrew the note he carried in his wallet.

"Via del Poggio," he read aloud.

"I think we've already passed it. We need to turn back."

They tried to do this, but going against the stream of people was impossible, so they were forced to wait until the flow had thinned enough for them to move against it.

Gina rang the bell of a simple brown brick house and they were greeted by their host, who introduced himself as Mauro. He was very large, with a big stomach, but a light way about him—someone, Duncan imagined, who'd gotten heavy only later in life.

"I expect for you," Mauro said, ushering them in and showing them to their room, which was on the small side but charming, with a window overlooking the street. Their luggage had just arrived, Mauro said, and pointed to the suitcases waiting in the corner.

"You're hungry now?" the man asked them. "My wife and I will make you dinner."

Duncan thanked him, and, after their host had left, explained to Gina what the clerk at the Hotel Duomo had told him—that all the restaurants would be booked and the city overwhelmed that night.

"Better to stay in," said Gina, "after all the traveling and heat and crowds. To be honest, my dizziness hasn't gone away and I think a calm night would be best."

Duncan gladly agreed, and after a shower and a change of clothes, they joined Mauro and his wife in the dining room. The meal was much too large: soup and pasta and fish, which Duncan ate slowly, occupied by his grim thoughts. Thankfully, Mauro distracted Gina with his chatter, only too pleased to make conversation with a pretty American girl.

"It's a pity my son can't be here to meet you. He lives in Rome now, or he did. Last month he left to Barcelona, chasing a Spanish girl. Who can know if he'll return?"

"Love has no respect for borders," said Gina.

"And no respect for fathers and their wallets," Mauro went on lamenting. "I am the one to lend him this apartment, and now it just sits there, empty. He doesn't pay even for maintenance."

"You ought to rent it out to tourists, then," Gina advised.

Mauro's eyes widened. "For the maintenance price *you* two could use this if you plan to visit Rome."

"Oh, I hadn't—" Gina looked to Duncan then, expectant, and he had to rouse himself to listen. "What do you say to heading to Rome next?"

"Why not?" He smiled at her as well as he was able, though the image he kept with him barred the way to thoughts of Rome or Paris or New York, or of any future anywhere. He was still seeing the awful scene on the campo, Frank Reinhold, forehead bloodied, that strong man dragged between the medics like a sack.

The image refused to leave him, was with Duncan still, even later that night, in bed, where he knew better than to hope for sleep to visit him. He couldn't keep the questions from coming.

Where was Mr. Reinhold now? How badly off was he? People died from accidents with horses—and if he had died?

Only a villain could go on by Gina's side without knowing if her sole remaining parent had been lost because of him.

Several times now on their trip, he'd snuck out in the middle of the night while Gina was asleep, but this time was surely the most dangerous. Tiptoeing downstairs, he'd been surprised to find Mauro awake so late, and told his host he was merely taking a walk, as he stepped out with the map from his guidebook to lead him to the hospital. The unfamiliar streets were mazelike and unsettling, populated by wandering drunks and lit only by dim lanterns. It seemed a miracle when he reached the limit of the old city and found a taxi waiting.

"Azienda Ospedaliera," he instructed the driver. "Viale Mario Bracci."

"Fifty thousand lire," the driver demanded; Duncan informed him he had only thirty.

They reached an agreement, though Duncan sensed he was still being overcharged, and worried how he'd manage to get back if he spent all his money now. He quickly dismissed the concern, unsure whether he ever *would* be getting back. There was so much that could go wrong. Gina's father might not be alone. If he and Graham were united in their search for Gina, Graham might be with him. Perhaps they'd brought police along and Duncan might be caught. As he approached the hospital, he understood that walking in might mean he'd never leave this building freely, and yet he rode on, in the vague hope that somehow matters would turn out all right.

The hospital was plain and modern. The line for reception

stretched nearly to the door, teeming with visitors, and every seat in the waiting area was filled. Duncan had a hard time getting anyone's attention, even after he'd waited his turn for half an hour.

"Does anyone speak English? I'm here to inquire about Franklin Reinhold. He was hurt in the race."

"Non capisco," said the nurses, until an older nurse who'd been standing off a ways took notice of him.

"Who you are, then?"

"Frank Reinhold's son-in-law."

Duncan received no response. Instead, the older nurse muttered something to the others in Italian. *"L'Americano dalla corsa di cavalli."*

As the nurses chatted, Duncan tried to gather whether he was their subject—*That's the one responsible, the criminal!*—and he began to fear he'd been reckless to admit who he was, though after a few minutes of being ignored, it seemed that he was less a wanted man than one who'd been forgotten.

"Excuse me?" Duncan asked tentatively.

"Reinhold, trecentoquarantatre," said one nurse, and, seeing Duncan's confusion, scribbled the room number onto a piece of paper.

In the elevator riding up, Duncan braced himself for what might be awaiting him. Outside the room he paused to peer through the pane of glass, relieved to see no visitors, no activity inside. The room contained three beds, though he couldn't tell which belonged to Gina's father until he stepped in and saw Mr. Reinhold in the center bed, asleep. The man was hooked by monitors to a machine that beeped beside him, and a feeding tube was in his arm. In the eerie glow of the fluorescents, his skin looked yellow, waxy, deathlike.

Duncan had entertained the thought before that Gina's father might not survive, but as a sort of experiment, daring himself to imagine the worst—only now did it strike him as a real possibility.

As Duncan drew closer to him, Mr. Reinhold began to stir. His sleep was light, or else he'd merely been resting, because abruptly, the man's eyes opened and fixed on Duncan, shining with greater fire than it seemed that battered body could contain.

"That was *you*, in the mask." Mr. Reinhold addressed him, neither surprised nor frightened to see Duncan suddenly appear. For a moment, Duncan feared the man would shout for an orderly or the police, but the way Reinhold slurred and blinked his bloodshot eyes let Duncan know that he was fighting through a fog of medication. Possibly Reinhold wasn't sure whether this meeting was more than a hallucination.

Mr. Reinhold's focus remained squarely on Duncan, as Duncan searched for what to say. "I hope you know how sorry I am that you got hurt." He'd have gone on, but Mr. Reinhold appeared not to be listening, was craning his neck to see out of the room.

"You're here by yourself?" There was sadness in his face when he said it, as if in order to proceed he had to overcome the wish—as improbable as he knew it to be—that Gina had come too, and he would finally be reunited with his daughter.

"Yes, it's just me. Gina's fine, don't worry. But you understand I had to leave her back at our room."

"You're asking me to . . . *understand?*" Mr. Reinhold was struggling to sit up straighter in bed, but the pain of it led him to collapse back down again.

"I only mean that I wish Gina could see you, that there were some way for all of us to accept—"

"Accept that you've stolen her? Is that what you're . . . what you're hoping I'll do?"

The words were labored, and Reinhold's lids drooped, so that Duncan came to feel discussion was impossible. Even if the man calmed down and they made headway, anything that passed between them would likely be forgotten.

"This might not be the right time to explain myself—"

"I ought to wring your neck!" Reinhold bellowed, with such sudden fierceness that Duncan was taken aback. He could see in the man's raving expression that he was not under control, that his judgment had been overthrown by medication, pain, and shock. "I should have gotten rid of you the first time you tried to take her from me!"

"I didn't try to take her from you," Duncan replied calmly, hoping to bring him back to reason a little. "It was Gina's decision to come home to New York."

"New York wasn't her home! She was lost there and you just about wrecked her." Mr. Reinhold struggled to breathe. "She came running back to me in pieces. And then you had the nerve to show up at my house to try to tempt her away from me again!"

The man was speaking from a very different place than he had then, thought Duncan, on that day in Santa Fe when he'd stood on his lawn, surrounded by flowering cacti and bougainvillea, sounding like the responsible and evenhanded father, the caretaker with only his daughter's best interests at heart. A different man showed himself to Duncan now, almost barbarous as he went on, rasping, spittle forming on his dry, cracked lips.

"You think you've got her this time, but don't delude yourself. Once she knows the truth she'll drop you and come back home with me again. Graham told me what the doctors in Berlin had to say. She clearly doesn't understand what's happened, what a sick bastard you are. But I know, and I'll see to it you end up rotting in a jail cell, wishing you'd never dared to take her. I'll see to it that you do!"

Mr. Reinhold's face was red: Duncan could see a vein bulging in his forehead, the cords straining in his neck. Hatred was coming off of him like heat, and Duncan could find no words to calm him. He must have been startled by the man's rage, because only now did it occur to Duncan that their heated exchange had attracted attention. An orderly came charging in, addressing Duncan roughly in Italian. Security might be arriving any instant. Without a word, Duncan dashed past the orderly and out the door, pain bolting through him as he raced through the hall, voices shouting in Italian behind him. Bounding down the stairwell, his ribs throbbing, he burst into the lobby, where a pair of revolving doors was all that stood between him and freedom.

The walk back to the apartment took hours longer than the trip by taxi, punctuated by breaks to recuperate from pain. The way was dark, the street names hard to see, and twice Duncan became lost, absorbed in his distress.

It had been frightening, and pitiful, to see Gina's father in this state, the wishes hidden away in his heart laid so bare. In all the years he'd grumbled over Gina's father, suspecting the man might be against him in some way, he'd always assumed that their rivalry was of the common sort. Even as he'd lied to Gina, mere days ago, inventing an argument between Gina and her father, it hadn't occurred to him that the reality was worse than he'd imagined. He'd pretended Gina's father had wished to keep her, and now it appeared that was the truth. Their conversation had left him dazed, in part because the man's condemnation of him had landed hard, but also because the same accusations could be made of Reinhold too. All along, this man who appeared to want his daughter to live as a free spirit hadn't, in his heart, wanted her free. What Mr. Reinhold wanted—profoundly, perversely, maybe even more so than Duncan—was to keep Gina for himself. And so it seemed to Duncan that, through his selfish act, he might also have rescued Gina from a kind of confinement he hadn't even known she'd faced.

By the time Duncan arrived at Mauro's house, the night sky was turning blue. He came in silently and climbed the stairs to find Gina asleep in bed. Lying beside her, exhausted, achy, soulsick, he had the wish to take her in his arms, to protect her from all the forces, even those within him, that aimed to keep her bound.

But if this was really how he felt, and if he loved her the way he believed he did, he must tell her, immediately, what he'd done to make her his again. He must allow her, in full knowledge of the facts and with full freedom, to decide if she wanted him or not.

There in the brightening room where Gina lay peacefully sleeping, he reached out to tap her shoulder. She rolled over, opened her eyes, and looked straight at him, the way her father had done just hours before. He was afraid of what she was seeing, but lacked the composure then to pull himself together, to smile and fake the way he had been. He was convinced that Gina must know something was wrong, and yet the expression on her face was pure lightness, a kind of radiance he was startled by, transfixed. In that moment, as he was about to confess, Gina spoke first, silencing him with her two brief words.

"I'm pregnant."

Thirteen

Gina // Siena, Rome

July 1996

In the moments after she'd made her wonderful and frightful admission, she'd awaited Duncan's reaction, but had been met only with silence. He'd been stunned, and then, when he'd come back to himself a little, he'd kissed her and held her while they lay in bed, still speechless, as the sun brightened the shades over their window. After they'd risen, while they dressed, he finally began to talk, though what he had to say had nothing to do with his feelings, as she'd hoped. He expressed concern over the practical side of things. She ought to be seen by a doctor. There were tests that should be run, supplements she should be taking.

"I'm thinking in that case," Duncan went on, "we definitely ought to leave Siena and head to Rome."

"So soon? They do have hospitals here too."

"Small facilities that are bound to be swamped right now. No, no. We won't take a chance on that." His tone was firm. "You'll need a doctor who speaks English, which you're bound to find some-where like Rome. Didn't Mauro offer his apartment last night?"

She was taken aback by the speed with which Duncan hatched this plan. "Yes, but he'd had a few glasses of wine. We can't be sure he meant it."

"So let's ask him." Eager to have the matter settled, Duncan pulled on his shirt and headed downstairs. After she'd also finished dressing, Gina caught up with him and Mauro in the kitchen, where Mauro was fixing their breakfast.

"He thinks Rome's a great idea," Duncan began.

Mauro picked up from there. "We'd love to keep you here with us, but truly Siena's not very nice now—too many tourists. And you can always come here again to visit. Only three hours on the train." As he spoke excitedly, Mauro fished through the kitchen drawers, pulling out a pair of keys. "For you, take these. The apartment is very pleasing. I can make you a promise you'll enjoy it."

"And are you sure paying maintenance is enough?" she asked him, though neither Duncan nor Mauro seemed especially concerned over the price.

"Enough, yes. Only look after it a little. I love this flat. I lived in it myself as a young man." Mauro paused, long-lashed eyes flashing, and Gina could see in the jolly old flirt the handsome youth who'd moved from adventure to adventure in that city. It might have been Mauro's nostalgia for his time there that stirred up longing in her too.

"Well, all right, then. I guess we'll be heading on to Rome."

Duncan reached for her and squeezed her. "Mauro says there's an eleven thirty train. If we're quick we can still catch it."

Once they were up in their room again, Duncan set about packing, hurrying around, tossing items into the suitcase, all the while focused on the tasks they would now be required to perform—they'd need to get more lire to pay for the room and for the taxi, then in Rome he'd call the hospital and see about scheduling an appointment. Gina watched him, struck by his busyness, and by what, through this sudden move, he was avoiding discussing. Since she'd made her big announcement, he'd still said nothing of his feelings.

Of course there was so much she wished to ask him. It terrified her not to know if this child she wanted dearly filled Duncan with joy or dread. But as much as she'd have liked to prod him, she told herself she must give him space at first to sort out his reactions, and so she resolved to spend the day not speaking of the pregnancy at all, if it came to that.

Around ten, they left Mauro's apartment and walked together with their luggage to a stand where they might find a taxi. There, they parted ways with their host, taking the keys to the apartment and a card with Mauro's number.

"Divertitevi a Roma!" Mauro shouted, waving, as the car backed out jerkily and raced up the steep road.

For three hours, they rode together through the Tuscan countryside, surrounded by patches of cultivated green, olive and cypress trees, vineyards. The day was perfect, blue sky and fleecy clouds, and from her first sight of Rome through the train windows, Gina found it incomparably lovely, belonging to some more perfect future, some life she now felt she was meant to lead. She gasped aloud, from a combination of excitement and fear, and finally had to stand and walk the aisles of the train to discharge the nervous energy inside her.

Mauro's apartment was on Via Mazzarino, in Rione Monti. The address turned out to be near the train station and very central too, roughly equidistant from the Trevi Fountain and the Roman

Forum. The street itself was quiet, with residential buildings no more than five or six stories high, and the occasional small restaurant with umbrellas and chalkboard signs out on the pavement.

They followed the street numbers to a great wooden door that opened with their largest key. Inside was a vestibule leading to an elevator and stairs. The small space was presided over by a very large statue, a male nude, as if sculptures of high quality were so abundant in Rome that they might be placed at the entrance of even minor buildings. The apartment itself was charming, with fans hanging from high ceilings, wooden floors, and a balcony off of the living room. To Duncan's delight, a small piano stood between the living and dining areas, and on the widest wall, across, stood a giant canvas containing a detailed portrait of a woman's face.

Gina stood observing her, this woman with a quiet smile, while Duncan phoned the hospital and returned to announce they would be seen if they could get there right away. There wasn't time to settle in, therefore, as much as Gina would have liked to, and, just minutes after they'd arrived, they were heading back to the Metro to ride to Tor Sapienza in the Municipio 4.

There, at Rome American Hospital, Gina was examined by a young obstetrician, a woman who'd been born to American parents and who narrated for her, in perfect English, the meaning of the image that Gina saw during her ultrasound. Duncan stood beside her in the room, holding her hand and kissing it to calm the nerves that wouldn't leave her until the doctor had told her several times that all looked well and the pregnancy was advancing normally.

"And how far along is it, can you say?" Duncan asked, while Gina turned to look at the wall.

"Hard to be precise about these things, but I'd guess under six weeks."

When Gina turned to face him, Duncan was nodding, relieved.

"A citizen of Europe," Gina piped in brightly, and shortly after, she and Duncan made an appointment to return in three weeks' time, which implied that they would still be there in Rome, a declaration, in effect, of their intention to settle, for a while at least.

That evening, back at their new apartment, they set about unpacking, and Gina had the sensation that now, after so many weeks spent in hotels, they'd arrived at a kind of home. The portrait of the woman overlooked them, and Gina wondered aloud to Duncan who she might be. "Mauro's first love? A daughter?"

"Our guardian angel," Duncan proposed, kissing her cheek, and at last she could see in him the delight she'd been awaiting.

Was it possible Duncan wanted what she wanted? That image she'd carried for so long, of the three of them, her and Duncan and their child, starting a home together—might it be here? In this city that had entranced her already?

Over the next days she and Duncan seemed genuinely happy, and she began to trust that he was as quietly pleased at the prospect of this new future as she needed him to be. Now and then she'd notice him smiling a boyish smile that wouldn't leave him, that reminded her of their earliest days together, back in school, when she'd catch him trying to conceal the grins that would suddenly overtake him.

They fell easily into a cheerful routine. In the morning, they ate their breakfast out on the balcony, then spent the early part of the day exploring the city. In the afternoon, when the heat was too great to be outside, Gina read and Duncan sat at his desk with his composition sheets or played the piano. He'd decided to try to get back to composing, since in Rome they were finally in no hurry, and conditions were calm enough for him to concentrate again. To get his mind back on his music, Gina bought them tickets to a performance at the Accademia Nazionale di Santa Cecilia, one of the oldest conservatories in all Europe.

The next day, she and Duncan took the train to Vatican City to visit St. Peter's Basilica. She'd been overwhelmed when she'd entered, and had to look down at the floor to get her bearings. The church was far larger than she'd imagined, dizzyingly so, and every foot of it contained such an abundance of artistry. In the past, beautiful things would often make her sad. They seemed to belong to the more beauteous realm of her childhood, and so recalled her loss. Here in Rome, though, her reaction was different. She felt instead a stirring hope that she might live beautifully again. They would both be better here, she and Duncan, away from the reminders of their former, lesser selves, now that Duncan had let go his fear and inhibition and she'd thrown off her own uncertainty about his readiness. Standing inside the basilica was like awakening to the fully alive existence she'd longed for since her childhood had ended.

She began to fantasize about a future there in Rome, and images came to her, solid and persuasive: of her pushing a stroller along the local streets to pick up Duncan from rehearsal; her coming to see him perform inside a grand concert hall, like the one at the Accademia Nazionale.

One morning, while Duncan sat down to compose at the small piano, she took a walk to the Accademia—the ancient and elegant stone building joined by modern structures, performance halls that, from the outside, resembled enormous silver disks. The grounds were otherworldly, the students passionate and serious, so much like Duncan, when she'd first seen him, that she knew he belonged here. She found her way to the admissions office and there spoke with a woman on the staff about the requirements: there was an application, and then an audition in the fall. The greatest obstacle to Duncan being accepted to the program was the language. He would need to be proficient in Italian. Gina collected the application materials and carried them home to give to Duncan.

His initial reaction was disbelief.

"You mean for me to apply? For us to stay in Rome. You're serious?"

"And why not?"

"We'd need money, for one thing."

"And we have it." He was perfectly aware that she had several hundred thousand left from her mother, which, if they took care, might last them as much as a decade. "And we can work here too, why not? You can give piano lessons. I can teach and, eventually, after the baby, start dancing again. We can compose, create new work, do everything that we did in New York before."

"Could you really go on this way?" he asked her, finally. "You wouldn't miss home?"

Even as the events of the past came to her more clearly each day, she by now felt so removed from her own history. At the least, she felt strangely little pull to return. Her colleagues in New York were getting on just fine without her. None of her other friendships rivaled what she had with Violet, and Violet was no longer there. The only person she would miss and who would suffer her absence, deeply, was her father. "There's just my dad, and he's across the country as it is. Plus, we're not on good terms, you say. That I've been wanting distance from him."

"Right, yes." Duncan spoke a bit too firmly, a bit too fast, but before she could press him further, he continued. "All I'm saying is, moving abroad is a big step. It can be lonely. I mean, I'm for it, I think *I* could do it. I don't need more than you. But I'm not sure that in your case it's the same."

In fact the prospect of such isolation did make her skittish, but she took pains not to show it. She could see the anxiety in Duncan's expression, the need in him to believe that she was equally content with only him, and would continue to be so, without end. "It won't just be you and me anymore," she pointed out. "You, me, *and* our child. I can't think how I'd need more than that."

Duncan reached for her and held her, apparently persuaded. Already the next morning, she'd found him at his desk, working on his conservatory application. She went off on her own then, to visit the Pantheon at the Piazza della Rotonda, a lovely square with the temple looming at one end. She'd been struck to see such an ancient building built on so grand a scale: columns as thick as five men standing side by side. Inside, a giant dome opened up onto the heavens. It was fantastical, really, to think that she might go on living in a place where a ten-minute walk brought her to a Roman temple, or to the Trevi Fountain, or to Trajan's Forum. So many wonders all around her, she might have gone on to see more, but she was feeling how her energy was fading and a small cramp was forming in her belly. She bought a bottle of cold water and walked slowly back to the apartment, where she found Duncan at the desk beside the balcony, so caught up by something he hadn't heard her come in.

She crossed the floor, wondering if he might be in the grips of a musical idea—but no, he was on the phone.

He wasn't speaking, only seated, his head leaning on one hand. His leg bounced tensely, and the phone cord was tangled around his forearm. When he saw her, he swiveled to face her and assumed a more neutral expression, but she had seen, in the instant that preceded, a look of despair. In her panic, she ran through the possibilities regarding what he might have heard. Could the hospital have phoned? Could there be a problem with her? With the baby?

"What? What is it? Was that the doctor?"

"The doctor? No, no." He set down the phone and rose to kiss her. "Don't worry. Nothing like that." Yet his face betrayed his distress.

"Something upset you."

He raised his hand to his forehead, massaging it, making the skin fold and straighten beneath his fingertips. "I didn't want to bother you about it, really. But . . . it's my mother, if you need to know." Reluctantly, he admitted that he'd phoned in for their messages. "She's taking it badly, my being away. Though I couldn't have expected any other reaction. But it doesn't change anything. The only place I want to be is here with you."

He sat down and pulled Gina onto his lap. As he held her, silent, gripping her tightly, she could feel him taking solace from her. She didn't assume that what he'd told her was the truth—it might be—but whatever he'd heard over the phone must have left him shaken.

"And was that all of it, then?" she asked him.

"All of it?"

"There weren't any messages for me?" She was pressing him a little, could feel him squirm beneath her.

"No, this time there weren't."

"This time? Were there other calls for me before?"

"No," he hurried to say, his tone hardly convincing. "People know we're away. There wouldn't be any reason to call."

"You're sure you're not protecting me from something? Maybe something unpleasant from my father?"

Duncan looked struck. Abruptly he stood, pushing her off of his lap, and began to pace the room. "I guess I can't blame you for being suspicious, since I wasn't straight with you before. But I wish I had your trust back."

"Relax, Duncan, you do." She smiled, choosing to relent, to put him at ease again. There was no point in pressuring him this way. She dropped the subject of her father after that, though privately she did find herself thinking of him, feeling that she couldn't let him go on without some reassurance. Eventually she'd have to tell him of her plans to stay abroad. She didn't inform Duncan of her intention to call home—he'd only object, and anyway, she didn't require his permission. The next day, she first tried her father from a pay phone in the Galleria Borghese, where she'd gone while Duncan stayed behind, composing, in their apartment. Having gotten no answer, she tried again the next morning when Duncan ran out for milk. Again, after four rings, her father's recorded voice came onto the line: *"You've reached Frank Reinhold. . . ."*

That morning she chose to leave a message. *"Dad, it's me. I'm sorry for not calling sooner. I should have, I realize. It's all been complicated, but you should know that I'm fine, really better than fine. I sent you a letter, though I'm not sure you received it. I hope you're all right. I've tried to reach you several times now and, well, I'm starting to get nervous. I'll try you again soon. Hope you get this. I love you."*

In bed, later that night, she found herself thinking back on a painting she'd seen in St. Peter's Basilica, a work by Raphael: Lot's wife turning to look at Sodom, burning, as she fled. There the woman stood, frozen, a pillar of salt, unable to move on with her family. This seemed to her a warning. Don't look back. Don't cry salt tears when you've been saved. She and Duncan were going to start a family together, an exciting new life in a great city, and he seemed so contented with this that he'd put his own concerns behind him. She'd heard nothing more about calls from his mother; he'd expressed no further doubts about continuing on as they had been. In the last week, Duncan had completed his application to the Accademia and contacted an Italian language school that ran through the summer—he'd missed three weeks, but if he hired a tutor to help him catch up, and with his background in French, the teacher was confident he'd manage.

Duncan was moving forward; she ought to do the same, and yet she couldn't get over her worries—especially regarding her father. Where was he?

It crossed her mind, rather darkly, that there was only one person who would know if her father was okay.

She waited before she made her move, knowing she'd be setting in motion something that would not easily be stopped. There would be consequences, and so for several days, she carried the number with her in her purse and periodically removed it, had a look, considered, then put it away again. It was a risky thing that she was doing, and on the morning that she resolved to act, she'd been up for the whole night, standing and circling the bed, unable to stop moving. Finally, at eight that morning, when Duncan went in to register for his Italian lessons, Gina withdrew the slip of paper and dialed the number she'd been given over the phone in Vienna, by the clerk at the Hotel de Rome—the number for Graham Bonafair.

Fourteen

Duncan // Rome

August 1996

O*n Fridays,* Duncan and his fellow Italian students were let out early and would go walking together across the balcony that overlooked the courtyard, down the stone steps through the gate onto the sidewalk. The Italian course was run out of a small grammar school on Via Del Vaccaro, a lovely little cobblestone street with a passageway forming an arch between the buildings. There were several restaurants in the area, and on this afternoon, the students were proposing they go for lunch together.

"Can't, I'm sorry," Duncan told them, already backing away. But today his classmates were determined.

"Perchè no?"

"Come on, it's early."

"Who will mind if you stay longer?"

"Mia moglie," Duncan answered, making use of the phrase he'd learned that week: "my wife." This was the first time Duncan had pronounced the words, the first time among his

classmates that he'd acknowledged having a wife. It seemed a mistake as soon as he said it. He was, perhaps, growing too relaxed in Rome.

"You're married?" asked a Welsh girl with huge, pale eyes. He'd taken off his ring for class so as not to prompt questions about Gina. "We all just assumed you went home and sat in your apartment alone."

He laughed at himself, and even thought he managed to blush like the shy sort they took him for. During lunch break, when the others gathered in the courtyard, he'd go off to eat his sandwich and write letters on a bench. He liked his classmates well enough, but he didn't think it prudent to let them get too close. Whenever the class exercises involved answering personal questions— *Where do you come from? What brought you to Rome?*—he chose to make up stories. In the course of that week, he'd invented a whole fictional account of his previous life in Michigan, son of a factory worker and a nurse of Italian descent who'd aroused his curiosity about this country. He'd even chosen to go by his middle name, Maxwell, or Max. No one knew him as Duncan, and since he'd begun growing a beard, soon it would be hard for any new acquaintance to be sure that the Duncan Lowy of his old photos, were they to surface, was him.

"Max has a wife," the Welsh girl spread the word to the Spaniard. "He's just full of surprises, isn't he?"

"Is she for real, then?"

"She is, and she hates it when I'm late." He was in a hurry to leave, suddenly. He'd made a mistake admitting he was married. That might cause trouble for him in the future.

"Why don't you bring her back here? She can join us for lunch too!"

"Sorry, but she's even more of an introvert than me. Anyway, I've gotta run. Good weekend to you all. *Ciao!*"

Finally, he managed to jog off. He couldn't allow Gina to mix with these students, and now he'd have to keep making excuses for her absence. The unnecessary complication bothered him, but after he'd walked for a few minutes, his irritation faded. In general, he found it hard to be annoyed in Rome; everything was just too lovely. The light here was so vibrant, the streets so charming—paradise seemed to lie around each corner. Just then he was passing by a row of pretty ivy-covered houses on his left, and on his right a grocery selling pyramids of brightly colored fruit. He bought some yellow plums to eat on his way and couldn't recall, back in the States, ever tasting fruit so sweet.

Pleasure like this had its costs, he thought, and one cost of remaining in Rome would be holding himself aloof from people. As much as he might prefer to settle in, make friends, live a normal life here with Gina, he knew he couldn't take the risk. Not since he'd learned how much more was at stake. Gina was pregnant. The pressure upon him was twice as great now. An innocent soul hung in the balance. He must remain under the radar as long as there was still a chance that a story about him might run in the paper or crop up on TV, still a chance that the hunt for him might reach from Siena to Rome. If the past weeks had taught him anything, it was not to underestimate Mr. Reinhold's resolve.

He reached the flat around twelve thirty and found that Gina wasn't home. He'd assumed as much, that on a nice day like this one, Gina would be out sightseeing for several hours and he'd have use of the apartment to attend to his own dealings.

His first order of business this afternoon was to call in to his home answering machine. Lately he'd been checking in as often as he could, ever since the shock he'd suffered when, after a lapse, he'd listened to his messages during his second week in Rome.

One after another, everyone who'd played a part in his previous life—his employer at the dance studio, his landlord, Blake, his father—all of them had called him in a panic:

"Duncan, I've just gotten the most insane phone call about you. . . ." "Duncan, Gina's father called me. . . ." "Duncan, what's going on?"

He'd felt the breath leave him, though he'd tried to remain calm, to tell himself that such a moment was inevitable and must be faced. Stoically, he'd listened until he'd come to the recording from his mother.

"My God, God help me, what have you done? Is it true? Gina's father called from Italy. He says he's gone off searching for you. That you've taken Gina hostage; he says she's not well and that you've used her weakness to turn her into your prisoner. Her father even believes that you hurt Gina yourself. He's asked me to urge you to turn yourself in. He tells me if you don't, he won't be able to protect you from a prison sentence, which you'll have to serve in Berlin, where I can never see you. My God, Duncan, this is a nightmare! I think I must be going mad!"

His mother sobbed into the line, so that Duncan felt his insides plummet as he listened. This was worse than he'd imagined. Though he'd recognized something like this might happen— Graham had reached out to his mother, so Frank Reinhold might do the same—he'd assumed more care would be taken with an old woman who was innocent in all of this. Apparently Mr. Reinhold had spared her nothing, had been perfectly willing to inflict suffering if some part of that suffering would stir Duncan to experience anguish of his own, and anguish that Mr. Reinhold must have felt Duncan had caused him. His anger at Gina's father allowed for some relief of his own guilt. He wouldn't have been forced to do this thing if Reinhold hadn't kept Gina from him and made her a prisoner himself. And so he must resist manipulation, survive the man's crueler tactics, or else Gina's father would disrupt his peace so greatly that, if Duncan didn't simply cave, he would make some fateful mistake.

He'd called his mother later that night, while Gina was asleep.

"Mom, I swear, what that man says, it isn't true. Gina and I are back together, yes, but very much willingly. We've reconciled. And she isn't sick. The one who's sick is Gina's father. He's so enraged to have lost her to me, he'll say anything to bring her back to him."

"Duncan, are you sure? I wish I could believe you, but he's got lawyers, police."

"He's got nothing but lies and the money to back them up. He's trying to hurt you to get to me, Mom. That's what this is. Please, please listen to me. Please believe me and not that man and the stories that he'll tell you. I'm not in danger, nor is Gina. We're both happy—except that I can't be happy if I think that you're upset."

He was persuading her, he sensed, and supposed this gave him courage to press on. Or else perhaps what gave him courage was the rage he felt toward Gina's father. A spirit of defiance rose up in him, which wiped away all hesitations, the stickiness left by his guilt. His resolve was redoubled. Gina would remain with him.

"There's something more you need to know, Mom." He swallowed. "There's a chance that Gina and I won't return."

"What do you mean you won't *return?* To New York?"

"To America."

"For how long?"

"I don't know."

"You don't mean ever?"

"I guess. I don't know what I mean." He could hear the nervous strain enter his voice, and could feel the small part of him that wished to come to his mother like a child would, tell her he'd gotten in over his head and needed help. Instead, he quickly shored up his resolve. "It's possible that I'll live here. For a while, at any rate. But it will be fine."

"Live where? Where on earth are you, Duncan?"

"I'm where I should be—with Gina."

"Duncan, that girl is not the only person that matters, not the only person who loves you and deserves a place in your life. You can't just shut us out," his mother insisted, her voice becoming shrill. "Your father and I need to have a way to reach you. To get in touch."

"I promise I'll write you soon and explain more. Until then, please don't worry about me and I won't worry about you. You can handle this. We both can."

He hung up the phone, briefly relieved, but knowing this would not be the end. Every day he called in to his messages again, awaiting another from her, a next breakdown, some threat or tug upon his conscience. None came. Not from his mother, nor from the others he'd responded to with letters. The letters he'd sent out to his acquaintances offered much the same explanation: he and Gina had gone off together, and her father, unable to accept the fact, too possessive to let his daughter go, had spun a wild narrative to try to stop them. He'd written all these letters in the course of the week, during his lunch breaks at school, every letter except the one to Blake. Blake, he knew, would require a different argument.

Blake, he'd written finally, *I apologize for failing to call you and for the fact that I can't agree to meet. At the moment, a meeting would be too risky for me, for reasons I bet you can guess yourself. I can't be sure Gina's father wouldn't send someone to follow you, or that you wouldn't allow it, out of a sense of loyalty to me, and a conviction that you're saving me from making a huge mistake. I know you mean well, and so I hope you know that my failure to trust you isn't an insult. If at some point I think you've come around on this, I'll be glad to see you again. For now, all I can say is that I'm wishing you the best, and I hope you can find your way to wishing that for me—even if for me, that means being with Gina.*

When he'd read his letter over, he couldn't say that he expected Blake would be convinced. Nevertheless, it was the best he could come up with, and he'd chosen to send it, several days before, in lieu of no response at all.

Now, having skipped lunch with his classmates, Duncan was famished, so he stepped out to the corner store and bought some bread, cheese, tomatoes, and cured ham, along with a newspaper to keep him busy until Gina returned. Upstairs again, he ate his lunch as he read the major stories: the Summer Olympics had ended and America had taken gold in the decathlon and set records in the two-hundred-meter race. Meanwhile, in politics, Bob Dole had picked Jack Kemp as his vice presidential running mate. Duncan had nearly forgotten the election coming up in November. These stories of America felt so disconnected from him now.

Bored by the paper, he looked up at the clock. The time was half past three, around when he came home from a regular class day, and typically, Gina was back before he was. He put on music to relax him, and then, feeling sleepy, chose to lie down. Without intending to, he fell asleep, and when he woke again, the time was half past four.

It wasn't like Gina to be gone this long. If she knew she was going to be late, she'd have left a note or called. He checked the phone, making sure it was on its base, and then he went across the hall to ask the neighbor on their floor if he'd seen Gina at all that day or knew where she had gone. When the neighbor said he hadn't, Duncan made another quick trip to the small grocery on the corner, the same one where he'd bought lunch. "Have you seen *mia moglie*?"

"*Non l'ho vista da ieri.*" Not since yesterday, said the old woman at the counter. Duncan thanked her and hurried home, fearing that it would be in the time when he was gone that Gina would try to call. On his way up the stairs, he kept hoping to hear ringing. No one called, though, not then and not in the course of the next hour, as Duncan paced the apartment, by then unable to distract himself from thoughts of what might be wrong.

Another accident was possible—he returned to the horror of that afternoon spent in Berlin, in the lobby of the Hotel de Rome. He remembered that feeling of despair on the ride over to the hospital, of preparing himself for the realization that he'd lost her utterly, that Gina was gone. If he hadn't suffered such a shock then, if he hadn't felt the bareness of his life without her, he wasn't sure he'd have been able to do what he'd done next, pretend she'd never left him, cling to her through his elaborate lie.

And what if today was the day, he thought, that Gina had uncovered the lie? What if today a missing part of her memory was magically restored and she'd realized how her love and trust had been abused? Or what if the day he'd been fearing most had arrived? Mr. Reinhold had found his daughter. Duncan recalled now a particular morning when he'd woken early and stepped out to find Gina in the living room, holding the phone. He hadn't heard her speaking, and she'd hung up as soon as she'd spotted him.

"A wrong number," she offered. "I guess it woke you too?"

He'd shrugged, truly uncertain what had happened, only now the meaning of that small event shone clearly. She'd been on the phone with her father, plotting her escape.

His imagination was running wild. He tried to contain it, to convince himself that all that had happened was that Gina had lost track of time in a museum or gone to see a movie in a theater she'd walked by on her way home. There were a dozen stories more plausible than Gina's father tracking her down, and yet he couldn't stop himself from speculating how this could have happened.

Had Mauro led Gina's father to them? Duncan had been aware this was a danger as soon as he'd proposed they stay in this apartment—for the first time, someone from their previous destination knew the precise address where they'd gone next.

He'd been a fool to stay put for so long. He'd let his fantasies overcome his reason, and as a result, he'd lost Gina, maybe forever. She was gone and there was nothing he could do! He couldn't call the police. Gina hadn't been absent long enough to raise alarms and, even if she had been, he couldn't show up at the station and insist a woman already reported missing, who might be on file as having been kidnapped by him, was now missing from him. His hands were tied: he was stuck and would remain stuck. Gina's father would deliberately keep him in the dark, as Duncan had done to him. So days would pass with Gina gone and his not knowing if she was alive and well, if she still loved him or hated him, what would become of their infant. Until his not knowing would make him so crazy he'd bring himself to the police, and there be arrested and receive his due.

Five thirty and still Gina hadn't returned. Duncan was by then seated with an open bottle of wine, half empty. In the background, he played the local news on the rare chance that whatever had become of Gina was being covered in the press. As unlikely as he knew it to be, he kept imagining her face or her father's appearing on the screen, and more than once, he thought he'd seen them, he was in such a suggestible state. He was sitting this way, lost in frightened reverie, when he heard a key in the lock. He looked to the door in stunned silence, not sure what to expect, and couldn't quite believe Gina was back even when she stood again before him, smiling at him as if it were an evening like any other.

"Oh no, you were worried, weren't you?" She was taking in his ragged face, the wine. "I'm so sorry. I lost track of time." She came close to him and kissed his cheek. As she drew nearer, the scent of cigarettes wafted from her hair and clothes.

"You smell like smoke," he muttered, still in shock.

"Do I? I wonder— Well, yes, I stopped in a café. I didn't realize how late it had gotten. I'm sorry."

"You don't need to be sorry. I mean, you're free to do whatever. I just worried."

"I'm fine."

She smiled, then quickly crossed the floor to turn off the TV. Rather than rejoin him, she stopped at the balcony, looking outward.

"Gina?"

She turned back, trying to appear easygoing, but her distress was palpable. Gina could never hide her feelings from him—this was one of the things he'd always loved about her, how passionate she was, and how transparent, by comparison.

"Something is going on, I can feel it. Whatever it is, you can tell me." He watched her slump her shoulders and slowly shake her head. When she looked up, she was laughing at herself.

"You're right, I'm a useless liar, aren't I? The whole point was not to worry you."

He came after her, trying to stay steady, reassuring. He took her hands in his, looking her in the eyes. "Please. I don't want secrets between us."

"Of course. No secrets." She hugged him tightly, her head against his chest, so that, as she spoke, he couldn't see her face. "I wasn't feeling well this morning, so I paid a visit to the hospital. It started after you left, cramps, awful ones. I wasn't sure how to reach you, and I didn't see any point in scaring you if it was nothing. Thankfully, the doctor said it was just dehydration, to be expected in the heat of a Rome summer. I just need to drink plenty of water and not exert myself too much. He let me go with this advice and a few pamphlets." Gina removed a stack of leaflets from her bag and set them upon the coffee table. "I should read them, but I'm too beat to do it now. I think I need to rest."

He walked her to the bedroom and she lay down on the bed. Duncan sat beside her. He was feeling a mixture of terror and gratitude—how fragile was his happiness, but he held on to it still. This woman he loved and the tiny creature forged out of that love—they were with him, safe. Or as safe as he could keep them.

He sat beside her, holding her hand and kissing it over and over, finding it hard to leave her side until, finally, Gina asked if he might close the curtains. The light remained strong into the evening, so he did his best to dim the room before stepping out to let her rest. In the kitchen, he filled a pot with water to boil pasta, and then recalled how Gina had said she ought to drink throughout the day. He reached for a pitcher, and the pot began to overflow.

He cursed, feeling his irritation. There seemed so much to manage at times, he couldn't think how he would do it—a child to care for, a new city to navigate, a home to make away from everyone they knew. And on top of all this he had his elaborate ruse to protect: from his parents, from Gina's father, Violet, Blake, Graham Bonafair, even his fellow classmates—the list went on. How would he ever manage to compose? How would he hold on to the person he'd once been?

Water had spilled onto his arms and shirt. He dried himself as best he could and returned, with the pitcher and a glass, to Gina's room.

When he reached the door, Gina was out of bed, standing by the window. The curtains had been drawn aside and she was looking down into the street. She quickly became aware of him and turned.

"Nausea. I needed air."

"Right, sure. And I brought you water too. That might help."

She thanked him and returned to the bed, smiling up at him sweetly. He set the pitcher and the glass down beside her, stroked her cheek and stepped away, choosing to say nothing of his misgivings, of his intuition, groundless perhaps, that as she stood staring out that window at the street, she was looking for someone.

Fifteen

Gina // Rome

August 1996

Hours earlier, when Duncan had left for school that Friday, Gina had set off for the Metro, riding all the way to Tor Sapienza, where she exited and took the same walk she'd taken on her first day in Rome, when she and Duncan visited the hospital. She rode the elevator to obstetrics, chatted mindlessly with the receptionist—confirming her appointment for three days from now, asking a few very obvious questions she had in advance of the checkup—and then set out to do what she'd come to do. After thanking the receptionist, she stopped by the door to collect several pamphlets—on prenatal care, nutrition, and the like—which she'd need later to prove to Duncan she'd indeed gone to the hospital, that that was where she'd been all afternoon.

She left the hospital around eleven thirty, which gave her half an hour to reach the café where she would meet Graham Bonafair.

She was nervous walking over, uncertain whether she was doing the right thing. She couldn't help but feel that skipping off behind Duncan's back was a betrayal, and she couldn't anticipate what the outcome of this meeting would be. Reaching the café, she recalled how elated she and Duncan had been when they'd come here, after the hospital where they'd witnessed the miracle of the beating heart inside her belly. She stood to lose so much.

It was a typical Italian café, with a dark wooden bar and marble-topped tables, red wallpaper, and a checkered floor. Most of the patrons here were older, locals reading newspapers and chattering. The staff spoke no English; the menus were only in Italian.

Her heart was beating fast as she peered around the room, afraid to be faced with Graham after all this time and to discover what sort of feelings might be stirred, what memories revived. She'd recalled enough by now to make this meeting momentous. She was so tensely anticipating seeing him, was seeking his face so exclusively in the small crowd dispersed among the tables, that she didn't recognize, right away, who was seated there, waiting for her, instead.

He waved at her from a table in the corner. Blake Flournoy.

She was alarmed. How had Blake come to be here? Was he traveling with Graham? She tried to think what it could mean, what sort of setup she'd walked into and if she ought to simply turn around and leave. Blake continued to watch her. He was dressed in a pink button-down shirt and jeans, his legs crossed casually, and he was drinking an espresso, which he swished around in its small cup. Nothing about his manner suggested confrontation, yet she knew Blake well enough to be wary.

"This is a surprise," she said, taking a seat.

"I'd guess it is," Blake replied, grinning.

He was still handsome, but his straight blond hair, slicked back, was starting to thin, and there were bags under his eyes. He'd aged since she'd last seen him, over a year ago. Even when Blake had still lived in New York, he and Duncan had typically met without her. None of Blake's girlfriends ever lasted long enough to warrant outings as couples, and she was perfectly grateful for this, as she imagined Blake was too.

"Graham told you I'd be here?"

"He did, yes. And I asked his permission to speak with you first. I assured him I'd help explain things to you, so you'd be better prepared for meeting him."

"I had no idea you two had ever spoken."

"Thanks to recent events. He'd reached out to me, along the way, for clues as to where Duncan might be. We've all been trying to pin you down, but you haven't made it easy." Blake was watching her closely, a faint smile on his lips.

Just then the waitress came by to get her order. Gina asked for an orange juice, Blake for another espresso. Once the woman had stepped away, he continued. "Graham's been knocking himself out to reach you, as I'm sure you know, and I've had a hell of a time getting in touch with Duncan. I've left him ten messages on his machine but he hasn't been responding. I'd been trying to fathom why, until recently, it hit me. That machine used to be both of yours. You must know the pass code too."

"You say *used* to be both of ours? Isn't it still?"

"Right. Right. You've supposedly no idea about all that, all forgotten. That's what Violet's been saying. Just tripped and forgot. That's what I'm meant to believe."

The situation was becoming clearer to her now. They must all be in communication at this point, Violet, her father, Graham, and now Blake as well. She looked across at him, this man who had always sought a reason to condemn her and must be thinking he'd found one now. Just how much of the truth had Blake managed to guess? There was a bitter quality in his expression, a tightness around the mouth, even as he smiled.

"So you're doubting my brain injury?"

"I'd doubt any story that came from you."

She had to think how to handle this, how much she must admit to recalling in light of her choosing to reach out to Graham. "I can assure you that losing my memory was very real, and very scary. There's still a lot I can't remember and a lot of what's happened I can't make sense of either."

"Maybe we can fill in some blanks for one another. For example, I'd like to know how, in your disorientation, you were mindful enough to erase all the messages I left for Duncan. All the arguments for why you're a lying manipulator bent on ruining his life."

"Does it occur to you," she replied calmly, "that this could be why Duncan doesn't call you back? He has your number. He's a free man. If he hasn't called, he must not want to." Catching a flicker of irritation in Blake's expression, she pressed on. "Maybe it's finally hit him that your mistrust of me is pathological. And maybe he finally realized that he doesn't need a friend who insults the woman he loves any chance he gets and accuses her of the craziest things."

"I've only begun accusing you," Blake said, leaving off as the waitress returned to lower Gina's juice and his espresso onto the table. *"Grazie mille,"* he said flirtatiously, with his fading charm. He didn't look well, Gina observed, and she had the thought that Blake's self-concern and isolation had already started to corrode him. Love was what kept a person young and fresh, but Blake stood contrary to love, at least where she and Duncan were concerned. She'd wondered about this in Blake, whether his own desires for Duncan might lie, unacknowledged, in him. Possibly this was why, from the very beginning, he'd set out to destroy the love between Duncan and her.

It calmed her to recall that today's allegations against her were hardly his first, and yet, in all these years trying to stain her reputation, what progress had Blake made? He'd perhaps learned she'd told a few lies as a child—stories to conceal the state her mother was in, or other fantasies she'd invented for her own escape from pain. Or maybe he'd reached the conclusion that Gina had pushed Duncan to want the things she wanted. Well, if Blake believed that any of this would turn Duncan against her, he wouldn't have hesitated to share it. That he hadn't done so meant he'd known that Duncan would side with her, and he'd come off as the jealous and untrustworthy friend.

"Did you read Violet's letter?" Blake demanded as she took a slow sip from her juice. "Is that the point at which you knew?"

"I never received any letter from Violet. I don't know what you're talking about."

"Oh, come on now!" Blake was growing impatient. He banged his fist on the table. "I know what I'm talking about. Violet and I went over it. She knows I'm here, and believe me, she's about as eager to confront Duncan as I am to have it out with you. She and I may not have anything else in common other than wishing to see you two separated, but I know she's not lying to me. You got that letter." He stared but Gina's face did not waver. "She left it for you at your hotel in Prague, right before you suddenly insisted on leaving. And then you wrote Violet that letter of your own. You gave her an address in the South of France. You were trying to throw her off your trail, weren't you? While you and

Duncan headed to Siena. And all this time she's worried sick and you haven't even spoken to her. Some friend you are!"

"I really don't know what you're after. Duncan and I changed our plans together. We started for France, then heard about the Palio."

"But obviously you were trying to get Violet off your case. You told her you couldn't handle seeing her; you gave her this whole story about how you were pregnant."

"Did Violet tell you *that*?" It surprised her and frankly hurt her to think that her best friend would betray her confidence— with Blake of all people, and on such a delicate matter. "That's really none of your business."

Blake seemed to recognize her genuine annoyance. "Jesus, it's not actually *true*, is it?"

"Who would lie about a thing like that?"

Silence stretched between them, Blake clearly taking this in, what this would mean for his friend. "You're serious. You're going to have a child like this? Under these conditions?" He began to laugh mirthlessly. "You really are insane."

She could feel her temper rising—nothing about her choice to have this child was insane. At times, it seemed the only clear and good motive she possessed. "I don't need to sit here for this. Why don't you get Graham to step out from wherever he's hiding? I didn't come here to explain myself to you." She began to stand, but Blake took hold of her arm.

"Oh, don't act so shocked. It's not as if you haven't heard this before. I laid it all out for Duncan in my messages."

"I've already told you that I didn't listen to them." She spoke with such conviction, such indignation, that she might almost have believed this herself.

"That tape ought to be full by now. Someone's been erasing."

"And why not Duncan?"

"Because if Duncan heard the things I'd said, he couldn't go on with you the way he is!"

Blake was becoming exasperated. The other café patrons were looking over and she hoped someone would soon come to inquire if she was all right. In fact, she hoped Blake would go further and provoke a stranger to intrude, at which point she would tell the person that she didn't feel safe, that she was pregnant, returning from the hospital, and that she felt threatened by this gentleman whom she'd never before met.

It began to concern her, her exit from this meeting. She wasn't sure how she'd get rid of Blake if he refused to let her go, or if he should insist that she take him to see Duncan. And there was still the matter of Graham.

Reaching into her purse, she removed a pen and began writing on her napkin. "I'm done here. If you have something more to say, say it to Duncan. This is the phone number where we're staying."

Blake let go of her arm to take the paper, folding it up and stuffing it inside his pocket. From his other pocket he withdrew several bills and laid them on the table. "Let's you and I take a short walk. I saw a pay phone on the street. We'll try this number together." Blake rose from his seat and stepped over to pull out her chair.

"Oh, for God's sake. Is this a test? I can't guarantee that Duncan will be home and answer."

"I'm sure you can't."

She peered around her, considering her next move. There were two young men seated, smoking, by the window—maybe she could enlist them in her defense. She doubted Blake would talk as tough with men his own size. For the moment, she felt safer staying here than venturing outside.

"I've had enough of this meeting. I think you should go."

"Not without you," Blake spat. He stepped closer to her but then halted—he was looking behind her, his attention frozen. She turned and saw the man moving toward them, taller than she recalled, every bit as handsome and gracious. He paled when he caught her eye, and his step slowed.

"Hello, Gina," he said, drawing up beside her. She felt so relieved at his arrival, and so moved to see him after everything that had happened, she had to restrain herself from throwing her arms around him.

"Hello, Graham."

She and Graham walked together along Via Collatina on the way back to the train. The road was plain, suburban, with boxy, modern housing, a road that might have existed not in Rome, but on the outskirts of almost any city, even Santa Fe. Strolling now alongside Graham, she had recollections of such walks in the fall and early winter of that year, when she was still dwelling on her mistakes, struggling to keep her thoughts from drifting into dark regions she'd lingered in too long.

"I'm sorry I let Blake meet you alone," Graham offered, head hung in apology. "He said he just needed a few minutes in private, that he was concerned about Duncan and wanted to find a way to help you both. He was awfully persuasive."

"I'd imagine Blake would be."

"But believe me, Gina. I had no idea he'd be aggressive with you. I never would have predicted . . . But then, there's been so much lately that I couldn't have predicted."

Sweet, innocent Graham. She chose not to respond to this, not to address the events, in all their complexity, that had intervened since she and Graham had last been together in Berlin. She couldn't know how much of the story he had gotten or pieced together on his own, if Blake had told him Violet believed Gina was pregnant, if he understood how radical her new plans were—to start a family with Duncan, here in this foreign place, cut off, indefinitely, escaping from the life she and Graham had planned before. Right now she meant to keep their conversation focused on the motive that lay behind her contacting Graham to begin with: "I need to know about my father. If he's okay."

Over the phone, Graham had already told her of the accident back in Siena, reassuring her that her father was on his way to a full recovery—he'd called Graham from the hospital and relayed his encounter with Duncan.

"He's doing much better," Graham assured her. "Of course he wanted to come with me to meet you, but I told him what you said, that you'd be returning with me and that he shouldn't risk his health."

She nodded, avoiding Graham's gaze, guilt-struck. The feeling stirred up memories of so many guilty moments in Graham's presence, times when her affection had felt forced or when, in bed, she'd been distracted by his difference from Duncan, put off by his eager, overly direct touch. And now all her past remorse was compounded by the new hurts she had caused and would cause next. Graham still imagined he might leave Rome with her. Her father was awaiting her imminent return. But she would not be going anywhere.

She felt at a loss for words, but thankfully, anticipating such a moment, she'd written a letter, which she removed from her purse and handed to Graham now. She'd spent several days trying out phrases, explaining herself without overexplaining, and above all trying to persuade her father to stop persecuting Duncan. Graham took the letter from her, and she felt both gratitude and sadness, thinking whether she ought to have written an explanation for him too. How gentle Graham was. At times she'd thought him too even-tempered—there were depths of emotion she'd been sure they'd never reach—but in the days they were together that had seemed a gift.

She remembered clearly now her father's private art showing—how he'd so obviously brought her and Graham together. She could recall the painting on display of her and Duncan, and how, as she'd stood before it fighting back tears, this other man had come up beside her, while someone, maybe her father, had taken a picture of them from behind. She'd looked over at Graham, who was handsome with light eyes that sparkled warmly. He'd introduced himself as a friend of her father's.

"Graham Bonafair. Your father's said a lot about you."

"Has he?" She'd been annoyed at the transparency of her father's motives. He thought her too absorbed by her feelings for Duncan at that time—doubt, pain, regret—and this pretty friend was intended to distract her. She'd had an urge to be unfriendly to Graham, and had avoided him that afternoon. A few days later, though, Graham had come to the house, bringing by some canvases he'd picked up for her father. They'd spoken for a while in the living room and she'd learned that Graham had taken a teaching position in the university art department. He'd moved, he said, after a breakup with his fiancée, and she supposed that her father must have told him of the breakup that she had just endured.

It had all felt very contrived, but though she'd resisted at first, she found she enjoyed Graham's company. At first she felt perhaps he was a stand-in—another object for her to invite into her private world, draw into her hopes and dreams. But Graham brought his own cheerful disposition, so much easier and more hopeful than Duncan's, such a relief after so many grim months. They started taking walks, usually into the old town of Santa Fe, among the red adobe buildings, or else they'd drive out to Abiquiu Lake or Jemez Falls, swimming together, as she and Duncan had never done, floating on their backs under the huge blue sky. It wasn't necessarily that her feelings for Duncan had vanished—they'd just grown paler in the light emanating from this brightly smiling, unfamiliar man before her.

At times she spoke of staying on in New Mexico. After four months at home, she'd taken a job at the dance studio where she'd once trained, and Graham began to encourage her to audition for the larger troupes in Albuquerque. A new fantasy began to form—of their moving somewhere together, finding work, sharing a house. But no matter how many details she might assemble to make such a future sharper, it remained lifeless. Her work in New York far surpassed anything she could find there, and her past with Duncan had more vibrancy and reality than any moment ever did with Graham. Each time she awoke in Santa Fe, there was always a first instant when she expected to be waking in New York, with Duncan, and then the disappointment when she realized all of that was gone. She thought maybe this would pass—and she indeed tried to will her affections for Graham to bloom. But there was always the thought that dogged her—that at any moment she'd gladly erase her present to be back in her past.

"I hope you know I never meant to have this happen," she told him. "For you to be forgotten."

"Oh, I know you didn't." Graham was smiling. She recalled his tendency to smile, especially when he was hurt, that affability that had, toward the end, begun to feel slippery. Just how deep were feelings that could be graciously brushed aside?

If she'd needed someone like Graham for a time, these past weeks had proved that her connection to him was one born out of a rather short-lived need. She found, now, that need—for stability, for comfort, for his ease of emotion—was no longer there. Someone else—someone who had always been in the background of her mind, if she was being truthful—had stepped back into the picture and usurped Graham's power.

"It just happened to you," Graham went on, overly kind to them both. "It wasn't about me."

"No, definitely not," she agreed. All of it made easy by Graham's avoidance of the insult. "The whole year was wiped out. More, even."

Graham paused, briefly wondering. "Did you feel the gaps at all? Or did you not miss what wasn't there?" Obviously such thoughts must have plagued him, and he must now be curious to hear how it had been. As uneasy as the subject made her, she felt that she owed him some answers.

"I had a sense that certain things were missing. More recently."

"And how did it come back, then? Was it gradual?"

"At first, yes. There were flashes here and there. An image as I woke in the morning. Sometimes, even, I'd find myself thinking or saying your name. But no more than that until a sudden shift. One morning in Prague."

"Violet told me she left you a letter. So you did read it?"

"That's right," she said, a painful admission—for Graham to hear her admit she knew the truth and had decided to run from it anyway. She wondered if he was coming to understand this now. While she'd been careful with her lies with Blake, it seemed to her that Graham deserved the truth, or at least a half-truth. She *had* gotten and read Violet's letter at the hotel in Prague—though by then she'd already known more or less what it contained. Graham didn't require the whole story, though; all he had to know was this. "It was a shock and I was furious at Duncan at first. Only then I had to admit that I'd been happy with him. That my feelings for him were still alive and strong."

"I see." Graham looked off and she waited for him to take in the meaning of what she'd said. "I think I understand now," he muttered sadly. "You won't be coming back with me."

"No, I'm sorry, but I won't."

He nodded, with more equanimity than she had imagined. Deep down, she thought, perhaps he'd known she hadn't loved him. Perhaps he'd wondered at how easily her memories of him had been erased, and this news that she was choosing Duncan surprised him less than either would have guessed.

"I can't say it makes sense to me," he said after a moment. "But I suppose you know what's best for you."

How very decent he was being, and how grateful she was for it, and yet this behavior only confirmed her choice. Despite all these weeks spent worrying and chasing after her, Graham was prepared to respect her feelings and simply walk away. Faced with losing her, Graham was rational and steady, whereas Duncan had been reckless and desperate. Love, she believed, had nothing sensible about it.

The Metro station was just up ahead and she was already late to meet Duncan. He would be worried and full of questions for her when she returned. As difficult as that return might be, she was eager for it, to be away from here and back with Duncan in their home.

"Goodbye, Graham," she told him, and he leaned down to kiss her, lightly on the cheek, before turning away, the long, lean back of her memories fading into memory once more, this time for good.

Sixteen

Duncan // Rome

August 1996

*L*ater on that evening, while Gina rested, Duncan prepared dinner and set the table in the dining room. A cool breeze blew in from the balcony and the setting sun cast a gold band on the back wall, which formed a halo over the face in the giant portrait. The woman—faintly smiling, with deep-set, thoughtful eyes—peered back at him from the wall. A guardian angel, he'd called her when he and Gina had first arrived, and though he'd been joking then, more and more he did believe it.

He still wasn't a religious person, had never had faith in higher powers and certainly not in angels, not in anything like the fat cherubs he'd been lucky enough to see in person on the Sistine Chapel ceiling. Yet despite his doubts, now that he found himself living so beautifully, being so fortunate, he had the distinct sense that someone must be looking out for him. He had no other explanation for why fate had gone his way so often in the past weeks—no other way to understand why, scarcely an hour after he'd gone into the Prague synagogue, certain that Violet would reach Gina and expose him, Gina had announced an urgent desire to leave the city that very morning. Nor could he explain how it was that, in Siena, at the precise moment he meant to confess to Gina what he'd done, she'd chosen to cut him off with the news that she was pregnant.

Since then, the child bound him to his course. He hadn't known it would be this way at first—he'd felt, on the contrary, that he couldn't allow a baby to be born under false pretenses. But then he began to recognize how much Gina wanted this, and wanted him to want it, and he understood it would be cruel to be honest with her now. The time for such a confession would have to be in the far future, once they'd become parents and they'd built a solid life together, and she'd learned that he really was capable of giving to her what she wanted; then he could admit the deception that he'd found it necessary to maintain at the beginning.

"*I know it must seem awful, what I did,*" he'd say, falling upon her mercy. "*I took advantage of you, I went against the wishes you'd expressed in the past. All I can say in my defense is that when you looked up at me in the Berlin hospital that day, I felt that you had chosen me, that this strange act of fate was precisely what was needed to bring us back to our feeling for each other, precisely what was needed to erase all the mistakes and all the rancor. I faced this moment, this impossible temptation: the paradise that I'd been longing for more than I'd even admitted to myself, and all I had to do was acquiesce, not deny it. So I didn't. And from there, messily, with plenty of wrongdoing, but all done out of love for you, we arrived here.*"

When he recited this speech in his head to future Gina, he was quite persuaded by it. Put this way, and with years of good history between them to lessen the harm of what he'd done, it might almost seem romantic. See what he'd been willing to go through, what knots he'd twisted himself into to keep that one going?

My God, you really do love me, he knew Gina would think. Not all women might feel that way, but Gina of the grand gesture, Gina who considered her father's obsessive devotion the hallmark of true love, didn't she crave precisely this sort of madness? Wasn't that what she'd always wanted from him, to stop being so cautious and to lose his head a little? So now he had, that much was certain—he'd ceased to be the timid Duncan of the past and had lost his head.

The meal was ready, and Duncan set it onto serving plates, which he carried to the dining room. The places were set. A small bouquet he'd picked up stood in the center of the table. The curtains blew in from the open balcony, and he could hear the muffled sounds of the city: the honking taxicabs, the whirring Vespas, shouts in Italian. He peered down into the street, seized by the fear he'd had the night before: that someone might be outside, watching them. A man walked by with a dog. An old couple passed under the window, holding hands. Not Gina's father, not Graham, not the authorities, not God. Only maybe, somewhere unseen, his guardian angel. He felt the urge to laugh.

He was going to get away with it.

"Duncan, what did you do?"

He turned to see Gina, who'd stepped out into the living room and was admiring the table. She was wearing a white dress, her face aglow with sunset light. He thought he'd never seen her look more beautiful than she did then. Such freshness and innocence— that he should be awarded this, after all his lies and failings, it wasn't fair, it wasn't just, but he would at least never take for granted this gift that he'd been given.

"You did all of this for me?" Gina, smiling, came up beside him.

He wrapped his arms around her, his hands upon the belly with the tiny heartbeat inside it, which, one day, would beat more strongly than his own. "I did this for all of us."

Seventeen

Gina // Rome

August 1996

O_n *her* train ride back from Tor Sapienza she had a fearful sense of how narrowly she'd escaped Graham and Blake. After being careful for so long, correcting for Duncan's recklessness, she was the one who'd been sloppy this time, by agreeing to meet Graham without considering the risks. Naturally, he might be contacted by Blake, or others might use him—sweet, simple Graham, who was too kind and naïve to realize it—to get to her. Still, she couldn't rid herself of the fear that Graham hadn't successfully chased off Blake, or any others he might have tipped off to their meeting. Every few minutes, she rose and walked down the center aisle of the train, looking at the passengers in the neighboring cars, seeking Violet or Blake or her father. None of them appeared, though, and after a time, she calmed down enough to take her seat.

She ought to relax, really, prepare herself for meeting Duncan, and yet she couldn't get past the agitation Blake had caused her. She'd been stunned by him, not only by his ingenuity in persuading Graham to let him meet her but by all that he'd managed to deduce from the information that he'd gathered. He'd been right about so much: how she'd pretended not to have read Violet's letter but left it for Duncan to read, how she'd come up with the visit to the Palio after calling the train stations and learning that getting there would require their leaving right away. On the trip, she'd written to Violet and given her the French address to throw her off, as Blake had guessed, and after sensing that Siena wasn't safe for them, she'd encouraged Mauro to offer up his place in Rome so that Duncan might accept it. Part of keeping the game going involved letting Duncan believe, at every point, that he was the one to manage their escape.

She'd been so expert in this, really, that Duncan seemed completely unaware of her efforts—all the more reason it shocked her to hear, on one of the early mornings before Duncan was awake when she'd called into their answering machine, that Blake had figured out so much.

She knows everything, Duncan. Her memory is coming back to her, if it was ever even gone at all. She knows she left you, knows you're lying that you're still a couple and that people are after you to stop you. I can't say if she's always known, but at the very least since the day she got you out of Prague. Think about it and you'll realize I'm right. You'd have been caught by now, if Gina weren't helping you. There's too much that can't be explained any other way. Why did she lie to Violet about where you were headed? Why didn't she ever insist on calling her father? Why haven't you ever called me? I keep trying you, though a part of me knows she'll never let me reach you. She won't let you hear this, and you don't want to hear it either— you're determined to see Gina as some innocent being, when that's the last thing she is.

This final insight of Blake's struck her the most. What a relief it had been for her to find Duncan convinced of her innocence, so convinced that he managed, for a time, to convince her of it too. For their first weeks together in Europe, she was the Gina of their pure past with him again, and, once she'd known the feeling, she'd known this was the only Gina that she ever wished to be. She chose not to see this as her being false, but as her returning to the person she must be—cheerful and loving and without guilt—to be a proper mother to her child.

For the child's sake, she'd done what she had to do, she told herself, and in a way, the real agency in all this wasn't her own, but belonged to this creature deep inside her. As if in some fairy tale, she'd slipped into forgetfulness so that the child could be conceived, and then, after it was, it had wrenched her back into full consciousness again.

It was the pregnancy that brought the past back to her, the sensations lodged in her body's memory. She knew with certainty that she'd felt this way before—tired, dizzy, tender. Suddenly, waking in her Prague hotel room, the details of that time returned to her: Vienna, the festival, the dinners out with her fellow dancers and the Frenchman, and the night she'd felt so ill that the Frenchman insisted he take her to a doctor. At the doctor's office the next day, she was given a test that left no doubt what was happening. She'd purchased a plane ticket to New York that very day. There were five shows left to perform, but she couldn't tell Duncan this news over the phone.

She hadn't informed Duncan she was coming. At the time, she'd hoped to make her arrival part of her surprise, though in retrospect she wondered at this choice. Might she have been afraid to tell him the news? She and Duncan hadn't discussed any changed feelings over having a child, but they'd taken fewer precautions in the weeks before her departure. She'd been testing his resistance; she thought he might want this, but she hadn't had any means to be sure. And yet, for all her nervousness, she'd run up the stairs, eager to see Duncan, not suspecting that anything could be wrong.

The lights were on in the apartment, though low, and music was playing, loudly enough that Duncan must not have heard the door open. Duncan was by the sofa, looking distractedly toward the kitchenette, where Marina Du Bellay was standing holding a wineglass. Marina spotted her first and, lowering the wineglass with a clink, stared back at her, her lipstick smeared and her shirt open, looking so pale and guilt-stricken that Gina knew at once what sort of scene she'd interrupted.

She'd left her bag and run out of the apartment before Duncan had even noticed she was there. Outside she'd darted into a taxi and had gone to stay at a cheap hotel near her dance studio. All the next day, she'd stayed in bed. She had the feeling like she'd lost her adult self, like standing in the doorway witnessing Duncan's betrayal, she'd become again the little girl standing before her fallen mother, suddenly so frightened and alone. What she'd done next had felt like a necessity. She could not trust Duncan. She could not trust herself to have the baby on her own.

She found the clinic, endured a short interview, and was given pills. This had seemed the least violent method. She hadn't counted on the blood. Yes, at the clinic they had said there would be bleeding, but in the night when she had woken up on bloodied sheets she'd been so horrified she'd spent an hour in the shower, and then another hour washing herself again after she'd cleaned up the mess, shoved all the sheets into bags that she set out with the trash.

She'd left for Santa Fe with the conviction that there could be no coming back. That pain, the blood, the guilt—it had all been too terrible to bear remembering. She'd done this mad, impulsive thing in a moment of rage, which, had she considered more deeply, she'd have known was bound to pass. She knew Duncan didn't love Marina, that Duncan didn't wish to leave her. This wasn't the danger she faced—the danger was in allowing herself to become hopeful, the danger was in becoming a mother, and loving anything as much as she would love that child, as much as she had loved her mother, only to know she might have it torn from her.

In her panic she'd destroyed that hope. Duncan she could forgive, but she could not forgive herself, and that meant punishment, eradicating all that made her happy, all that she'd been able, with Duncan or since her mother's death, to give herself: a thrilling career, a loving life with Duncan—all that she'd said goodbye to, so that she might embark on a new romance that was empty from the start. In its emptiness, she was able to hide. Graham knew nothing about her, and it had been far easier to be someone else with him, flat and new and without fault. A man like Graham was too kind, and too uninterested in the truth, to bother to ask more. With Graham, she began to invent a new half-believed-in future in which Duncan had no part.

Possibly that future might have come to be, and the past with Duncan might have been truly erased, if not for the strangest twist of fate. Everything she'd worked so hard to forget had been simply and effortlessly erased for her.

In those first days following the accident, when the past was emptied from her mind, for all that it had been scary and unsettling, she'd also felt so very light. She'd loved Duncan without restraint. She'd had no reasons not to love him. Here was this sweet and caring boy doing all he could to please her, to take her mind off of anything that troubled her—and what could she want more than that? Maybe her mind had known better than to recover, maybe some part of her recognized that this happiness hadn't been with her before and should be clung to, and she could have stayed in that state of naïve bliss forever if she hadn't woken in Prague to that sore, gnawing, nauseous feeling that she was sure she'd had before.

That morning when she'd woken inside the Prague hotel, she'd lain in bed, on her back beside Duncan, the room around her spinning, and all the memories and images that had been cast loose had begun falling into place.

She'd stepped out onto the Prague streets, feeling as if she no longer knew what was true and what was false. The brightly painted houses looked like toys. Nothing was as it had seemed, not her loving Duncan and not her own lovable self. A letter from Violet was waiting for her in the hotel lobby, and she knew her friend would be meeting her in an hour or so, at which time she'd be rescued from Duncan, and this mad hunt that she'd unwittingly been caught up in would end. After today, she might never even see Duncan again.

She continued her walk, heading into the old city. Her thoughts were too much of a maelstrom for her to do anything but meander, half-blindly, until she ended up in front of a house that looked even stranger than the rest: the little old-fashioned cottage with the Star of David out front. She might have been hallucinating—for an instant she imagined that she was—how could it be that Duncan stood before her, like a ghost?

Had she not seen him then, so humbled, eyes glassy with tears, would she have gone on to meet Violet? Would she have run off with Violet, rather than escaping Violet and running off with him? She might have—yes—she'd felt so insulted and betrayed. He'd preyed upon her weakness; he'd exploited her affection; he'd destroyed her yearlong efforts to get past him and be free.

How it had surprised her, then, when she'd seen Duncan and felt a shift, a sudden strange urge to laugh, right there on the sidewalk. Duncan, how in the hell could you have done this? You wily bastard, how did you dare?

She was moved then by the magnitude of what he'd done, the many details that she'd disregarded earlier, but which attained their proper meaning now: the missing address book, the wedding band that slid too easily off of her ring finger, the sudden move out of Berlin. For her, to get her back, he'd schemed and risked almost everything he had: his career, his connections to friends and family, his reputation, his safety. He'd tossed aside every other commitment, drowned out every moderate objection— he'd thrown himself off of a balcony, for God's sake—for her, for their love!

All those voices in her that had doubted him for being seduced by Marina, or insisted that he'd lose his faith and disappoint her, were silenced, on that day, by what Duncan had done. Her cautious, pragmatic Duncan, whom she always feared lacked the madness required for great art and great love—he was crazy to the core! Weren't they meant for each other? Duncan was just the liar that she was, and Duncan's love for her was just as true.

When the train reached the station nearest to their apartment, the time was nearly five. Gina was almost two hours later than she'd intended and surely Duncan would be home and worried by now—with questions. On the walk home, she had to keep herself from hurrying and growing flushed, and, at the apartment, she took the elevator up rather than the stairs, so as not to appear breathless at the door. She must seem pale and slow moving when she entered, since the story she'd prepared involved her feeling ill. She'd learned early that, with lying, the key was to remain attentive to the smallest details, and to inject into the lie as much truth as possible. For this reason alone, she'd arranged to meet Graham near the hospital, and had collected the leaflets she'd present Duncan, as evidence, before announcing she was tired.

In fact, she wasn't tired in the least, was very much the opposite—she was coursing with adrenaline, too restless to stay put. She still felt compelled to come and look out of the window to be sure she wasn't being watched, checking whether she recognized a face hidden away in a parked car. She was standing by the window when Duncan entered, carrying a pitcher of water, looking on from the doorway.

She stammered that she'd been feeling off, and Duncan led her back to bed and poured her a glass of water. He was starting dinner, he let her know. "Do you feel well enough to eat?"

"Well enough to try."

Dinner was set out for her with flowers, and she was relieved, seeing this, that Duncan must have believed her. During the meal she ate less than she might have, in light of the story that she'd given. Since she'd claimed to be tired before, she suggested they go to sleep early, and they awoke at dawn the next morning, when the sun began shining in and the room warmed, until she found herself shifting in bed, searching for cool spots in the sheets. It would be a hot day, so she advised they get up and out before the heat became too strong. She wanted to walk a bit, since they'd done no sightseeing together all that week. She proposed a stroll down Via dei Fori Imperiali, the road that had formed the spine of ancient Rome, running from Trajan's Forum to the Coliseum.

She'd made the trip several times herself, moved both by the grandeur of the way and by the poetry of the ruins. The road was wide, with paths for pedestrians to pass under the umbrella pines so common in the city. Statues lined the way, and at the bottom of the road the Coliseum rose like a great sun on the horizon. Walking at dusk, as she sometimes did, she would see the light hit the amphitheater so that it seemed to glow.

Trajan's Forum was the least preserved of the famous ancient structures, but it was the one that drew her most. Nearly all of the original marketplace was gone, and what was left were excavated foundations and grassy paths with columns planted in rows, or fragments lying on their sides. She hoped Duncan wouldn't find it disappointing. To her it was mystical, walking on ground where ancient Romans had walked before her, taking in the columns standing where a building had been, where a single stone marked a wall that had contained inhabitants of another rich and complete world, now vanished.

These ruins felt close to her. She'd grown up inside a ruin. Her mother was a ruin, her father and her house. Every corner, word, or look was a fragment left of some better time. And she, too, accumulating losses of her own, had become her own barren space, a field of fragments and absence. Only now something in her had shifted. The emptiness had filled. She contained a life. An extraordinary life—this creature that had willed itself into being. She would be a mother. She would raise a child with Duncan, and he'd go on to write music and she'd return to dance, and their lives would unfold in perfect collaboration, in a way even wilder and more romantic than she might have imagined on her own.

Duncan came to stand beside her, with his arms wrapped around her. There they stood, under the cloud-shaped trees that shaded a brick wall, peering out at the excavated ground.

She placed her hand over her belly, unthinkingly, and leaned back against him. Duncan was bound to her. She knew this now. It had taken her discovering his madness to be certain, but today she felt it in his grip. However battered, however deserted by family and friends, however like a ruin they might become, she and Duncan would endure.

"I love you," he said, squeezing, hands laced over her belly.

She entwined her fingers with his. "And I love you."

Duncan would never let her go, she thought. Not with her to help him. She'd never let him let her go.

The End

Acknowledgments

My deepest gratitude to the wonderful team at Simon and Shuster, who did such beautiful work on behalf of the book. Special thanks to Adam Eaglin, whose vision and encouragement have guided me for years and made this novel happen in the first place; to Zack Knoll, the most talented, dedicated, and generous editor a writer could wish for; and to Sylvie Rabineau, whose faith in me has fueled my creativity and expanded my sense of what's possible. Thanks also to my daughter, for her patience and radiance.

About the Author

ROBIN KIRMAN studied philosophy at Yale before receiving her MFA in writing from Columbia, where she also taught for several years. Her curiosity about human psychology has led her to combine work in psychoanalysis with writing fiction. Her first novel, *Bradstreet Gate*, was published by Crown in 2015, and her television series, *The Love Wave*, is currently in development.